The Future of European Social D

The Future of European Social Democracy
Building the Good Society

Edited by

Henning Meyer
Senior Visiting Fellow, Government Department, London School of Economics and Political Science, UK

Jonathan Rutherford
Professor of Cultural Studies, Department of Media, Middlesex University, UK

Editorial matter, selection, introduction and conclusion © Henning Meyer and Jonathan Rutherford 2012
Preface and Appendix © Jon Cruddas and Andrea Nahles 2012
All remaining chapters © respective authors 2012

All rights reserved. No reproduction, copy or transmission of this publication may be made without written permission.

No portion of this publication may be reproduced, copied or transmitted save with written permission or in accordance with the provisions of the Copyright, Designs and Patents Act 1988, or under the terms of any licence permitting limited copying issued by the Copyright Licensing Agency, Saffron House, 6–10 Kirby Street, London EC1N 8TS.

Any person who does any unauthorized act in relation to this publication may be liable to criminal prosecution and civil claims for damages.

The authors have asserted their rights to be identified as the authors of this work in accordance with the Copyright, Designs and Patents Act 1988.

First published 2012 by
PALGRAVE MACMILLAN

Palgrave Macmillan in the UK is an imprint of Macmillan Publishers Limited, registered in England, company number 785998, of Houndmills, Basingstoke, Hampshire RG21 6XS.

Palgrave Macmillan in the US is a division of St Martin's Press LLC, 175 Fifth Avenue, New York, NY 10010.

Palgrave Macmillan is the global academic imprint of the above companies and has companies and representatives throughout the world.

Palgrave® and Macmillan® are registered trademarks in the United States, the United Kingdom, Europe and other countries.

ISBN 978–0–230–29093–8 hardback
ISBN 978–0–230–29094–5 paperback

This book is printed on paper suitable for recycling and made from fully managed and sustained forest sources. Logging, pulping and manufacturing processes are expected to conform to the environmental regulations of the country of origin.

A catalogue record for this book is available from the British Library.

A catalog record for this book is available from the Library of Congress.

10 9 8 7 6 5 4 3 2 1
21 20 19 18 17 16 15 14 13 12

Printed and bound in Great Britain by
CPI Antony Rowe, Chippenham and Eastbourne

Contents

List of Tables and Figures   vii

Preface: Social Democracy in Our Times   viii

Acknowledgements   ix

Notes on Contributors   x

Part I Introduction

Building the Good Society   3
Henning Meyer and Jonathan Rutherford

Part II Social Democracy in Europe

1 Social Democratic Trajectories in Modern Europe: One or Many Families?   13
Stefan Berger

2 The Europeanization of Social Democracy: Politics without Policy and Policy without Politics   27
James Sloam and Isabelle Hertner

3 The Preconditions of Social Europe and the Tasks of Social Democracy   39
Stefan Collignon

Part III A New Political Economy

4 A Decent Capitalism for a Good Society   57
Sebastian Dullien, Hansjörg Herr and Christian Kellermann

5 As Much Market as Possible; as Much State as Necessary   74
Colin Crouch

Part IV Re-Framing Social Democracy

6 The New Language of Social Democracy   93
Elisabeth Wehling and George Lakoff

7 Social Democracy and Trade Unions *Dimitris Tsarouhas*	107
8 The Greatest Happiness Principle: An Imperative for Social Democracy? *Christian Kroll*	120

Part V Political Futures

9 Dispossession *Jonathan Rutherford*	137
10 The Challenge of European Social Democracy: Communitarianism and Cosmopolitanism United *Henning Meyer*	152
11 Not without a Future *Jenny Andersson*	166
12 The National in the Network Society: UK Uncut, the English Defence League and the Challenge for Social Democracy *Ben Little and Deborah Grayson*	177

Part VI Conclusion

The Way Ahead *Henning Meyer and Jonathan Rutherford*	195
Appendix: Building the Good Society – The Project of the Democratic Left	198
Bibliography	209
Index	224

Tables and Figures

Tables

8.1　Comparison of prominent approaches to quality of life　　124

Figures

8.1　Life satisfaction across Europe (European Social Survey data)　　129
8.2　Subjective well-being after 1990 in Romania by income decile (1 = poorest, 10 = richest)　　130
8.3　Objective well-being (material need) and subjective well-being (psychological need)　　131

Preface

Social Democracy in Our Times

We first met in 2008, in Berlin, at the beginning of what became the biggest economic crisis in 80 years. In spring 2009 we launched our declaration, Building the Good Society, which started a debate about new ways to achieve social democracy in Europe after the crisis. After a series of Europe-wide seminars and conferences, now we have an academic book that is developing what we began. The Good Society project has been an extraordinary achievement. The essays here explore the depth and range of the changes to our economies and societies over the last three decades. They issue a challenge to us, as politicians, to re-connect with our values and the people. They begin to formulate a new kind of politics for European social democracy. The great strength of Building the Good Society has been the give and take between politicians and academics. This project has developed in the best of our traditions of bringing together theory and practice.

Social democracy across Europe is in grave difficulty, but it is precisely during this time of political crisis that we look beyond a narrow concept of state, market and society. Our declaration, Building the Good Society, which you can read at the end of this book, begins a new period in the fortunes of European social democracy. We hope that it will continue to be read and debated widely, and that in this dialogue a new movement for democracy and the good society will grow. There is a long road ahead, but we will travel it together.

Andrea Nahles and Jon Cruddas, MP

Acknowledgements

This book is part of a larger political project, which we have called Building the Good Society, and there are too many people involved in it for it to be possible to name and thank them all. But thank you to the original group, which met in Berlin in the winter of 2008 and began the project, in particular Gavin Hayes, General Secretary of Compass, and Thorben Albrecht, who at the time was running Andrea Nahles' office. It was Andrea Nahles and Neal Lawson, from Compass, who first met and agreed that the SPD and Labour needed to create a new relationship, out of which a pan-European dialogue could grow. Karl-Heinz Spiegel, who directs the London office of the Friedrich-Ebert-Stiftung (FES), made this happen. A special thank you goes to Karl-Heinz, whose generosity, political good sense and organizational skills are greatly appreciated by those who know him and work with him. And also thank you to Jeannette Ladzik, the project manager of the FES London Office, who organized the conferences and seminars. It is the daily work behind the scenes that keeps everything going and out of which this book arose.

Notes on Contributors

Jenny Andersson is a CNRS research fellow at the Center for International Studies, Sciences Po, Paris, and an associate professor at the Swedish Institute for Futures Studies, Stockholm. Most recently she has authored *The Library and the Workshop: Social Democracy and Capitalism in an Age of Knowledge* (2009), andersson@ceri-sciences-po.org.

Stefan Berger is Professor of Modern German and Comparative European History at the University of Manchester, where he also acts as Director of the Manchester Jean-Monnet Centre of Excellence. He has published widely in the field of comparative labour history, the history of historiography, historical theory, nationalism and national identity. His most recent book publications are *Friendly Enemies: Britain and the GDR, 1949–1990* (with Norman LaPorte, 2010); *Nationalizing the Past: Historians as Nation-Builders in Europe* (with Chris Lorenz, 2010); and *Kaliningrad in Europa: Nachbarschaftliche Perspektiven nach dem Ende des Kalten Krieges* (2010).

Stefan Collignon is Professor of Political Economy and the founder of the Euro Asia Forum at Sant'Anna School of Advanced Studies, Pisa. He is International Chief Economist at the Centro Europa Ricerche, Roma, and served as Deputy Director General for Europe in the Federal Ministry of Finance in Berlin in 1999–2000. He is the author of numerous books on monetary economics and on the political economy of regional integration.

Colin Crouch is Professor of Governance and Public Management at the Business School of Warwick University. He is also an external scientific member of the Max-Planck-Institute for the Study of Societies at Cologne. Previously he taught sociology at the London School of Economics, was Fellow and Tutor in Politics at Trinity College, Oxford, and was Professor of Sociology at the University of Oxford. He is a Fellow of the British Academy and of the Academy of Social Sciences, and a founding member of Compass. He has published within the fields of comparative European sociology and industrial relations, on economic sociology and on contemporary issues in British and European politics. His latest book is *The Strange Non-Death of Neoliberalism* (2011).

Sebastian Dullien is Professor of International Economics in Berlin. Previously he was economics correspondent at the *Financial Times Deutschland* and worked at the United Nations Conference on Trade and Development.

Deborah Grayson is a professional activist and writer. She is currently co-writing a book about drug harms with David Nutt, former chief scientist on the UK's Advisory Council on the Misuse of Drugs, and she works for the Yes to Fairer Votes campaign. She was previously an organizer for Climate Rush, The Spartans, and The Cuts Won't Work, and she is a member of the False Economy working group. She also directs opera.

Hansjörg Herr is Professor of Supranational Integration at Berlin School of Economics. He is the author of one of Germany's leading textbooks in economics, *Volkswirtschaftslehre: Paradigmenorientierte Einführung in die Mikro- und Makroökonomie* (2002).

Isabelle Hertner is Lecturer in European Studies and German at King's College, London. She is currently completing her PhD at Royal Holloway, University of London. Her research interests include the Europeanization of national parties; party organizational change; and the role of Europarties in European legislative politics. Before coming to the UK, Isabelle completed her MA at the College of Europe (Bruges) and worked in Brussels for a German welfare non-governmental organization.

Christian Kellermann is Director of the Nordic Office of the Friedrich-Ebert-Stiftung (FES) in Stockholm. Before joining the FES he worked as a financial market analyst in Frankfurt and New York.

Christian Kroll is a visiting scholar at the Harvard Kennedy School of Government whilst completing his PhD at the London School of Economics. His research focuses on quality of life, happiness and social capital. He also contributes to the current debate around the measurement of progress and well-being beyond gross domestic product and acts as consultant to various stakeholders on these issues. Previously he worked at the United Nations Headquarters in New York, in the budget committee of the German Parliament and at the Friedrich-Ebert-Stiftung in Madagascar.

George Lakoff is Richard and Rhoda Goldman Distinguished Professor of Cognitive Science and Linguistics at the University of California, Berkeley. He is the author of the influential book *Moral Politics: How Liberals and Conservatives Think* (1996) and of the *New York Times* bestseller *Don't Think of an Elephant!* (2004), in addition to books on cognitive science, linguistics, philosophy, mathematics and poetics. His research centres on cognitive linguistics, especially the neural theory of language and the application of cognitive linguistics to political discourse.

Ben Little is Lecturer in Media and Cultural Studies at Middlesex University. He writes for, and is on the editorial board of, *Soundings Journal*, and he is editor of the ebook *Radical Future Politics for the Next Generation* (2010) and of an online debate for the journal. He also co-founded the discussion forum Left-Over Lunches and writes about the relationship between politics and comic books.

Henning Meyer is Senior Visiting Fellow at the Government Department, the London School of Economics, and co-founder and editor of the *Social Europe Journal*. He holds an MA in British and European politics and government, a PhD in comparative politics and an executive MBA. Previously he was head of the European programme at the Global Policy Institute in London and Visiting Fellow at the School for Industrial and Labor Relations at Cornell University.

Jonathan Rutherford is Professor of Cultural Studies at Middlesex University. He is editor of *Soundings Journal* (www.soundings.org.uk).

James Sloam is Senior Lecturer in Politics and co-director of the Centre for European Politics in the Department of Politics and International Relations, Royal Holloway, University of London. He has published widely in the fields of political parties, German politics and youth participation in democracy.

Dimitris Tsarouhas is Assistant Professor at the Department of International Relations, Bilkent University. He is the author of *Social Democracy* *in Sweden* (2008) and of numerous articles on European politics. His main research interests include European social democracy, comparative European politics and social policy.

Elisabeth Wehling studied sociology, journalism and linguistics in Hamburg, Rome and Berkeley. In 2007 she joined the PhD programme of the Linguistics Department at the University of California, Berkeley. Her research emphasizes political language and cognition in Germany, Europe and the US, as well as the role of gesture in political discourse. She is co-author, with George Lakoff, of *Auf leisen Sohlen ins Gehirn. Politische Sprache und ihre heimliche Macht* (2007).

Part I
Introduction

Building the Good Society
Henning Meyer and Jonathan Rutherford

This book is both academic and political in its making. It represents a larger process of reconfiguring and renewing European social democracy. Both of us were part of a group of people who met in Berlin in the winter of 2008. The meeting had been organized by Karl-Heinz Spiegel of the London office of the Friedrich-Ebert-Stiftung and Neal Lawson the chair of Compass the pressure group and part of the British Labour Party. Leading the initiative were two rising political stars: Andrea Nahles who was then the elected Vice-President of the SPD and Jon Cruddas Labour member of parliament (MP) for Dagenham and Rainham. Cruddas had established himself as a politician of national significance during the 2007 campaign for the deputy leadership of the Labour Party.

The purpose of the meeting was to explore the prospects of a new alliance between the SPD and Labour that would revitalize a failing European social democracy and would make a break from a decade of Third Way politics. In June 1999 Tony Blair, prime minister of Britain, and Gerhard Schroeder, chancellor of Germany, had published a joint declaration of European social democracy. Their statement brought together the ideas of the British Third Way and of the German *Neue Mitte*. Blair and Schroeder wrote that their model of social democracy had found widespread acceptance: 'Social democrats are in government in almost all the countries of the union.' By the time of our meeting in Berlin the situation was entirely different and social democracy was losing elections across Europe.

The task we set ourselves in Berlin was to write, collectively, a new joint declaration of European social democracy and to publish it on the anniversary of the Blair–Schroeder statement. It was published in April 2009, under the joint authorship of Andrea Nahles and Jon Cruddas. Its title signalled a major shift towards a politics that placed democracy and society before the market and before the state.

In the press release announcing publication we said:

> We have a vision of the good society and a more egalitarian economy that will create a secure, green and fair future. But to achieve it capitalism must now become accountable to democracy; and democracy will need to be renewed and deepened so that it is fit for the task. A good society cannot be built from the top down, but can only come from a movement made by and for the people. Creating the good society will be the greatest challenge of our time and it will shape the lives of generations to come.

In January 2010, Compass and the Friedrich-Ebert-Stiftung hosted a London conference: 'Building the Good Society – A European Perspective'. The event brought together social democrats from 19 countries to debate the new declaration and to establish a pan-European network to build a movement for change. Preceding the event, *Soundings* journal and *Social Europe Journal* ran the first pan-European online debate on the future of European social democracy. The wide-ranging discussion lasted for seven weeks and included 80 leading thinkers, politicians and activists. It gave shape to the parameters of future debate. Following the 2010 conference, there have been a further series of workshops in Sweden, Turkey, Germany and England. The book has grown out of this activity. Many of its contributors were involved both in the online debate and in the conferences and workshops.

As the book nears completion, the situation is arguably much worse for European social democracy. In the German federal election of November 2009 the SPD's support collapsed to a catastrophic 23 per cent. Labour narrowly avoided a similar collapse in the 2010 general election, after managing 29 per cent of the vote – its worst election result since 1918. In the same year, in the Swedish general election, the social democrats registered their worst result since 1911. Britain, Germany, Sweden, Holland, Italy and France form the collective home of European social democracy. They are currently all governed by centre right parties. As former Labour foreign secretary, David Miliband said: 'Left parties are losing elections more comprehensively than ever before.' Change is essential. But the question for social democracy is: What kind of change?

We begin with Stefan Berger's history of social democracy in Europe. Stefan identifies what appeared to be a social democratic renaissance in the second half of the 1990s, associated with the 'unlikely contestant of the British Labour Party setting the agenda'. As we now know, the renaissance was short-lived and social democrats found themselves with little to counter the advances of neo-liberalism. Their parties were reduced to representing brittle coalitions of public sector workers, the poor and the liberal middle classes. James Sloam and Isabelle Hertner add substance and detail to Stefan's history by focusing on some of the organizational and political structures of the EU. They argue that, as Social Democratic Parties have sought to reconfigure themselves at a European level, they have become disconnected from their supporters and voters, who remain distant from the Europeanization process. James and Isabelle write that the ideal of a 'social Europe' can be the unifying theme that revives European social democracy and re-connects it to its national voters.

Stefan Collignon takes up the cause of social Europe and sets out the political and philosophical pre-conditions for its realization. His chapter is an example of the central importance of political economy in the formation of European social democracy. The revival of its fortunes will not come about through a series of new policy initiatives, but it will require the excavation of social democracy's founding values in order to build new foundations. On these foundations social democracy can reconstruct itself for a Europe which will 'belong to all of us'.

Stefan's discussion of money leads into Part II of the book, on political economy. At the heart of the crisis of European social democracy is the absence of a viable alternative to the neo-classical economic theories that have dominated the last three decades and provided intellectual legitimacy for the neo-liberal model of capitalism. Globalization and the influence of the Third Way led to the uncritical embrace of markets and corporate-driven globalization and to a fundamental shift away from Keynesian economics. Now, with neo-classical theories discredited and the neo-liberal model a ruinous disaster, social democracy is bereft of a political economy. Sebastian Dullien, Hansjörg Herr and Christian Kellermann begin to remedy this situation in their chapter 'A Decent Capitalism for a Good Society'. They remind us that, for a long period, social democracy did not have anything to say about the contemporary model of capitalism. Its ideologues and politicians talked about markets and globalization, but they steadfastly avoided any analysis of the dynamic of capital accumulation, of the drive downward to the bottom line and of the tendency to corporate monopoly. Nothing captured the ultimate problems of New Labour more than its naïvety around financial capital.

In our first meeting in Berlin, we English and Germans tentatively explored out differences and sought out a common ground. The discussion began to sag a little. Would we begin to talk in circles, thinking in tandem but not together? The pivotal moment came when the question of capitalism was introduced. Let's talk about the capitalism we all live in, and let's try and understand what it has done to our societies and how it has transformed the fortunes of the left in Europe. We had a conversation. As the authors of *A Decent Capitalism* say, capitalism is back on Main Street. Its attempts to commodify money, labour and nature fundamentally fail, and they cause great damage to people and society in the process. Markets need clear rules, clear tasks and clear limits if they are to provide the basis for the development of the good society.

Colin Crouch focuses on the central problem of modern capitalism – not so much the market or the state, but unaccountable corporate power. The decades of neo-liberal dominance did not deliver the perfect competition and self-regulating markets of its fantasies. It created monopoly and an economic system that increasingly evaded democratic accountability. As Colin argues, the consequence of an economy dominated by giant global corporations has been 'a rise in overall inequalities of wealth and income in advanced societies, reversing a longer-term trend in market economies towards reduced inequalities'. What is needed in order to begin to reverse the trend is the invigorating power of civil society. Colin quotes J. K. Galbraith's call for groups of 'employees, consumers, savers and shareholders' to exert a balancing power against corporate might. Imperfect maybe, relying on the power of the powerless certainly – but, as Willy Brandt, said we must dare more democracy.

Who dares might win, but current senior social democratic politicians are not renowned for taking risks. They have proved to be tentative about embracing new ideas, wary of changing direction, and lacking in inspiring leadership. They err on the side of caution, calculating the electoral arithmetic, the future always only a few weeks ahead, the task of the next tactic that will secure today's political advantage. That now has to change. Across Europe, Social Democratic Parties are going to have to create structures and spaces within their party organizations that unleash a transformational intellectual and political dynamism. They will need new words that create a different vocabulary of social democracy, networks that link parties with social movements, and new ways of organizing in communities and workplaces.

We begin Part IV of our book with Elisabeth Wehling and George Lakoff arguing for a new language for social democracy. Their reasoning is straightforward. Political success does not lie in trying to argue better than one's opponent. It comes from fundamentally reframing the terms of the debate and arguing differently. They cite the simple example of how left politicians fail to break with the right's negative language of tax. 'Phrases they use when talking about taxes – such as "tax burden", "tax relief" and "tax refugees" – reflect this moral reasoning, and more: they evoke it in the listener's mind'. As a case study, they examine Labour's 2010 election campaign.

Nowhere has the negative language of the right attracted more than in the trade union movement. Dimitris Tsarouhas begins his chapter with the question: 'Are trade unions still relevant for social democracy?' He reminds us that social democracy grew out of the working class struggle to create trade unions and that this is an extraordinary question to be asking. But in the last few decades, as Social Democratic Parties shifted to the right, they disengaged themselves from the labour movement. Dimitris argues that 'the Third Way fallacy of excluding the unions from the attempt to build a progressive alliance betrays a dangerous neglect of the labour movement's foundations as well as a disregard for the practical realities of the labour market. A good society needs a strong trade union movement.'

If Dimitris' chapter is less about re-framing the argument in favour of unions than about reminding people of their essential role, then Christian Kroll's chapter on happiness pushes social democracy towards the new language of well-being. For the last century, gross domestic product (GDP) has guided politicians in their search for a better society. But it is not a good compass if we wish to create a good society. As Christian points out, GDP as a metric may actively promote the wrong decisions, such as allowing the financial sector to pursue short-term profit. Christian's alternative is to find ways of measuring quality of life by using subjective indicators of well-being. Asking people how they perceive their living conditions encourages a bottom-up rather than a top-down approach. Their responses allow for a subsequent statistical analysis of what factors correlate with high well-being. The good life is what people define as such, rather than something that is imposed on them.

As we reach Part V of the book, 'Political Futures', we have set out a context for the electoral failures of social democracy, identified the central importance of developing a new political economy for the good society and identified three key strategies for renewal – a new language, a new and different relationship with the trade unions and a new metric by which to measure the value of social democratic policies. In the final section we incorporate these elements into a wider imagining of what political shape the future might take.

Jonathan Rutherford argues that social democracy must return to the local and to people's everyday lives and construct a new politics and language out of people's everyday lives and experience. European societies have changed significantly in the last three decades, and we lack a sociological understanding of the kind of societies we live in. Social democracy has to go back to the people, in order to reconnect with their hopes and fears and thus to rebuild active popular support. Henning Meyer's chapter identifies how the neo-liberal model of capitalism undermined community and compares New Labour's neo-liberal-influenced decisions on the economy with Germany's social model. He addresses one of the central debates in Jonathan's appeal to a more conservative tradition of socialism: the contrasting demands and claims of communitarianism and cosmopolitanism. He argues that social democracy must explore the paradoxes in its traditions in order to evolve a new politics for today.

Jenny Andersson looks to the future not so much as to a glimmer on a distant horizon as to an active presence. The future is defined in our daily lives, and politics gives it expression. Nothing does so more than New Labour. As Jenny writes, '[n]ew Labour embodied this futurity more than any other political movement, constantly geared towards the management of the potential of the people and with the governing of aspirations and hopes of people'. Its emphasis on aspiration and opportunity relocated political content to the future. This progressive politics has, she writes, 'a tremendous paternalism', an authoritarianism that says 'I know what future is best for you and what you are destined to become'. It is, she argues, an 'inherently utilitarian approach to people as becomings of future use'.

This analysis is a devastating moral critique of the progressive politics that overtook Social Democratic Parties. As Jonathan argues, it brought with it a contempt for settled ways of life and a disparaging of the love of country. Those who valued tradition were dismissed as dinosaurs, and those who called upon the radical traditions of socialism were accused of romanticism. Life was to be lived facing the future, in an ever intensifying pursuit of personal gain and self-recognition, as if the project of social democracy had foundered in fear and denial of loss.

The final chapter is a challenge to social democracy to change or to lose political relevance. Ben Little and Deborah Grayson look to the future and see some fundamental changes in the nature of political organizing. Political activism has shifted away from its connection with the party towards networks. And these networks, particularly those associated with identity politics, are beginning to re-constitute the national in politics. Ben and Deborah write that social democracy needs to re-articulate the relationship between the local, the national and the global. It can learn from the way in which social network technologies enable connections between people and things. The cultural shifts around the new digital network technologies offer the potential for a more social and more democratic politics and society. In Part VI of the book, Henning Meyer and Jonathan Rutherford conclude that political power is increasingly being wielded by those who embrace the network logic. But the future belongs to those who are capable of harnessing the energy and innovation of the networks and of reconfiguring them into new institutions with a degree of permanence. Can social democracy achieve this kind of political transformation? Does it have a future as a moral and cultural force for good? Will it recover its historic role as defender of society against the destructive dynamism of capitalism? These are the questions that lie before us, waiting for our answers.

Part II
Social Democracy in Europe

1
Social Democratic Trajectories in Modern Europe: One or Many Families?

Stefan Berger

The social democratic movement in Europe has been a consciously internationalist and transnational movement from its inception. The conceptual confusion around the terms 'social democratic' and 'socialist' indicates at times simple homologies and at times ideological differences. But, from the early socialists of the nineteenth century to Karl Marx and the leading socialists of the nineteenth and twentieth centuries, they were always clear about one thing: they represented the interests of workers and ordinary people everywhere. Hence they also founded Internationals to which socialist movements affiliated. However, such internationalism always co-existed with a very effective nationalization of Social Democratic Parties right across Europe. As political parties organized themselves within national frameworks and sought representation in national parliaments, their 'natural' constituency was made up of national publics (Schwartzmantel, 1991; Sassoon, 1996).

Such nationalization of their organizational activities led to the nationalization of socialist consciousness, which was so impressively underlined by the support of (almost) all Socialist Parties for the war effort of their respective countries at the beginning of the First World War. It is this tension between nationalization and internationalist commitment that has characterized European social democracy from the nineteenth century to the present day, and it will form the backdrop of this brief essay on social democratic trajectories in Europe. How many trajectories were there? As many as there were nationalized Social Democratic Parties? Or can we in fact talk about only one trajectory, taking into account the strong internationalist commitment of social democrats and their self-perception as sharing basic principles and values? I will divide the discussion chronologically into (a) the period before the First World War; (b) the interwar period; and (c) the post-Second World War period; and I will conclude with some brief comments on the situation after the end of the Cold War.

Learning from Germany? The German social democratic model before 1914

Socialist ideas go back to the early nineteenth century, and some short-lived socialist organizations also existed during the first two thirds of the nineteenth century (Lenger 1991; Breuilly, 1994, chap. 3; Pilbeam, 2000). But most of the Social Democratic Parties, as we know many of them today, were in fact founded during the last third of the nineteenth century. The German *Allgemeiner Deutscher Arbeiterverein* (ADAV) was one of the first in 1863, and it led the early historian of social democracy, Gustav Mayer, to talk about the early separation of 'bourgeois' and 'proletarian democracy' in the German lands. In 1875 the ADAV merged with a rival socialist organization to form a united socialist workers' party, which became the forerunner of the contemporary *Sozialdemokratische Partei Deutschlands* (SPD). Many other parties across Europe were founded shortly afterwards: the Danish Social Democratic Federation in 1876; the Czech SDSD in 1878; the French *Section Française de l'Internationale Ouvrière* (SFIO) in 1880; the Dutch *Sociaal Democratische Arbeiders Partij* (SDAP) in 1881; the Belgian *Parti Ouvrier Belge* (POB) in 1885; the Norwegian *Det Norske Arbeiderparti* (DNA) in 1887; the Swiss *Sozialdemokratische Partei der Schweiz* (SPS) in 1888; the Austrian *Sozialistische Partei Österreichs* (SPÖ) in 1889; the Swedish *Socialdemokratiska Arbetarepartiet* (SAP) in 1889; the Bulgarian Social Democratic Workers' Party in 1891; the Italian *Partito Socialista Italiano* (PSI) in 1892; the British Labour Party in 1900; and the Finnish *Suomen Sosialidemokraattinen Puolue* (SDP) in 1903.

In the 1890s and 1900s many of those parties looked towards the German SPD as a model, because it was in those decades that the SPD became organizationally the largest, electorally the most successful and ideologically the most theoretical of all the socialist parties in Europe (Nettl, 1965). Furthermore, it achieved all this after going through a ten-year period of severe repression under the anti-socialist laws between 1879 and 1890. During this time the party was still allowed to stand for elections, but all organizational and propaganda or electoral work was prohibited. Social democratic newspapers and pamphlets could not be published. Thousands of activists were imprisoned, and thousands more had to go into exile. However, electoral support for the SPD grew under the anti-socialist laws and exponentially after it was lifted, so that, by 1912, it was by far the most successful Socialist Party in Europe. Building up a socialist milieu that cared for its members 'from cradle to grave', the SPD founded a large number of ancillary organizations – from kindergardens to youth groups to sports and leisure organizations to burial associations (Berger, 1994, chapter 4).

The SPD was also widely regarded as the leading party within the Second International, which had been founded in 1889. Its very name indicated that it saw itself as a continuation of the International that had existed between 1864 and 1876. Inspired by the Polish uprising of 1863, that First International united organizations that represented between 5 and 8 million members, many of them trade unions rather than political parties. It was characterized by ideological divisions between followers of Bakunin, Proudhon and Marx, all attempting to achieve ideological dominance within the organization. The meetings of the International were characterized by vociferous debates whether to favour mutualism or collectivism and whether to prefer trade unionism or political action. Ultimately it was those divisions that destroyed the First International. Yet the principle of internationalism did not die with it, which is why a new International, explicitly linking its existence to this First International, came into being in 1889. It was, again, characterized by ideological heterogeneity, even after the anarchists were expelled from the organization in the 1890s. After all, the International contained the British Labour Party, for which Karl Kautsky found the famous compromise formula that, although it did not subscribe to socialism, it was actively pursuing the class struggle in Britain. And at the same time it also incorporated Vladimir Ilyitsch Lenin. Despite such big ideological differences, the new International was more successful than its predecessor in uniting people around specific iconic events and campaigns such as May Day, the International Women's Day and the Eight Hour Day campaign (Joll, 1955; Braunthal, 1966–1980; Haupt, 1986).

The prestige of the SPD, including its heroic resistance against the anti-socialist laws and its organizational, electoral and theoretical prominence, gave leading social democrats – such as Karl Kautsky, Eduard Bernstein and Rosa Luxemburg – prominent voices in the councils of the International. However, the model character of the SPD was not undisputed before 1914. The French socialist leader Jean Jaurès was one of the most vociferous intellectuals leading the charge. He accused the SPD of what the labour historian Dieter Groh would later call 'revolutionary attentism' (Groh, 1973). In other words, the SPD preached the revolution, but it did nothing to bring it about. Quite the contrary, it concentrated on building up its organization, and the more beautiful and elaborate the organization became, the less likely the SPD was to risk anything that might endanger its organizational empire. Instead, it became more and more dogmatic in its theorizing and in its demands for ideological superiority in Europe – unable as it was to realize that socialists elsewhere might have different priorities and problems. Jaurès was in fact hinting at different trajectories for different Socialist Parties in Europe, thereby denying the claim of leading German social democrats that it presented the only true model for Socialist Parties (Goldberg, 1962). If the criticism of the SPD started well before 1914, it was the support of the German social democrats for the war effort of the imperial government that led to a deep disillusionment with the SPD elsewhere in Europe. Charges of militarism and Prussianism echoed throughout Europe (e.g. Sanders, 1918).

The struggle against communism and fascism and the attempt to maintain social democratic internationalism in the interwar period

Despite the deep divisions of European social democracy during the First World War, attempts to revive the International started again before the hostilities ended. British social democrats were instrumental in mediating between the French and Belgian comrades on the one hand and the German ones on the other. The first post-war meeting of the International took place in Berne in 1919, but the strong enmities from the war years were difficult to overcome. Hence it took until 1923 before the Labour and Socialist International (LSI) was founded in Hamburg. It was significantly different from the pre-war International in that the LSI no longer aimed at making binding resolutions for all member parties. Instead it explicitly endorsed the political sovereignty of its member countries (Kowalski, 1985).

This was, at least in part, in explicit recognition of diverse trajectories of Social Democratic Parties in Europe. An increasing belief in national exceptionalisms came to characterize the self-understanding of European social democracies. Whether it was the phenomenon of pillarization (*Verzuiling*) in the Netherlands, the tension between early male suffrage and continued repression of the workers' movements in France, the strength of anarchism in Spain, Lib-Labism in Britain or the subversism of the Italian working class – to mention just some prominent examples – the idea that national peculiarities resulted in nationally specific trajectories was strong after 1918. It was, however, not just the idea of nationally specific paths that divided socialists in the interwar period; this was, after all, a phase in which ideological divisions ran deep. On the far left of the pre-war socialist movement, sympathies with the Bolshevik revolution were considerable, and Lenin's theses divided the socialists: some were to join the Communist Third International and began to form Communist Parties in their respective countries of origin. Others were unhappy with the Bolsheviks' ideas of a 'proletarian dictatorship' whilst at the same time being sceptical about the social democrats' moderate post-war stance. They formed the so-called Second-and-a-Half International, which attempted to steer a middle course between social democratic reformism and Bolshevik radicalism. Ultimately, the debate became so dichotomous that this attempt to find a middle ground failed, some joining the Third International, whilst the rest united with the social democratic moderates to form the LSI in 1923 (Wheeler, 1970; Rees and Thorpe, 1998).

Many national social democracies in Europe were engulfed in struggles to combat Communist Parties on their left whilst at the same time battling with extreme right-wing and fascist parties, which rose to prominence in many European countries in the interwar period. Across Europe social democracy became the most prominent defender of liberal democracy, struggling to keep ailing democracies from falling to right-wing governments whilst at the same time defending itself against charges of 'social fascism' from the Communist Parties after 1929. The LSI coordinated attempts to arrive at common policies on vital international issues through the setting up of a number of commissions that formulated standpoints on disarmament, international politics and labour politics. As we can see, there clearly were still common denominators that united social democrats in the interwar period; the transnational networking that had been such an important element of social democratic internationalism from the middle of the nineteenth century onwards continued throughout the interwar period, and indeed it found a high point amongst the circles of exiled social democrats – who all assembled in London and other extra-European centres of exile during the Second World War. Yet, as the debate surrounding the reasons for the success of national socialism amongst German Social Democrats in London shows, national concerns still figured prominently even in a transnational exile community (Horn, 1996; Tombs, 2003; Berger, 2006).

In the 1930s, a new model of a Social Democratic Party began to emerge in Sweden. In 1920, the SAP formed its first ever coalition government, in alliance with the Agrarian Party, which looked after small-scale agricultural interests. From 1932 onwards, over the next 60 years, the SAP was almost continuously the party of the government, initiating a series of reforms that pushed Sweden more in the direction of social equality than any other European society. In Hjalmar Branting it had a charismatic leader, who managed to sell the SAP's programme to the electorate, and in Per Albin Hansson it had an important theorist, who popularized the idea of the Swedish 'people's home' as the basis for a fairer and more just society. As Social Democratic Parties in Norway and Denmark also began to make important advances, the focus of attention of European social democracy began to shift from Germany to Scandinavia between the 1930s and the 1980s (Berman, 1998; Misgeld et al., 1998; Redvaldsen, 2011).

European social democracy during the Cold War

After the end of the Second World War European social democracy had to position itself vis-à-vis the new post-war order, which saw the continent divided into two spheres of influence dominated by the new superpowers – the United States in Western Europe and the Soviet Union in Eastern Europe. Winston Churchill, in his speech of 5 March 1946 at Westminster College, Fulton, Missouri had famously remarked that an iron curtain had come down to divide Europe – with the dividing line running through the defeated Germany. In northern Europe Finland managed to stay on the Western side of that divide, and in the Balkans the Western allies, above all the British, helped to defeat an indigenous communism in a bloody civil war to prevent Greece from falling into the Soviet sphere of influence. Yugoslavia, alone amongst East European Communist countries, managed to stay a course independent of Stalin – largely thanks to the fact that the Red Army did not 'liberate' the country, but that Tito's partisans managed to drive the German occupants out by their own strength. Some social democrats rejected the emerging bipolar world and championed the idea of a 'third way' – a democratic socialist way, which would reject both the dictatorship of the proletariat that the Soviet Union pushed through across Eastern Europe and the ruthless capitalism that they associated with the USA (Eley, 2002, 295–8).

However, by 1947 and 1948 third-way socialists were in a distinct minority everywhere in Western Europe. For reasons of international diplomacy, social democrats in Austria and in Finland stressed the neutrality of their respective countries and were keen to ensure good diplomatic relations with the Soviet Union, but they belonged squarely to the West European social democratic camp. It was the fate of East European social democrats that brought about a greater distancing between West European social democrats and the Soviet Union. Any residual sympathies among left-wing social democrats in Britain, for example, and the erstwhile war-time ally melted away as it became clearer and clearer that Social Democratic Parties in Eastern Europe stood little chance of survival. Their leaders faced the choice of accepting mergers with Communist Parties in which the communists would play the leading role or risking persecution, imprisonment, exile and even death. In his memoirs, the then International Secretary of the Labour Party, Dennis Healey, remembered how depressing it was for Western social democrats to stand by helplessly as independent Social Democratic Parties across Eastern Europe were crushed (Healey, 1988).

The process by which West European social democrats settled into the bipolar world order ensured that, once again, social democrats came to be staunch defenders of political liberal democracy. However, with notable exceptions, they did not come to dominate post-war politics in Western Europe. True, in Scandinavia social democratic parties expanded their power base amongst voters, and in Sweden and Norway they began to implement extensive welfare states and other reforms geared towards producing more equal societies. In the Netherlands, social democrats were in government continuously between 1946 and 1958. In Britain, the Labour Party surprisingly won the elections in 1945 and began to implement a range of important reforms, including the introduction of the National Health Service, which transformed British society. But in Germany the social democrats embarked on long years of being in opposition, which was all the harder as they felt that their resistance to national socialism gave them the moral mandate to shape a post-war Germany. The West German voters, however, did not agree with them. In France it was the figure of de Gaulle that dominated the reconstruction process, and in Italy social democrats were squeezed in-between the dominant Christian democrats and a powerful Communist Party. In the Iberian Peninsula the end of the Second World War did not bring an end to repression and persecution for social democrats, as the right-wing authoritarian dictatorships in Spain and Portugal continued into the 1970s (Berger and Broughton, 1995).

Persecuted in Eastern Europe as well, and unable (with notable exceptions) to put a decisive stamp on many of the West European societies that re-emerged from the ruins of war, social democrats were nevertheless keen to rebuild internationalism for the third time since the collapse of the First International. As after the First World War tensions between social democrats in Germany and in those countries that either had fought against Germany or were occupied by Germany ran high. The uncompromising and undiplomatic stance of the post-war leader of the SPD, Kurt Schumacher, did not help matters. Schumacher had been imprisoned in a concentration camp by the national socialists. As a staunch antifascist, he felt that he was not tainted by national socialism and could therefore speak up for German interests in the post-war world. This, however, did not go down well with many social democrats in other West European countries who felt that Germans should perhaps be more humble after 1945 and less overbearing (Edinger, 1965, 177ff.).

Yet European social democracy did not only have leaders that polarized the centre-left, it also had a number of important bridge-builders. In 1951 the Socialist International was finally founded in Frankfurt/Main. In its early years it was to develop into a platform on which European social democrats discussed the rebuilding of Europe. Mistrustful of the Europe that was being built by Christian democrats and centre-right politicians, social democrats set out a different vision, of a social Europe that was not only about freedom of movement for capital and goods and for the abolition of tariff barriers, but also about the benchmarking of good social policies. However, social democrats did not play an important role in the initial phase of the European Economic Community, and it was only in later decades that they succeeded in making, in the European Union, a set of institutions that paid due attention to social rights (Devin, 1993; Dimitrakopolous, 2011).

The other big issue that dominated post-war social democratic discourse within the International was decolonization. Considerable energies were invested in coming to a common position on this issue, but ultimately all these attempts came to nothing, as the French socialists under Guy Mollet embarked on an extremely violent war in defence of Algeria in the latter part of the 1950s. There were also considerable efforts of European socialists to work together in order to formulate common positions on European integration and European security in the 1950s (Imlay, forthcoming).

In the 1970s, under the chairmanship of Willy Brandt, the International embarked on two major new initiatives. On the one hand, it now actively promoted an engagement with the problems of the developing world. A dialogue between the developed northern hemisphere and the underdeveloped southern hemisphere was to be the first step on the road to greater global equality. On the other hand, it put considerable resources into helping those southern European countries that had emerged from dictatorships in the 1970s, namely Portugal, Spain and Greece. The socialists were ultimately the main beneficiaries of the Portuguese revolution in 1974, and the influence of the International went in the direction of channeling the revolutionary energies into liberal democratic and reformist waters. In Spain the long transition to democracy after Franco's death saw the emergence of the *Partit Socialista de les Illes* (PSI) after many years of repression. However, it was widely feared that the new PSI might be dwarfed in electoral support by the more outspoken and more prominent Communist Party. With the help of the Socialist International (SI), the Spanish socialists under Felipe Gonzales, a protégé and friend of Brandt, managed to outflank the communists, becoming the biggest party on the Spanish left and ultimately a long-standing party of government. And in Greece a similar success story can be told of the Panhellenic Socialist Movement (PASOK) after the generals had paved the way for a transition to liberal democracy (Karvonen and Sundberg, 1991).

Under the conditions of the Cold War, social democratic parties everywhere were shedding their remaining Marxist principles and developed into 'catch-all' or 'people's parties' – attempting to appeal to the electorate beyond their traditional working-class support base. This ideological re-orientation was most successful in Sweden and the wider Scandinavia, but social democrats elsewhere struggled to break into the more middle-class or at least lower middle-class vote (Bartolini, 2007).

In some places such as Germany, social democrats played an influential role in managing industrial crises and de-industrialization in the 1960s and 1970s. Their mixture of Keynesian economics, social plans, tripartism and welfarism allowed them to move towards structural economic reforms, which were planned in the long term and prevented rapid change, with its consequences of impoverishment and migration. The West-German social democratic Chancellor Helmut Schmidt embodied such a pragmatic approach to managing industrial crises. His nickname, 'the fixer' (*der Macher*), symbolized – or evoked the image of – a hands-on, no-nonsense approach to economic reform that still allowed high levels of social security (Carr, 1985). The British Labour Party, by contrast, failed to bring about a similar tripartite consensus, which could have helped to change the image of Britain as the 'sick man of Europe' throughout the 1970s. The best hope for such change was Barbara Castle's 1969 White Paper 'In Place of Strife', which was, however, comprehensively rejected by a self-confident trade union movement that thought it could defend working-class interests without any interference from politics. In the 1980s Margaret Thatcher was to demonstrate how wrong they were (Dorey, 1995; Tomlinson, 2009).

The 1980s was a decade of deep crisis for European social democracy. Its key beliefs, including in a powerful role of the state for setting macro-economic frameworks for the development of the economy, in social engineering to produce a more equitable society, and in welfare statism all came under sustained criticism from a neo-liberal, neo-conservative right that seemed to sweep everything before it. What is more, social democracy was challenged from the left too, by a host of new social movements and green parties that positioned themselves to its left on issues such as disarmament and the environment. As de-industrialization accelerated, social democracy's working-class electoral base shrunk more and more, and in many places the social democrats struggled to gain support among other groups of the population. The collapse of communism in Eastern Europe at the end of the decade on the one hand finally ended the long-standing rivalry between social democratic and communist trajectories in the labour movement: the social democrats could feel vindicated by these developments. On the other hand, capitalism lost its main rival, and some voices now proclaimed triumphantly 'the end of history', in other words the victory of liberal capitalism over all forms of communism/socialism (Fukuyama, 1992). The existence of the communist threat in Eastern Europe had facilitated the creation of a social democratic welfare consensus in Western Europe during the Cold War (Hobsbawm, 1994, Part 2). Would the absence of communism allow the neo-liberals to unravel the social democratic achievements even more quickly than during the 1990s? There were many reasons for social democrats to be wary of the post-Cold War world.

Quo vadis, social democracy? What role do social democrats play in a post-industrial and post-Cold War world?

The collapse of communism in Eastern Europe marked a wider crisis of Communist Parties, which also affected Western Europe. In Spain and France, communist mass parties once powerful declined further in importance, whilst the flagship party of Euro-communism, the Italian PCI, split into a more hardline orthodox party (*Rifondazione*) and a more moderate Party of Democratic Socialism that was, to all intents and purposes, a Social Democratic Party. For many years until then, PCI leaders had more cordial relations with the Socialist International than with the Communist Third International. The disappearance of the Italian socialists under a cloud of corruption (*tangentopoli*, 'bribesville') in the early 1990s helped the reformation of the social democratic milieu in Italy (Bull and Heywood, 1994).

In some parts of Eastern Europe social democratic parties emerged in opposition to the ruling Communist Parties. Thus, for example, the SPD was refounded in the German Democratic Republic (GDR) in 1989 by dissident groups, in the middle of the terminal crisis of the *Sozialistische Einheitspartei Deutschlands* (SED) regime. In other parts of Eastern Europe the ruling Communist Parties transformed themselves into Social Democratic Parties seeking to shed their dictatorial and authoritarian pasts and moving to more democratic forms of self-understanding. Overall, the landscape of Social Democratic Parties in Eastern Europe remains extremely diverse: the social democrats can be found in the vanguard of liberal economic policies in some places, whilst elsewhere they are engaged in more traditional Cold War social democratic policies. In Germany the successor party of the Communist East German SED, the Party of Democratic Socialism (PDS; now *Die Linke*), occupied positions to the left of the SPD, which had great affinities to social democratic positions as they had existed between the 1950s and 1980s – with their distinct commitment to social welfare, macro-economic policies and social engineering (Fülberth, 2009).

Given the manifold differences between Social Democratic Parties in contemporary Europe, to what extent was it still possible to talk about a social democratic milieu in the post-Cold War world? The dominant neo-liberalism of the 1980s celebrated a major triumph with the fall of communism. The deregulation of markets continued throughout the 1990s and 2000s, and flagship social democratic governments, in particular the Labour Party governments in Britain between 1997 and 2010, even increased the liberal deregulation of markets. It was only the massive financial crisis after 2008 that put a question mark behind the wisdom of such deregulation and brought demands for more control. However, so far, few commentators have come up with feasible ideas about how global financial markets can be regulated in the absence of any effective forms of global governance (for some suggestions, see Griffith-Jones et al., 2010).

The electoral fortunes of Social Democratic Parties since the end of the Cold War were mixed. If some commentators had foreseen the terminal decline of Social Democratic Parties, they were proven wrong: the second half of the 1990s witnessed what appeared to be a social democratic renaissance across Europe. In 2000 Social Democratic Parties found themselves in government in all but four West European countries; but there was very little agreement as to what a new social democratic project might amount to. Were social democrats only to manage neo-liberalism better than their rivals? There was renewed interest in debates surrounding ideas, the unlikely contestant of the British Labour Party setting the agenda. Tony Blair's 'third way' generated a lot of interest, as did Anthony Giddens' ideas, which were closely associated with 'New Labour'. A 'stakeholder society' was to overcome the traditional welfare orientation of social democratic parties and activate civil societies, in an endeavour to overcome state dependencies. Although the German Chancellor Gerhard Schröder and his close political ally Bodo Hombach sought to introduce something similar with their notion of *Neue Mitte*, the social democratic rank and file remained at best sceptical of such British redefinitions of social democracy, whilst the socialists in France were far more hostile to any 'third way' ideas (Giddens, 2001).

However, the renaissance was not to last either, and Social Democratic Parties found themselves back in opposition in most European countries as the first decade of the twenty-first century drew to a close. Even in that flagship social democratic country of Europe, in Sweden, the conservatives are finding themselves in government since 2010, as increasing numbers of Swedes turn their back on the egalitarian social democratic model. European social democracy was rooted in the attempt to overcome the glaring inequalities produced by nineteenth-century capitalism. During the twentieth century, social democracy learnt to live with a capitalism that held out the promise of social reform and equality of opportunities. In the German SPD and in the Swedish SAP it produced political parties that had, for much of the time between the 1890s and the 1980s, a model function for other Social Democratic Parties. But at the beginning of the twenty-first century there seems to be no model, no ideological or organizational distinctiveness, and no easily identifiable constituency. Given the wide variety of Social Democratic Parties in the post-Cold War world, it has become questionable, for the first time in more than one hundred years, whether it is still meaningful to talk about an European social democracy (Moschonas, 2002).

Conclusion: One family or many?

In the birds-eye, long-term historical perspective provided here, we have emphasized the cohesiveness of the social democratic model over much of modern European history. Most Social Democratic Parties came into being during the last third of the nineteenth century, and most were staunchly anti-capitalist. Marxism was an important, but by no means the only ideological influence. As political parties, they sought representation, on behalf of the working classes, in national, regional and local parliaments, and, as parliamentarians, their members worked hard to improve the social, economic and political conditions in their respective nation states. They built formidable organizations, which amounted to more than mere electoral machines but frequently described a way of life. Before 1914 the German SPD was an organizational and ideological model for many other Social Democratic Parties in Europe.

In the interwar period European social democrats were amongst the staunchest defenders of democracy against both communism and fascism. They sought to redefine liberal democracy by adding a social and welfare dimension to it and by introducing the concept of economic democracy, which was to transform the unfettered version of capitalism in the interest of the many. Swedish social democracy came to stand for this new reformist path to socialism, and it went furthest in transforming Swedish society in this image. The commitment to internationalism from the second half of the nineteenth century right through to the present day indicates that social democrats in Europe (and, later on, well beyond the European borders) were seeing themselves very much as members of one political family.

After the Second World War, most European social democracies abandoned their self-styled nineteenth-century commitment to the emancipation of the working classes. Instead, their attempts to maximize their electoral returns have led them to develop profiles as 'people's parties' or 'catch-all parties' that sought to gain support from an increasingly diffuse middle class. As people increasingly defined themselves through their purchasing power, as consumers, rather than through their workplaces, the rhetoric of class gave way to the language of equal opportunities and fairness. But this was a language that was by no means exclusive to Social Democratic Parties. Christian democrats and popular conservatives as well as various Liberal Parties came to share the same linguistic terrain, as political parties increasingly crowded together at the centre of politics, where elections were won.

If it was increasingly difficult to define Social Democratic Parties via their social constituency, they also became ideologically more and more indistinct. Towards the end of the nineteenth century many social democrats were, at least in theory, committed to revolutionary Marxism. In practice, most Social Democratic Parties were reformist already by the interwar period. The rivalry with revolutionary communism after 1917 heightened the commitment to the parliamentary road to socialism.

However, socialism – understood as the transformation of capitalism – still remained the end goal of most Social Democratic Parties. This began to change in the Cold War world, in which more and more social democracies became content to aim for capitalism with a human face. In some respects, social democrats claimed that they could manage capitalism better and produce a fairer, more equal society through social engineering, the control of markets and welfare policies.

As this social democratic managerialism was thrown into crisis by the advances of neo-liberalism in the 1980s, social democrats had little to counter it with. Pressed by various social movements on their left and by neo-liberal parties on their right, they increasingly came to represent marginal constituencies of the poor and underprivileged. They bounded back for a while in the late 1990s and early 2000s, but they failed to reformulate a convincing and lasting social democratic vision for the future. The lowest common denominator that unites social democratic parties in Europe today is their commitment to democracy and to social solidarity; and, if they can renew their century-old vision of a socially just and democratic society, they might still have a chance, in Europe, to form a transnational political force that transcends national differences and forms one political family.

2
The Europeanization of Social Democracy: Politics without Policy and Policy without Politics

James Sloam and Isabelle Hertner

Social Democratic Parties in Europe have suffered at the polls in recent years. The disastrous performance of the German Social Democratic Party (SPD) in the 2009 German federal election inspired a raft of political commentary, from *Der Spiegel* to the British *Financial Times*, which speculated about the 'end of social democracy'.[1] For some, the eventual defeat of the British Labour Party in May 2010 further supported this hypothesis.[2] The failure of Social Democratic Parties in national elections was replicated by their poor performance in the 2009 European Parliament election. Although social democracy is certainly in decline when compared to the highpoint it reached in 2000, when centre-left parties were in power in 12 out of the then 15 European Union (EU) member states, this dire narrative is exaggerated, because it ignores the cyclical nature of party politics (Paterson and Sloam, 2010). Between 1993 and 1997 social democrats were in opposition in the EU 'big three' (France, Germany, and the UK) (Merkel, 1992), and since the formation of the conservative/liberal democrat government in the UK in May 2010 we are back in the same situation. Today we should therefore talk of the retreat rather than the defeat of European social democracy, and certainly not about its end. A more interesting fact is that mainstream Conservative and Christian Democrat Parties have not profited very much from the decline in fortunes of their main competitors – indeed, voters have turned away in droves from 'catch-all parties' of left *and* right (Paterson and Sloam, 2010). Nevertheless, recent economic, political and social trends have proved particularly problematic for the centre-left across Europe.

Numerous authors have pointed out that European integration over the past three decades – resulting primarily from the Single European

Act and the Treaty on European Union – has been one of the main drivers of change in public policy (van der Hoek, 2005) and in party politics (Mair, 2008). The centrality of the EU for all its member states has been illustrated vividly by the ongoing debt and credit crisis in the Eurozone. In this context, it is crucial to explore the extent to which the Europeanization of social democracy has been part of the solution and/or part of the problem.

This chapter will examine the impact of European integration on Social Democratic Parties and social democratic policy, the gradual development of a transnational 'Europarty' at EU level and the promotion of the idea of a 'social Europe'. We first investigate the constraints provided by the EU in terms of changing polity, politics and policies: in particular, the completion of the Single Market (deregulation and the reduction of state subsidies within the Internal Market) has reduced the scope for traditional demand-side policy. Despite the increasing importance of the EU polity and increasing penetration of EU policies, the development of EU-level politics has been a slow process. This has led to a dysfunctional situation where we increasingly have 'politics without policy' at the national level and 'policy without politics' at the EU level (Schmidt, 2006; Mair, 2008). In response to common challenges – secular, European and international in nature and origin – efforts have been made to reconfigure social democracy on the European plane. In the second part of this chapter we turn to changes within social democracy itself – in terms of pan-European organization and policies. We then provide an in-depth investigation into the extent to which social democratic *politics* has been *Europeanized* in the light of the 2009 European Parliament election and of the debate around a social Europe. Despite the increasing importance of the European Union for Social Democratic Parties, there remains a dangerous disconnection between politics and policy in a multi-level polity.

Social democracy and European integration

If the European centre-left is in retreat and this is not entirely due to the electoral cycle, what are the reasons for the recent decline of Social Democratic Parties? Our argument is that – in many ways – the European Union is both part of the problem and part of the solution. Following Vivien Schmidt (2006) and Peter Mair (2008), deeper European integration has made it more difficult for national political parties to satisfy their voters when they come to power. Of course, the demands on public spending are not only European in their origin. Perhaps the two primary causes for the current debt crisis are common demographic challenges

(European Commission, 2008) – the costs of ageing societies for public services and the costs of the welfare state – and the need for austerity across Europe in the aftermath of the global financial crisis (due to the cost of saving the banking industry from collapse and to the ensuing recession) (OECD, 2010). However, EU competition policy has limited the extent to which national governments can subsidize national industries and services; the Single Market (without a common economic policy) has led to competition amongst national governments to reduce their tax base (to attract investment and jobs); and – in the light of the ongoing debt crisis in the Eurozone – the public spending constraints of the European Growth and Stability Pact will be significantly tightened (European Commission, 2010a, 2010b).

Taken together, these factors lead to a situation where there are less resources to distribute and deregulation becomes the default option; and this situation, in turn, prompts an identity crisis for social democrats (who have traditionally committed themselves to greater levels of public spending and social protection than their centre-right rivals). For Social Democratic Parties in particular, the reduced steering capacity of national governments has therefore resulted in 'politics without policy'. The consequences have been damaging. Social Democratic Parties often cannot deliver what they promise, which leads to an increasingly dysfunctional relationship with the electorate. Centre-left parties have found it difficult to adapt and have tended to follow one of two paths: (1) the path of revisionism, illustrated by the New Labour project in the UK (Shaw, 2008); or (2) the path of populism, marked by a large gap between rhetoric and reality on issues to do with public spending (especially in the current economic climate) – this approach is typical of the *Parti Socialiste* (Socialist Party) in France (Wagner, 2008).

Parallel to these developments, social democratic parties have been struggling for some time to maintain support in the context of social change. Given the individualization of values (Inglehart and Welzel, 2005), lifestyles (Giddens, 1991) and risks (Beck, 1992) in recent decades, the 'big tent' strategy for social democrats has become unclear. Initially, the shrinkage in size of the blue-collar working class was met with efforts to build support amongst (and an electoral alliance between) public sector workers and the less well-off (Padgett and Paterson, 1991). This attempt is no longer so viable. Whilst the centre-right can – as its default position – claim to be a better manager of capitalism, what is left for the left? (Paterson and Sloam, 2006).

As the EU has become more important and social democratic policies have become more difficult to achieve at the national level, Social Democratic Parties have sought to reconfigure themselves at the EU level (see below). But European party structures and EU policy initiatives have mostly been developed out of functional necessity. There has been little effort to embed these changes amongst voters and supporters, who remain distant from the Europeanization process. The reason for this attitude is quite understandable. Politics still takes place at the national level – European Parliament elections, and even referenda on the EU, are largely fought out on often unrelated national issues (Schlesinger, 1999; Garry et al., 2005; Hobolt and Brouard, 2010). Thus the Europeanization of Social Democratic Parties is somewhat covert and indirect, removed from social democratic supporters and sympathizers, and it results in 'policy without politics' at EU level.

One can see the increasing activity of Social Democratic Parties at the EU level as a work in progress. Indeed (as explained below), the establishment of pan-European party structures is a very recent phenomenon (Hix, 2002). Once a Social Democratic Europarty starts to deliver (which would result in social democratic policies in the EU), it could be argued that a more political character will emerge with supporters who recognize the importance of EU policy and with a demos that can better appreciate the interrelated nature of the EU (and hence can begin to develop a sense of pan-European solidarity and social justice). However, the ideal of a social Europe is difficult to achieve in practice, given the different starting points, different policy trajectories and different political cultures involved (Paterson and Sloam, 2005; see below). Social Democratic Parties are also faced with the practical problem that 'positive integration' (agreement on specific social policy measures/regulations pertaining to the Internal Market) is even more difficult to achieve than 'negative integration' (simply taking barriers away), given the numerous veto-players that exist within the EU's multi-layered and multi-faceted policy formation process (Scharpf, 1999). Therefore any initiatives towards social democratic policy are likely to be small and incremental rather than radical and dramatic, and they are unlikely to capture the public imagination.

In this sense, Social Democratic Parties are trapped in a vicious cycle. We argue that they must operate a dual strategy in order to break this cycle. First, they must, in Willy Brandt's words, 'dare more democracy', open up party structures and actively mobilize sympathizers and supporters at grass roots level. All these actions have been attempted by Social Democratic Parties in the past, often successfully, and they are also on the agenda today – from Labour leader Ed Miliband's promise to engage in 'a million conversations' to reconnect the British Labour Party to a disillusioned public to the promise of German Social Democratic

Party chairman Sigmar Gabriel (2010) to engage more widely with party sympathizers. Second, they must be more explicit and open in their aims to achieve social democratic policies at the European level within the context of economic globalization; solidarity at the European level can only be achieved if citizens understand that we face common external challenges.

Social democracy at the European level

In this section we will look at the reorganization of social democracy from a European perspective. We emphasize the lack of politics at EU level and the programmatic heterogeneity of Social Democratic Parties, features that – together with the existence of formal institutional barriers – prevent the emergence of a strong party government.

Whilst member states of the European Union suffer from having politics without policy, the EU makes policy without politics, as policies are made without the kind of debate along a left-right divide normally found at the national level. Schmidt (2006, 158) writes:

> EU politics is not really politics in any traditional sense of party and partisanship, since it is mainly about interests, whether the national interests projected by the member-states in the Council of Ministers, the European Council, and the IGC [Intergovernmental Conference]; the public interests defended by national representatives in the EP [European Parliament]; or the organized interests mediated by European Commission officials as well as, increasingly, by members of the EP.

Partisan politics is marginalized at European level because 'Europarties' are still relatively weak organizations. A Europarty can be defined as an institutionalized form of party organization at the EU level that has seen a partial transfer of sovereignty from national member parties (Johansson and Zervakis, 2002). However, the question of whether Europarties are political parties in the traditional sense is highly controversial. In the past parties have only existed at the domestic level, where they fulfil specific roles: vote-seeking, office-seeking and policy-seeking. Some scholars argue that Europarties cannot be regarded as parties in the traditional sense but as loose coalitions of national parties (Marsh and Norris, 1997). After all, vote-seeking is one of the goals of parties alongside office- and policy seeking. In the past, Europarties were not seen as vote-seeking because European elections did not designate an executive at EU level (Lightfoot, 2005, 7). Others believe that Europarties need to be interpreted within the context of the EU (Hix, 1993; Ladrech, 1993). Although linked to the European Parliamentary groups, the Europarties are distinct entities that exist to fulfil a different kind of role (Day and Shaw, 2006, 99). The Party of European Socialists (PES), which brings together the Socialist, Social Democratic and Labour Parties of the EU, was founded in 1992 following the Treaty on European Union and the formal recognition of political parties at a European level in Article 191 of the Treaty. It succeeded the Confederation of Socialist Parties of the European Community, which had been set up in 1974.[3]

Over the years, and due to constitutional change and enhanced financial regulation, the PES and the other Europarties have become more relevant actors at EU level (Johansson and Raunio, 2005). They now receive funding from the general EU budget, which means that the European Parliament is free to increase the money for Europarties without Council approval (Lightfoot, 2006, 307). The clarification of their financial status had an important impact on the activities of Europarties and on their internal organization. The regulatory requirement for Europarties to obtain a legal basis in a member state meant that they had to move into an office outside the European Parliament buildings and could no longer 'borrow' staff from the parliamentary group. All Europarties now have a permanent salaried staff, and this break with the European Parliament has significantly increased the number of professional party workers – all the staff currently working for the PES have only been employed since the adoption of the regulation (Lightfoot, 2006, 307). In 2007 the rules were further amended, and a crucial aspect has been clarified: Europarties can use the money from the EP budget to fund their electoral campaigns.

Yet we need to keep in mind that, despite the strengthening of their role, Europarties still do not form a European government. For the European election of 2009, due to internal divisions, the PES could not even decide on a common candidate for the presidency of the European Commission (EC). In the resolution of its party congress in December 2009 ('A new way forward, a stronger PES') the PES has committed itself to choose a common candidate for the European Commission presidency for future European elections. This could raise the European profile of future campaigns and politicize and personalize the debate.

Moreover, some developments have taken place with regards to individual membership. In the past, linkages between the PES and European citizens have been very weak (Day, 2005). However, in 2006 the PES introduced the 'PES activists' initiative as some kind of individual membership. Every member of a PES member party is automatically a PES activist, but he or she needs to register online with the PES. During the 2009 European elections, PES activists across the EU have led grassroots campaigns. Unsurprisingly, not all member parties have welcomed this development. For example, whilst the French Socialist Party has openly embraced the PES activists, the British Labour Party and the German Social Democrats were indifferent, or even sceptical. Hence the 'fear of capture' (Day and Shaw, 2006) of the national parties by the Europarties still needs to be figured out.

We can hence summarize that, due to constitutional recognition and financial regulation, the PES has become a more important actor at EU level. Nevertheless, there is still a lack of politics at European level that prevents social democracy from becoming a strong force.

To begin with, social democracy can only be a powerful force at European level if it is in government. After a honeymoon phase dating from the end of the 1990s until the early 2000s, the situation has changed fundamentally. In 2010 only five out of the 27 member states of the EU were represented by a social democrat in the European Council. Moreover, Social Democratic Parties in the EP lost nominally 2.3 per cent of the popular vote between 2004 and 2009, down to just 25 per cent of the vote, which translated into 184 seats (out of 736). The largest party was the centre-right European People's Party (EPP), at 36 per cent (265 seats). However, it has to be kept in mind that the 2009 European elections also showed decline for Conservative (−0.6 per cent) and Liberal Parties (−0.6 per cent), whilst nationalistic and populist parties gained votes. In this power constellation, the left can hardly set the political agenda.

Yet is has been argued that, even in government, Social Democratic Parties do not implement change at European level, as the phase between 1997 and the early 2000s has shown. During that period, social democracy underwent programmatic and policy renewal: it opened up to feminist ideas, minority rights and the protection of the environment and adopted a more positive stance towards European integration (Moschonas, 2009, 168). Moreover, most European social democrats came to recognize the need for modernizing the welfare state, for pursuing active policies to reduce unemployment, for maintaining budgetary stability and (to varying degrees) for increasing the role of the private sector (Paterson and Sloam, 2006, p. 234). However, at European level, during the late 1990s the success of social democracy can at best be described as 'modest' (Ladrech, 2003, 117). The single most notable success was the Employment Chapter in the Amsterdam Treaty.

It established employment as one of the goals of the EU in a high-profile manner. Promoting employment is henceforth one of the objectives of the EU and becomes a 'matter of common concern' for the member states (Article 2 of the EC Treaty). The new objective was to achieve 'a high level of employment' without weakening the competitiveness of the EU (Article 2 of the EU Treaty).

The final Employment Chapter was a compromise and has been described as 'Blairite' more than continental social democratic, because of its absence of any tough interventionist powers for the EU (Ladrech, 2003, 119). Apart from the Employment Chapter, European social democrats had no common programme for economic regulation at EU level; the economic strategies of the 12 socialist governments were too heterogeneous for effective coordination (Moschonas, 2009, 178). Yet, as stated earlier, changes in policy at European level are slow and incremental. Politics tends to be more consensual, and some of the policies introduced during the past decade (in areas such as equal opportunities and employment) are social democratic in nature – even if they have not been decided by a social democratic majority at EU level and social democrats alone cannot take credit for them. Furthermore, a large part of the EU's spending focuses on maintaining economic cohesion by financially supporting poorer regions through the Structural Funds. We also need to keep in mind that social democracy is a heterogeneous movement across Europe. This heterogeneity is reflected in the current discourse on 'social Europe'.

The debate around 'social Europe'

Although Social Democratic Parties are members of the PES and their voting behaviour in the EP is increasingly coherent (Hix et al., 2005), their policies at national level continue to differ considerably. This, in turn, makes it difficult to speak with one voice at European level and lead common European elections campaigns.

The debate around 'social Europe' is a good example of the heterogeneity of European social democracy. To be sure, 'social Europe' is a rather vague phrase and a precise definition does not exist. The phrase includes more than the classic notion of social policy. For example, the European Commission's social Europe campaign includes issues such as EU-wide social security, healthcare, gender quality, the promotion of jobs and workers' mobility. Part of the challenge in defining 'social Europe' is, of course, that national welfare states and social policies differ across the EU (Majone, 1996). The Maastricht Treaty had failed to establish a social dimension to its policies. However, Jacques Delors, President of the European Commission, also had social policy in mind when he wrote of economic co-ordination as one of the pillars of the Economic and Monetary Union. He elaborated this idea in the so-called 'Delors White Paper' on 'Growth, Competitiveness and Employment' in 1993 (Sloam, 2005, 130). Yet the failure to achieve deeper integration in economic and social policy formed the basis of Social Democratic Parties' criticism of Maastricht for the years to come. Today, 'social Europe' is still on the political agenda of European social democracy. During the 2004 European election campaign, certain socialist leaders – such as Poul Nyrup Rasmussen, head of the PES, and Antonio Guterres, then president of the Socialist International – used 'social Europe' as a slogan (Moschonas, 2009, 179). It has been chosen by the PES because of its diffuse meaning.

For the 2009 European election campaign, the SPD's motto was 'social Europe'. However, the SPD's credibility as the supporter of a social Europe had suffered in the past years. In government between 1998 and 2005, the SPD under Gerhard Schröder's pragmatic chancellorship was very hesitant about supporting social legislation at EU level, which caused major rifts with the French Socialist Party (Wielgoß, 2002, 74–112). In 2009, when the SPD was the junior partner in a grand coalition with the Christian democrats, selling 'social Europe' to the voters was no easy task: the SPD had lost many of its core voters due to labour market and pension system reforms under 'Agenda 2010'. Hence 'social Europe' did not dominate the SPD's election campaign in 2009. The French socialists, on the other hand, embraced not only the slogan but also the PES' common election manifesto. After all, since the 1970s, the Parti Socialiste (PS) has been one of the most ardent advocates of social legislation at EU level, although the Jospin government (1997–2002) took a more pragmatic approach than many socialist activists had hoped (Wielgoß, 2002).

Institutional obstacles for European social democracy

Yet the problem might be rooted more deeply: not only has the weakness of the Europarties and the programmatic diversity between national Social Democratic Parties made collective action at EU level difficult, but the EU's political system itself is challenging for political parties – be it national or European-level ones. Moschonas (2009, 169) argues that the political system of the EU operates as an obstacle to the 're-social democratisation of social democracy's programmatic options'. From his point of view, the EU is a fragmented system of powers where decisions derive from negotiations between the European Commission, the Council of Ministers and the Parliament, 'none of which manages to monopolize the leadership functions' (Magnette, 2005, 65, quoted by Moschonas, 2009, 170). At European level, the system of party government does not exist. In the absence of a European parliamentarian or presidential system, and also in the absence of partisan competition for the executive, Europarties exert neither the function of government nor the function of political representation. Even though political parties are firmly rooted in national political institutions, their influence at EU level is reduced through the competition between the different power centres, national and European. No partisan family simultaneously controls national governments, the European Council, the Commission and the Parliament. Hence the European macro-system is without a party coordinator. Moschonas argues that, while the EU poses a 'role' problem for each and every party family, the problem is more pronounced for social democracy. Moschonas (2009, 173) echoes Scharpf's (1999) explanation of the difficulties of implementing 'positive integration' in a federal context with many veto-players: 'Control of the market and capitalism', he posits, 'has always required both a strong central authority and a strong political force capable of pursuing policies that are different from the market's.' In short, Social Democratic Parties aim to correct or change the dominant economic paradigm and are therefore more in need of strong institutional and societal resources, which the EU does not offer.

As no central public authority exists, it is not easy for transnational social democracy to manage European governance – as the social democratic period at the end of the 1990s demonstrates. The EU, being a profoundly 'conservative' system, 'protects' the units (the states) that make it up and does not easily revisit institutional and political decisions it has taken (Moschonas, 2009, 173). In this political context, where change is, at best, slow and gradual and politics tends to be rather consensual, social democrats often take 'refuge in rhetoric', as the slogan 'social Europe' demonstrates. However, despite the challenging institutional make-up of the EU, a more social Europe is not out of reach for Social Democratic Parties. Radical policy change in the EU is hardly possible and the implementation of social democratic policy (especially within the current climate of budgetary austerity) is highly unlikely. Yet the context of economic interdependency (highlighted by the Eurozone debt crisis and the bailouts of member states of the

Eurozone) and of the global financial crisis may just provide the spur for social democratic consolidation in the EU. In times of austerity for budgets, when centre-right governments cut enormous amounts of public spending (as the conservative/liberal democrat government in the UK does), social democracy might become successful again. But it needs to offer credible alternatives to the voters.

Conclusion

In this chapter we have argued that the end of social democracy is not even close. The recent economic, political and social trends have proved problematic for the left, and there is no doubt that Social Democratic Parties have suffered at the polls in recent years. European integration, which can be perceived as an opportunity no less than as a challenge for social democracy, reduces the scope for social democratic policy-making at national level. At the European level, where a large amount of policies are decided, there is still no party government in the way in which there is one in national politics. Moreover, social democracy being a heterogeneous movement across Europe, it remains difficult to create a strong common narrative – as the debate around social Europe has pointed out. Nevertheless, European social democracy's future might not be as gloomy as predicted.

We have demonstrated that the emerging Europarties are still relatively weak actors in a system that does not (yet) allow for confrontational party politics. Yet some promising developments have taken place. The PES is a much stronger actor today than it was at the beginning of the 1990s. Social Democratic Parties have taken an increasing interest in influencing EU policies (even if this has been a frustrating process, and one in which national interest has often trumped common social democratic values). However, institutional change at EU level is always slow and incremental, and the PES and other Europarties are undergoing significant change. We argue that Social Democratic Parties must simultaneously become more local and more European: more local in order to engage broadly with supporters and sympathizers, who might more realistically see the fruits of their engagement at this lower level; and more European in order to achieve, at the European level, social democratic policies that have become more difficult and costly to implement at the level of the individual member state. Although this dual strategy might seem idealistic (given the poor recent electoral performance of Social Democratic Parties), the current climate of budgetary austerity and of current public focus on the global economy in the light of the recent financial crisis might just provide a window of opportunity for this strategy to succeed.

Notes

1. This phrase was originally used by Ralf Dahrendorf (1990) to interpret the poor electoral performance of Social Democratic Parties in the 1980s.
2. For a useful commentary on the electoral decline of European social democracy in 2008 and 2009, see Engels and Mass (2009).
3. For an overview of the PES' historical background, see Hix and Lesse (2002).

3
The Preconditions of Social Europe and the Tasks of Social Democracy

Stefan Collignon

European social democracy is in a crisis. Everyone feels it, electoral results prove it. Policy makers are torn between improving economic efficiency and correcting social injustices, between liberalizing European markets and reforming the national welfare state. But their dilemma is not programmatic. It results from the changed environment in which they operate and from a state-centred ideology that cannot cope with this change.

Social democrats have come to accept the market as the superior engine of wealth creation; they seek power, however, in the democratic state in order to turn it into a modern welfare state. Democracy is the key to the social democratic project, for it allows affirming the common good of society against the partial interests of market agents. This democratic tradition goes back at least over 100 years, when Eduard Bernstein pointed to the growing contradictions between revolutionary discourses and democratic practices and opted for the latter: 'Democracy is both a means and an end. It is a weapon in the struggle for socialism, and it is the form in which socialism will be realized' (1993 [1899], 142).

Social democracy became successful in the second half of the twentieth century, when it combined political and social struggles with Keynesianism and thereby showed that it could integrate partial interests with policies that improved general well-being. All that changed after 1973, when Bretton Woods collapsed. Lack of exchange rate management and huge international capital flows after the oil price shocks generated volatility and uncertainty in financial markets. Nation states lost control over the economy. Steering the macro-economy became increasingly difficult for small state governments (which includes all European states), and the social democratic model lost its lustre and legitimacy.

Faute de mieux, social democrats have joined the neoliberal bandwagon. Voters soon felt betrayed. The good society of 'equal citizenship, solidarity, social mobility, trust and strong community' seemed 'undermined and destroyed by an elitist, pseudo-cosmopolitan concept of the good society, built around neoliberal globalization, European Unification, permanent welfare state reform, ill managed mass migration, the rise of individualism and a knowledge-based meritocracy' (Cuperus, 2010). This perception of social democracy mixes facts with fiction, modern values with reactionary discourses. It misses the reasons and effects of the profound transformation that has followed globalization and Europeanization.

To understand the change, we need first to analyse the role of money in markets and then to look at the relation of money, markets and the democratic state. We then discuss the transformation of this system under the influence of European integration and globalization and conclude with some policy proposals. Finally, the title for this chapter was chosen to recall Bernstein's (1899) famous book, because, now as then, social democracy is torn between an outdated discourse and its commitment to democracy.

Money, the commanding heights of capitalism

Like so many times before, the 2008 global crisis was a crisis of financial capitalism. The collapse of the international monetary system of Bretton Woods in 1973 was also a financial crisis that led to the creation of the European Monetary Union, in an attempt to protect Europe's social model against financial instability.[1] Yet, many social democrats ignore that the European Monetary Union has transformed the role of the nation state not only as a guarantor of welfare but also as a political instrument for constructing the good society and a social Europe.

Part of the problem is the focus placed on the 'real economy' to the detriment of the 'parasitic financial sphere', because it prevents drawing the necessary policy conclusions from monetary union. This way of thinking has a long tradition in economics, from Smith to Marx and to the follies of modern neoclassical monetarism. For these economists, money only has value for what it can buy; it covers the utilities of goods like a veil. Financial assets are simply forms of representation that stand for something 'real'. And yet it is money that makes the world go round; it is money that allocates resources to their use. In short, money rules the economy.

Money is a social institution, which, like all institutions, depends on rules and *norms* that are collectively accepted and followed, even if individuals occasionally deviate in their behaviour (Searle, 1995). Such norms structure economic and political life and exist in a broad consensus, which emerges from the exchange of information, from discussions and debates and from listening to each other. A modern approach to social democracy must therefore critically question the norms that structure social reality and must inquire into how they become consensual.

The construction of a new social reality requires that political and economic norms are mutually consistent. Transformative strategies must redefine what the 'good society' is. But what is 'good', or morally acceptable, cannot be separated from the ways public debates are conducted in society; and these debates are structured by institutions and by their normative backgrounds. What people believe to be good in society is necessarily different in a market society – where individuals are used to making contracts as free and equal agents – from what they believe to be good in a *hierarchical society, where they are assigned a position* without choice. Insofar as money is created by financial contracts, it generates the moral economy of capitalism.[2]

John Maynard Keynes understood that money was not a veil over the real economy. For him, money was a means of payment, the asset that extinguishes debt contracts.[3] The exchange of goods often takes place over time, and this implies that people make promises and contracts about the delivery of goods and payment. While the notion of a contract can be stated simply to refer to an agreement between free and equal individuals, this conception of contractual relations has two important implications. The first is that contracts may be broken and promises not kept. Social relations in a market economy are therefore a source of uncertainty, and, to reduce uncertainty, society needs the rule of law, which guarantees the enforceability of contracts and the rights of individuals. Thus the modern market economy could not exist without strong institutions that regulate markets.

The second implication of the money-as-means-of-payment paradigm is that it allows us to understand the nature of property as the result of contracts, and this has consequences for the social democratic concept of social justice. Property has always been a key concept in socialist thought. Classical economics, starting with John Locke and ending with Karl Marx – but also the neoclassical property rights school, which has inspired neoliberal ideologies – treat property as possession. Possession means the right 'to do anything to anybody, and to possess and enjoy whatever [one] wanted and could get'.[4] Because economic agents exchange goods according to their relative utilities, *having control* over resources must be the essence of property. Thus, according to this paradigm, money has no role other than facilitating the circulation of possessions. However, in a capitalist economy, property is more than possession. When individuals make contracts, the control of resources is delayed until the promise is kept. A *promise to get access to possession* in the future generates a *claim* for the owner and an obligation for the possessor. This is not the same as *having possessions* and *controlling* their use. This claim is a property *title* and, if it is publicly recognized, it gives *rights* of ownership that emerge from contracts between free and equal partners. For Keynes, money was liquidity, which had the great advantage of *giving access* to possession by terminating the obligation of a property claim – that is, a liability – in financial contracts. Capital is nothing but a legally recognized property claim of this sort. Thus, because modern money is the liability of the banking system, it is generated by money and credit.

This reading of capital is different from Marx's approach, which has influenced socialists for a long time. By adopting the classical exchange paradigm, Marxist economists confounded the *claim* to possession with possession itself and thought that capital was identical with private property. For them, controlling the means of production was possession of resources. This view structured their concept of social justice. Expropriating the means of production simply meant grabbing resources and redistributing them so as to support those in need. Such redistribution may be justified by the norms of traditional society, where people barely survive at the subsistence level and 'big men' have the right to take and redistribute resources to ensure the community's survival (Scott, 1977). In modern societies, by contrast, where *rights of individuals* – whether private or collective – are the foundation of justice, expropriation is a violation of the normative system. The Marxist concept of justice ('from each, according to his ability; to each, according to his needs') contradicts the norms of a modern monetary society, which is based on contracts. Justice has to become *fairness*, as John Rawls (2001) has shown, and his is the best articulation of the modern social democratic concept of justice to this day. One must hasten to add, however, that it is not enough to establish the moral norms of fairness, which is the task of philosophers; it is necessary in addition to ensure that these norms acquire generalized consensus, and this is best facilitated by democracy.

In addition to creating its own normativity and sense of justice, money also generates an economic logic, which has turned capitalism into the most dynamic social system in human history. Understanding the mechanism behind this economic dynamism is important, because it has not only created more wealth than ever before and transported the modern values of freedom and equality across the globe, but money has also generated social inequalities that stand in flagrant contradiction with the monetary economy's own norms. When socialists treated property as possession, they had to explain capitalism by the motive of greed. However, Keynes' theory of liquidity preference explains the double-faced dynamics of capitalism by the interest claim in financial contracts: contracts set the norm of freedom and equality; interest claims in financial contracts propagate them in an ever-growing economy. Interest claims are justified because lenders need to be compensated for giving up the advantage of the liquid possession of money. The price for money is the interest rate. If uncertainty is high, the liquidity premium will also be high, and, unless lenders are paid this compensation, they will not make loans. Because money is needed to get access to resources and financial markets provide money through loans to firms, finance directs the allocation of resources. This is why financial markets represent the commanding heights of capitalism. But servicing the cost of credit and capital requires that borrowers generate income and profit commensurate with the degree of uncertainty in the economy. If the expected profits were higher, the demand for credit would increase; if they were lower, no loans would be made. Thus the profit motive is an incentive for entrepreneurship, but in the long run the system is ruled by financial decisions made in capital markets.

The surplus required to service the debt is produced by using real resources, especially labour. Marx' genius was to describe the logic by which the surplus is generated; his failing was that he did not see how liquidity preference and the interest for money determine the equilibrium for the capitalist economy. Keynes provided the tools to understand financial markets and money – and thereby transformed the way social democrats could conduct economic policies. Keynesianism was attractive for social democrats, because it taught that, if they managed the economy correctly, the market could be a source of prosperity and could augment the margins for income redistribution.

Nevertheless, in recent years we have come to see that, in a world with scarce resources, this system also poses problems for the sustainability of the planet's environment. The capitalist economy expands the monetization of real resources. If these resources are limited, the expansion must stop at one point. There are two ways in which this can happen. Either the interest rate goes to zero, which means that uncertainty becomes economically insignificant, or the ecological catastrophe throws the world into a crisis where the accumulation of capital goes into reverse. The first case describes a soft landing in socialism, the second the more likely scenario of a world in permanent crisis.

The policy implications for social democrats are clear: they must build a society that minimizes uncertainty, reduces economic shocks and reassures citizens that their future is secure. In short, they must pursue policies that are the opposite of neoliberalism. And they can only do this in a democracy, where citizens charge governments to put their preferences into practice.

The economic foundations of democracy

Because financial contracts are the foundation of the monetary economy, capitalism has a normative content, which distinguishes it from hierarchical economies. Contracts are concluded between individuals, who are free to say *yes* or *no*; and this freedom constitutes the equality between autonomous individuals. By contrast, in hierarchical societies economic relations are based on possessions and the allocation of resources is made by hierarchy. The daily practice of concluding contracts in market transactions generates the common knowledge that freedom and equality are the valid and dominant norms in a modern society.[5] Social democracy stands on this normative foundation. It recognizes citizens as free, equal and endowed with the right to choose their government jointly; and this makes it possible to think of justice as fairness. As Bernstein (1993 [1899], 141) already insisted: 'the concept of democracy includes an idea of justice, that is, equality of rights for all members of the community, and it sets limits to the rule of majority'. Without this sense of justice as fairness, free and equal citizens would not accept to be ruled by any government.

One hundred and fifty years ago, social democracy started out with the claim that freedom cannot exist without equality. This claim is still true. However, the validity of norms is one thing; the harshness of facts is another. Marx correctly described the mechanism through which capital is accumulated by those who have property. Unless it is counterbalanced by a government acting in the interest of all citizens, the capitalist system will inevitably make the rich richer and the poor relatively poorer (although not necessarily in absolute terms). Social democrats therefore sought to conquer power through the democratic state in order to re-establish material equality. In this they were opposed by liberals, who consider that governments interfere with liberty. Yet liberalism and socialism are, both, children of the modern market society, although they assign different importance to equality. For liberals, equality is a purely formal matter of rights; for social democrats, equality must be material insofar material living conditions determine the (in)equality of opportunities. The recognition of these *twins of modernity* may still offend some socialists – just as Bernstein (1993 [1899], 147) shocked the social democrats when he wrote, a century ago:

> a certain measure of restraint is to be recommended in describing war on 'liberalism'. It is indeed true that the great liberal movement of modern times has, in the first instance, benefited the capitalist bourgeoisie, and that the parties which took the name of Liberal were, or became in time, nothing but straight forward defenders of capitalism. There can, of course, be nothing but enmity between these parties and Social Democracy. But with respect to liberalism as a historic movement, socialism is its legitimate heir, not only chronologically, but intellectually.

Then as now, liberals and social democrats have stood at the forefront of progress, accepting the democratic state as a guarantor for individual freedom, while authoritarian conservatives have used the state to suppress liberty. However, being on the same side of progress does not mean that there is no deep ideological divide between liberals and social democrats. Liberals defend the formal equality of universal suffrage, while social democrats build the welfare state to realize material equality and equal opportunity. Liberals reject the interference of government and see the state as a rule enforcer for the system; socialists refuse the acceptance of material inequality and construct the welfare state to secure fairness. Both camps have derived their claims from the concept of free and equal citizens, but they give different weights to these values. Both these values are directly opposed to the conservative idea of the authoritarian state, which is based on order and hierarchy and the subordination of citizens to the authority of the state.

The focus on citizens is important, not only because welfare is necessarily a personal experience and the good society is there for individuals, but also because it defines the locus of sovereignty in modern states. Sovereignty is the power to set the ground-rules in a given society, and those who can do so legitimately are called 'the sovereign' (Collignon, 2003, 63). In pre-democratic states, this power was vested in the ruler; since the French and American Revolutions, the sovereign is the people, meaning all citizens together. As owners of the common good, citizens have a right to choose the direction of policies that affect them all. Without this shift to popular sovereignty and democracy, social democracy could never have accomplished the gradual construction of the modern welfare state. The power of universal suffrage is such that even conservative and liberal governments had to agree to legislation that strengthened the equality of citizens.

Put differently, the democratic concept of sovereignty says that citizens are the principal, governments are their agents. Hence neither governments nor states are sovereign; instead governments are the trustee of people, appointed for a limited period of time. Such a democratic concept of sovereignty has very far-reaching consequences for the modern understanding of the state. In the authoritarian state, individuals are subjects that 'belong' to the state, to which they must obey. They have to surrender their personal welfare to the imperatives of the community. After the French Revolution, this holistic concept was transferred to the idea of 'nation' to which individuals 'belonged', so that the nation state could again claim sovereignty over its citizens. By contrast, the theory of the republican democratic state considers free and equal citizens as owners of public goods who assume responsibility for the society they live in.

This republican idea has inspired many social democrats, from Lassalle to Jean Jaurès to Carlo Schmid.[6] Associating citizens to the public good is what socialism is all about.[7] The republican state focuses on the service, namely the public goods, which it must provide to citizens. These services are the *res publica*, which all citizens share. If we look at the state as the provider of public services and at government as the agent that manages these services, the issue of government is no longer one of 'belonging' to the state or nation, but one of 'being concerned' and affected by policies. Citizens are sovereign; governments, as service providers, fulfil their function as agents of the owners of public goods. Consequently, if the public goods have become European, European citizens need a government to sustain them. Thus a denationalized government is crucial for understanding the role of government for social democrats in the European Union.

Social Europe's precondition: An economic government

Although European unification has always been a political project of making lasting peace, it has really been driven by market integration. The single market has generated economies of scale, higher productivity and improved competitiveness in global markets, and it has strengthened Europe's capacity to survive the globalization shock. Unfortunately, the transformation of the European economy has not only created winners, but also losers. The old dilemmas of capitalism and social justice have re-appeared at the European scale, and this poses new problems for the legitimacy of the European Union and the practice of social democracy. The re-distribution of wealth is no longer simply an issue for states taxing the rich and giving to the poor. It now involves transnational solidarity.

In the early stages, European integration was about achieving synergies, positive sum games and win–win situations that justified the transfer of policy competences to European institutions. The benefits generated incentives for nation states to cooperate voluntarily, because everyone was potentially better off and losers could be compensated out of the net gains from integration. For example, Germany was willing to pay for the expensive agricultural subsidies to French farmers, because the common market eliminated barriers for German industry. However, only national governments could distribute the welfare gains through social transfers within the nation state.

With the creation of the single market and the common currency, the incentives of win–win situations can no longer be taken for granted, although they have not totally disappeared. Money makes a difference. The logic of voluntary coordination still works well in many 'old' policy areas like foreign trade, common agricultural policy, competition policy, and so on. However, with the euro, a whole new range of European public goods, called *common resource goods*, has emerged. The Maastricht Treaty gave the European Central Bank (ECB) the primary objective of maintaining price stability, and this implies that money is kept scarce; but the stability of the financial system requires that all banks in the Euro Area have unrestricted access to liquidity. This makes the euro a common resource good. As a consequence, all economic agents who need money in advance of making purchases have become subject to the same hard budget constraint, regardless of whether they are private or public, firms or consumers, investors or wage earners, so that the currency area has become the integrated unit for economic policy making. Economically, the Euro Area is the country; politically the situation is, of course, different, and this diverging perception is at the root of the present euro crisis and of the disappointing performance of Europe's economic governance.

While Europe's economy is integrated by markets and money, its politics is causing havoc. This is because common resource goods follow the logic of zero-sum gains. This makes redistributing benefits and compensating the losers much harder, and national governments are more easily tempted to free-ride on their colleagues than to cooperate. Voluntary policy cooperation between governments will no longer work because the gains obtained in one country inevitably imply disadvantages for others, and each member state will seek to reap the benefits and to avoid the costs. This often lamented 'national egoism' systematically undermines the welfare-enhancing capabilities of the Union. As a consequence, the so-called *output legitimacy*, whereby people consent to European policies because these improve their welfare, is losing its force. Europe's social model, the welfare state, is increasingly under threat, because distributive justice is framed in reference to states and not to citizens.

The recent debt crisis is an example of the uncooperative logic that emerges from common resource goods. Because money is scarce, excess borrowing by one government requires excess savings by another – otherwise interest rates shoot up and damage grows. Governments have therefore an incentive for free-riding. They seek to restrict the borrowing of their partners while increasing their own deficits. Not surprisingly, most member states have regularly violated the Stability and Growth Pact over the last ten years.

The dynamics of zero-sum games could be overcome by some form of loyalty of solidarity. Albert Hirschman (1970) has famously shown how societies can live with a certain amount of dysfunctional misbehaviour, provided that discontent can be 'voiced' and will be heeded to. Otherwise 'exit' or expulsion will follow. The bridge between voice and exit is loyalty. Hirschman describes 'loyalty' as a force that avoids 'exit' and strengthens 'voice', provided that (1) members are willing to trade off the certainty of exit against the uncertainties of an improved situation; and (2) they estimate that they have a reasonable ability to influence outcomes. These are precisely the conditions necessary for solidarity within the EU. They are essential for keeping the European Union alive, but they require institutional mechanisms for making sure that the people's voice has influence. However, the intergovernmental system of voluntary policy coordination between governments prevents the emergence of solidarity. Loyalty requires that citizens are able to influence a government that responds to their voices, preferences and complaints. The present political organization of the EU does not allow for the emergence of European solidarity because democracy takes place in the nation state and citizens' voices are directed at national governments that negotiate compromises among themselves in the European Council. The resultant policy consensus among elites is the opposite of citizens having influence over policy outcomes. There are hardly pan-European debates that give citizens a voice, because citizens cannot choose a European government.

To overcome the inconsistencies in a macro-economic government, socialists have repeatedly demanded an economic government. The idea was blocked by neoliberals and conservatives, who did not want to be constrained by regulations and could play the 'national card' in order to prevent market interference from European institutions. Hence neoliberal and conservative ideologies are preventing European solidarity from emerging. Conservatives argue that a European democracy is not possible because the degree of solidarity among Europeans is insufficient. But the conservative idea of solidarity is different from Hirschman's concept of loyalty through interest representation. Conservatives see loyalty as obedience to the state, because citizens 'belong' to their nation. They derive solidarity from the feeling of 'national identity' and conclude that governments have the paternalistic duty to maximize benefits for their subjects. This form of governance produces precisely the incoherence of policy actions that undermines the legitimacy of European integration. It allows member state governments to oppose a 'Transfer Union' and larger European budgets or a delegation of power to the European Commission on nationalist 'us'-against-'them' arguments, so that they can neglect income redistribution between winners and losers in the European market. If social democrats adopt these arguments and do not insist that in a democracy all citizens are the owners of public goods, irrespective of their identities, they fall into the conservative trap. A social Europe needs a European government that represents the sovereignty of all citizens.

Social democracy's task: A democratic Europe

A century ago, Bernstein argued that there are two preconditions of socialism: a certain level of capitalist development and the seizure of political power in government. The preconditions for a social Europe are more complex. The level of economic integration has effectively attained a degree where an economic government becomes a necessity for further advances in welfare. But, without a European government, there is no power to seize. If social democrats think they can seize power by winning a majority in the European Council, they are mistaken, as the painful experience of the Lisbon Strategy has proven (see Collignon, 2008). Thus, a precondition for a social Europe must be the creation of a European democracy. Only then can socialists struggle to seize power.

Two tasks need to be combined in order to construct a European democracy. The first is finding a principle for defining governmental competences at the European level. The simple answer is: the reach of a government is determined by the reach of public goods. For example, local public goods are only consumed by local communities; national goods by nations. European public goods affect all citizens in the European Union. Thus using the same currency turns interest rates, inflation and fiscal policy into European public goods. Because these public goods define the dimension of a good society, citizens must be able to appoint a government that administers them *on behalf of the citizens by whom it is elected* (see also Habermas, 2001, 65). National governments cannot legitimately make laws for people who have not elected them; nor should a European government make policies that do not affect all European citizens collectively. The right to appoint a government only makes sense if its competences coincide with the constituency that appoints it. Hence, the first principle is that a European government must be responsible for those public goods, and only for those, that affect all Europeans collectively.

The second task is to ensure that citizens can control the European government. One may argue that member state governments are the democratic organ for democracy in Europe. But this is a category mistake. By definition, *national* governments cannot represent all *European* citizens. They are elected on the basis of policy proposals that amalgamate national and European policy dimensions. Voters can choose between these packages, but they cannot distinguish between their national and European interests. Because the national dimension is dominant, the decisions are also dominated by national concerns, and this makes it impossible for citizens to choose between alternative policies at the EU level. As a result, citizens often feel that governments do what they want and that their own preferences are ignored.

The European Union does not have a government that people can change. Karl Popper (1996, 124) distinguished two types of governments: democratic regimes, where people can get rid of their governments through general elections; and those, which he called 'tyranny', where that is not the case. Europe's governance system introduces a strong portion of tyranny into European politics, because citizens cannot remove the intergovernmental consensus in the European Council that rules them. They can, of course, revoke their national government – which is the 1/27th part of the ruling power, and never a majority – but this is hardly the same as 'one man, one vote' in general elections. Who would call 'democratic' a system that only allows by-elections but never calls general elections? If European policies are not to be seen as 'tyrannical' and undemocratic, citizens and not national governments must elect a European government.

One may object that, in their national contexts, voters also have to accept policies they did not like, because their own preferred policies remain in a minority and they themselves cannot design policies without political parties. Yet the essential difference between democracy in nation states and the lack of it in Europe is that, in national politics, political parties compete for the office of government, and this makes them responsive to the debates and preferences of their potential voters; in the European Union this is impossible, because, by definition, member state governments are not accountable to the European constituency. Hence national solidarity has an institutional foundation, European solidarity has not. National governments need to satisfy only a faction of European citizens, while their policies affect all of them. By contrast, the existence of a democratically elected government at the European level would generate competition between political parties, which, in order to form such a government, would need to mobilize a majority and would therefore offer citizens a choice between alternatives.[8] This would not only strengthen the legitimacy of European policies, but also foster European solidarity.

The only institution that has the potential of allowing European citizens to choose policies collectively is the European Parliament (EP). Moreover, the Lisbon Treaty have opened the way for new democratic practices, which involve the EP. It has created the 'ordinary legislative process' (TFEU art. 294), which reinforces the EP's role as the representative of European citizens by putting it on par with the Council, although the area of the process' application is limited. This 'ordinary legislative process' sets a procedure for the interaction of Commission, Council and Parliament. It specifies how *legal acts* are adopted and whom they bind (TFEU art. 289 and 294). Because legal acts need the approval of the EP, which represents European citizens as a whole, the new procedure improves the democratic legitimacy of European policy making substantially, but it now needs to be extended to all European public goods.[9]

However, if only the EP can represent all European citizens, the efficient administration of Europe's public goods requires a government as their agent, one that executes their collective preferences. The Lisbon Treaty allocates this function to the European Commission (see TFEU, art. 17). But democracy requires that the Commission is elected by Parliament, which reflects political majorities that emerge from European elections. Voters do not only choose programs, they also want to know who will be in charge of implementing it. The Party of European Socialists (PES) must therefore formally nominate a person as the socialist candidate for president of the Commission prior to the election of the EP. The Lisbon Treaty opens the door to this procedure, because the EP must confirm the Commission president. While the election of the president by Parliament is a democratic imperative, transparency could be improved if the socialist candidate were chosen through a system of primaries that would involve citizens. But if social democrats want to venture more European democracy, then they must also organize themselves more efficiently at the European level.

Conclusion

Setting up a European government may sound unrealistic. But then, socialism has always been 'unrealistic'. The whole point of it is to make 'real' what does not yet exist because the old no longer works. Today one has to recognize that the nation state is no longer capable of managing the Euro-economy efficiently, particularly when markets are free and money belongs to all European citizens. Either the edifice of integration will be destroyed and Europe's welfare reduced, or Europe moves forward to a full democracy with a government that runs the common affairs of all its citizens. This is a matter of realism.

Today European social democracy is again in a crisis, not because its values and objectives are no longer valid, but because no one knows any longer how to turn them into reality. Over 100 years ago, social democracy was also in a crisis. Eduard Bernstein provoked a long debate about the best strategy to realize the values of social justice and democracy that constituted the social democratic project. He argued that dogmatic Marxism was no longer helpful as a guide, because the social realities in Germany and Europe had changed. Today the idea of using the nation state to build the good society is no longer useful. This is largely the consequence of the profound changes that have taken place in the European economy due to the creation of the Single Market and of the single currency and that were necessary in order to preserve the foundations of Europe's prosperity and social model. Yet only a democratic government, fully accountable to all European citizens collectively, would be able to act with the authority and legitimacy that is necessary for creating the conditions of a social Europe. The practical solution of how to deal with day-to-day policies in Europe will then emerge from Europe-wide debates; but, without the proper institutional framework, nothing can be done. Hence the task for Europe's social democracy is to create a democratic government. As Willy Brandt once said: 'It belongs to all of us, this Europe'!

Notes

1. For the contribution of the German social democratic Chancellor Helmut Schmidt to the creation of the euro, see Collignon and Schwarzer (2003).
2. See Collignon (2010).
3. See Keynes (1971).
4. These are the words by which Hobbes (1998 [1641], 28) described the 'state of nature', which he considered a 'state of war'.
5. When private property and property were abolished in the Soviet Union and other Communist countries, the contract principle and its inherent norms were subordinated to the hierarchy of party and state.
6. Ferdinand Lassalle founded the German SPD; Jean Jaurès was assassinated at the outbreak of war in 1914; and Carlo Schmid was one of the authors of the modern German constitution.
7. Bernstein reminds us that the etymological root of 'social' is the Latin socius, associate.
8. See also Lisbon Treaties, TFEU art. 10.4.
9. See TFEU, art. 10.2.

Part III
A New Political Economy

4
A Decent Capitalism for a Good Society

Sebastian Dullien, Hansjörg Herr and Christian Kellermann

A good society needs to be built on an economic system that differs significantly from the current financial capitalist models around the world. In light of the claim of personal freedom, emancipation and choice within and through a good society, a market system is the most functional, dynamic and feasible alternative on the table. However, a number of national, regional and global changes would be necessary in order to provide for the economic preconditions for a good society based on stable growth, equality and sustainability. In what follows we will sketch out the main arguments and pillars for a reformed capitalist model, which we label 'decent capitalism'.[1]

Main Street beyond mainstream

'Capitalism' as a term is back on Main Street. Crashing, dismantling, reforming, repairing, restoring – all kinds of approaches to capitalism are discussed in the wake of the recent crisis. The debate has gained far more momentum today than it had during the past decade, though we had already witnessed a number of such crises. In contrast to the debates of the first decade of our century, policy alternatives to a wholesale freeing up of the markets are suddenly being seriously discussed again. However, in practice, the gap between regulatory rhetoric and an actual reform of our economies is still considerable. Our systems remain at risk of ongoing instability. Crises will continue to be the norm rather than the exception, if we keep on working with the dysfunctions of current capitalism. Many of us will be unable to live a decent life under conditions of increased insecurity, inequalities and pressure in terms of wages, jobs, raising children and providing for old age. An excessive degree of unequal income distribution and personal insecurity is not only detrimental to a good life, it is also economically dangerous and inefficient. The reasons for economic crises and increasing inequality, which are symptom and root of personal and systemic insecurity and inefficiency alike, are manifold.

Most of today's mainstream economics books concentrate on the most obvious crisis factor: the financial markets (see for example Wolf, 2008; Krugman, 2009; Posner, 2009; Rajan, 2010). The sheer amount of books published in the wake of the crisis suggests a major shortcoming in this sphere of capitalism. And in fact finance has played a crucial role in most of the economic crises we have experienced since the 1990s. Financial markets are both gigantic amplifiers of imbalances within and between our economies and a root of imbalances themselves. Illuminating the cracks in finance is therefore the logical starting point for fixing or overcoming our current capitalistic system. Fundamentally correcting the influence and functions of financial markets is also the anchor of the political project of building a good society. However, one has to be very careful not to fall for the argument that the cracks are not that dramatic after all. Behind fancy finance talk of controlling credit default swaps and asset backed securities there is sometimes the hidden agenda of scapegoating single financial instruments or actors in order to be able to leave the basic structure of the system untouched. Like US economist Nouriel Roubini and historian Stephen Mihm, we think that a broader look at capitalism is necessary. We also agree that sticking to ideologies and taboos like the simple belief that free markets will always solve economic problems unduly narrows our perspective of what is wrong with today's capitalism. As Roubini and Mihm (2010, 6) put it: 'It's necessary to check ideology at the door and look at matters more dispassionately.'

A sober and encompassing approach to today's economic dysfunctions is necessary, because the excesses of finance are only one part of the fundamental problems that economies and societies are facing and that have contributed to the recent crisis. There are at least three dimensions of instability that are related to finance, but they go beyond the narrow instabilities of the financial system. First, imbalances between different sectors within economies have escalated. One expression of this is the case of private households and governments that are highly indebted as a consequence of real-estate and other bubbles, which were fuelled by the financial system. Second, international imbalances have never been as big as today – take for example the most prominent cases, the current account deficit of the United States and the current account surpluses of China, Germany or Japan. Third, together with financial deregulation, the shareholder-value principle of corporate governance became dominant. This led to a short-term orientation of management and high bonus payment for management at the cost of the long-term sustainable development of companies and firms.

Related to the shareholder principle are higher profit mark-ups enforced by powerful financial institutions and a decrease in the share of wages as percentage of national income. Beside these developments, the market radical globalization of the last decades led to a huge increase in wage dispersion and to an ever-growing low-wage sector, which had not been seen since the early times of brutal capitalism before the First World War. Labour markets in almost all industrial countries became more deregulated, whereas at the same time trade unions became weaker. In many cases collective bargaining on an economy-wide or sectorial level eroded. Firm-based wage negotiations or individual working contracts without any collective agreements started to dominate. These developments not only led to increasing wage dispersion, they also brought back the risk of deflation. When eroding labour market institutions and weak unions are not able to prevent cuts in money wages, the wage anchor collapses and a deflationary wage-price spiral is triggered. Japan came into such a constellation after its asset price bubble at the end 1990s; countries like Greece, Ireland, Portugal or Spain came into it after the subprime crisis; and without fundamental changes the whole of Europe and the USA are confronted with the danger of deflationary development.

Without doubt, a certain degree of inequality based on hard work or innovative entrepreneurship is the fuel of capitalism. However, when the degree of inequality becomes very high – as it is today – and the level of incomes loses all sensible relationship to an individual's effort or performance, the system begins to crack. It is not surprising that 'equality' is back on the agenda when discussing the successes and the future of market societies. Influential books in that matter include *The Spirit Level* by Richard Wilkinson and Kate Pickett (2009) and *Animal Spirits* by George Akerlof and Robert Shiller (2010). Increasing inequality is a phenomenon that can be found in almost every country. High inequality does not only provoke a feeling of 'unfairness' in and between societies; it also hinders social mobility and has negative impacts on health – and also on productivity. Hungry wolves do not hunt best – in fact, the very opposite is true for our economies of today. The American dream of high social mobility within society and of the opportunity for everyone to become rich if he or she works hard enough is in fact little more than a mirage. Today mobility within society is more of a reality in the Nordic countries of Scandinavia, where equality is higher than in the Anglo-Saxon world of capitalism (Lind, 2010). This is an important insight for redesigning capitalism in the sense of a good society.

Capitalism has other problems too: in the past it has led to a very special type of technology, production and consumption growth that is blind to ecological problems and to the fact that natural resources are limited. Prices systematically fail to incorporate ecological dimensions and the deterioration of nature in an adequate way, and they give the wrong signals for the direction of innovation as well as of production, of consumption and of the way in which we live. After experiencing a number of regional ecological disasters in the past century, the world is now heading for a global ecological disaster, unless fundamental changes take place very soon. This makes the search for solutions very complicated: the present crisis is not only a deep crisis of traditional capitalism, but it has emerged at a time when a deep ecological crisis is also evolving. To solve only one of the two crises is not enough in order to provide humanity with sustainable and acceptable living conditions.

Main features of a new economic model

A decent capitalism should include three interrelated dimensions. First, the model should be ecologically sustainable: it should incorporate preventing global warming, changing to a renewable energy basis and preventing other problematic developments such as a reduction in biodiversity. Second, it should be formed in such a way that the growth process is not jeopardized either by asset-market bubbles or by goods market inflation or deflation and does not result in the excessive indebtedness of individual sectors – or even whole economies, thereby leading inevitably to the next crisis. At the same time, such a model should promote innovation and therefore the technological development necessary both for solving ecological problems and, in the medium and the long term, for increasing labour productivity and hence for holding out the possibility of growing prosperity for all. Third, in our view, it is critical that all population groups have a share in social progress. Inequality of income and wealth distribution must be at politically and socially acceptable limits. Everybody should have a decent living, which is the basic thought of the 'good society' project.

Focus on demand and green growth

At first, we want to address the question of what are the drivers of growth in a decent capitalism. A society's volume of production is ultimately determined by its level of demand; the latter is made up of investment demand, consumption demand, government demand and exports minus imports. If the demand and production volume increases more slowly than productivity, employment falls. If working time and labour participation remain unchanged in such circumstances, unemployment rises. If development is to be lasting, the volume of demand must grow at a stable and adequate rate. This requires a certain proportion between the different components of demand to obtain. For example, it makes no sense to build up economic capacities through high investment if consumption and the other components of demand are too weak to make full use of these capacities. As consumption is the biggest demand element – usually it represents between 60 and 70 per cent of the gross domestic product (GDP) – it is important to have a regular expansion of the consumption demand on the basis of the incomes of households.

Of paramount importance is, of course, the investment demand, which comes from private sources and also from public households. Investment does not only create demand; investment goods embody new technology and are vital for economically sustainable growth in the future.

In order to allow for a sufficient demand growth on the part of private households, it must first and foremost be ensured that wages as a share of income increase again, and then that the wage bill – at least over the economic cycle – increases at the same rate as the GDP. It is true that, ultimately, most profit income also flows to private households. For most households, however, wage income represents the bulk of their earnings and therefore defines their consumption possibilities. Furthermore, experience shows that the propensity to consume is much lower in the case of profit income than in that of wage income. An increase in profits and thereby in household incomes with a high savings rate, without a corresponding increase in income in general, therefore does not suffice as a driver of demand. Also of importance for demand are wage dispersion and government policies that influence distribution. In a constellation where income distribution becomes rather unequal, a consumption demand based on income becomes a problem.

Government demand is also important. Governments deliver many important public goods, like education or health care, and in this way they structure consumption in a society in a positive way. Governments are also of key importance in delivering infrastructure, as well as for ecologically sustainable growth. Many of the economically most successful countries in the world have a high proportion of public expenditures of GDP, as do for example the Scandinavian countries. If governments have to deliver important public goods and also want to modify unacceptable market-given income distribution, public budgets cannot be made 'lean and mean'.

Such export-driven growth is, however, quite naturally, a zero-sum game, as the export surpluses of one country lead to import surpluses in others. Excessive and enduring export-driven growth strategies of single countries are therefore generally harmful for the rest of the world and would have to be limited by global regulations.

There is a fundamental conflict between the present method of production and consumption on the one hand, and ecological needs on the other. If we do not quickly begin to tackle ecological problems, the survival of large parts of the world population will be endangered, creating extreme conflicts about areas in the world in which to live and work, about water and food, and – last but not least – about natural resources like oil. It is clear that the notion of a good society is by definition a global project and cannot be pursued in an isolated way. What we see today is an enormous and lethal failure of the market mechanism to combine economic growth and ecological needs. This does not only involve present methods of production and consumption; it also involves the type of technological development that has been taking place over the last two centuries. That development is not the fault of individual firms and consumers. It is the failure of the price system that, for centuries, sent out wrong signals about technological development, production and consumption. In spite of this fact, we do not see a fundamental conflict between economic growth as such and ecological needs like preventing global warming or finding methods of production and consumption without depleting non-renewable resources. With radical changes in the structure of production and consumption and with technological developments that will, of course, deeply affect our way of living, green growth without negative ecological effects is possible. We do not assume that growth is needed forever. Whether growing prosperity based on technological development takes the form of higher consumption or more leisure time is a question that a society must ask itself once a certain stage of development and level of living standards have been reached.

The project of the radical globalization of the market has been combined with the unsustainable accumulation of debt in many sectors. For example, even if the private household sector as a whole has a creditor position, it is detrimental to the stability of an economy if a substantial proportion of private households have extremely high debts. Governments, too, have become highly indebted (measured in percentage of

GDP), as have whole countries. It also makes a difference which sector is in question. The enterprise sector, for example, can be indebted to a much greater extent than private households, because the latter cannot use the borrowed money to engage in production and in value creation on the market. However, enterprises and financial institutions in the radical era of the market have also neglected to increase their equity sufficiently.

The fact is that a growth in demand cannot be generated on a permanent basis if one individual economic sector builds up excessive debts, while other sectors accumulate surpluses. The same applies, in global terms, to individual economies. It is not necessary for the balance sheets of individual economic actors, sectors and economies to be balanced. But indebtedness (always measured as a percentage of GDP) should be kept within certain limits in order to avoid the over-indebtedness of sectors or of entities within sectors.[2]

Consumption demand and investment demand under a *laissez-faire* regime do not automatically develop in ways that allow stable and sustainable development. What is needed is a coordinated grip on consumption and investment demand, in the interest of the economy and society as a whole. Achieving steady and satisfactory demand growth without dangerous tendencies towards indebtedness requires the imposition of a certain framework and economic intervention by the state. The institutional framework must be worked out in a way that leads to a relative equality of income and reverses the redistribution that has worked to the heavy detriment of lower-income groups. At the same time investment has to be stabilized by government interventions. Public enterprises can play an important role here – as well as infrastructure investment, the cooperation between the private and the public sector and investment incentives set by the government.

To change production and consumption in an ecologically sustainable way will require a major change in the way energy is produced, mobility is organized and houses are built. Such a fundamental change will inevitably have to be combined with a massive wave of new investment. The next decades, if fundamental ecological change happens, will lead to new private and public investment and to GDP growth.

A financial system for economic prosperity and innovation

Financial systems represent something like the brain of the economic system. They are of crucial importance for dynamic development, although they can also drive economies to ruin. In fact in a modern economy a well-functioning financial system has at least four tasks that are indispensable for sustainable growth.[3]

First, by means of creating credit, it enables enterprises – and in particular innovative enterprises – both to invest and to produce. The credit system can create money and credit, so to speak, *ex nihilo*, without any need for previous savings. These funds can be made available to entrepreneurs, who can use them to purchase materials or machines for production. The circuit closes when the investments of an individual enterprise increase the capital stock and hence the production potential of the economy – as well as incomes and savings – thereby ensuring, almost retrospectively, the financing of investment. Since this process often goes hand in hand with innovation, the financial system supports the development of productivity in an economy at a crucial point.

The second central task of the financial system is the redistribution of risk. Although to a certain extent this function has fallen into disrepute in the wake of the subprime crisis, the redistribution of risk between different economic entities remains an important function of the financial system. Investments in individual projects often bear an enormous risk, up to the point of total failure. Individuals would therefore be reluctant to bear such risks alone, or would do so only with the promise of substantial returns. However, since the financial system makes it possible to spread the risk among many investors and, moreover, individuals are not compelled to commit their entire assets, the aggregate willingness to invest in such projects increases.

Banks' credit allocation is an important part of the liquidity and risk transformation of the financial system. The banking system amasses the short-term deposits of the general public, while at the same time granting long-term loans to investing enterprises. Stock markets can take on this function because shareholders buy a long-term investment in the form of a share, which they can sell at any time on the secondary market. Non-bank financial institutions such as investment banks, which are usually more risk-prone, also finance risky activities and can (on condition of being properly regulated) support growth. A society in which the financial sector offers more liquidity and risk transformation will have a higher capital stock, and thus higher labour productivity and also higher material prosperity, than a society that lacks such a financial sector.

The third task of the financial sector is to make capital and credit available to the sectors and enterprises that offer the most promising investment projects. By exploiting economies of scale in the procurement of information, the financial system tends to judge better than individual investors which projects are likely to bear fruit. The allocation mechanism for the distribution of financial resources to their most efficient application is compatible with low general returns. Thus the general rate of return could fall to almost zero, and income from technology for innovative companies could become the sole substantial source of higher returns.[4]

The fourth function of a financial system consists of accumulating the assets of small investors and using them to enable much bigger investments.

Against this background there can be no question of striving for an economic order that tries to manage without a financial system or without the indebtedness of individual sectors. The problem is that, over the past few decades, a financial system came into being that either does not carry out the above-mentioned functions or does so only in a form that leads to instability. In our view, there are five basic dimensions with regard to the necessary regulation and reform of the financial system.

First, risk-taking non-bank financial institutions like investment funds and hedge funds should be separated from commercial banks. The latter should not be allowed to give loans to non-bank financial institutions, the selling of loans by commercial banks to non-bank financial institutions has to be limited, and there should be no proprietary trading by commercial banks and no cross-ownership between commercial banks and other financial institutions. Such a framework would still provide sufficient capital for riskier ventures as risk-loving financial institutions can attract funds from the public.

Second, it is not acceptable to allow the development of a shadow banking system that, by exploiting regulatory loopholes and shifting activities to less regulated areas of the financial system, or even to states with wholly unsatisfactory regulation, systematically withdraws transactions from the regulated financial system. All financial institutions have to be regulated. Financial institutions have operated not only with ever-greater leverage, but also in a riskier, more short-term, more speculative and more return-demanding manner, which yield expectations climbing to irrational heights. It is equally unacceptable that financial institutions have been able constantly to reduce their capital adequacy ratios, ending up with little in the way of an equity capital buffer when crisis hit. The capital adequacy standards of commercial banks – but also those of other financial institutions – must increase again.

The third dimension consists of the creation of anti-cyclical instruments for macro-economic governance in general and for the financial system in particular. In financial markets especially – even with the best regulation – excesses regularly arise that have the potential to destabilize the rest of the economy, unless the state intervenes. This tendency of financial markets has been intensified by misguided supervisory regulations and accounting reforms. The rules of the game in the financial market, therefore, must be substantially rewritten in order to make the financial system once again capable of performing its important functions in the economy.

Within the framework of anti-cyclical policies, the central bank as well as the finance ministry attains a key position in the financial system. As soon as matters appear to be going off course, as in the case of a real-estate bubble, it must be possible to counter the situation by administrative means. Interest rate increases to stop bubbles are not sufficient, and are potentially harmful for the whole economy. Other policies should also be deployed more robustly in order to correct certain macro-economic mistakes. For example, tax policy can combat excesses in real-estate and stock markets by taxing speculative profits.

Fourth, all financial products (especially all types of derivatives) need to be approved by a supervisory agency before they are allowed onto the market. Trading has to take place in organized exchanges only. These rules would allow sufficient opportunities to hedge risks and do not increase costs for firms in any relevant way. Rating agencies also should be supervised by public authorities as well as by institutions defining international accounting standards.

Fifth, international capital movements pose another problem. Individual central banks are barely able to influence them by means of interest rate policy, but they can lead to huge current account imbalances and to destabilizing exchange rate turbulence. Here, too, central banks are in need of additional instruments to enable them to intervene in international capital movements. On the whole, the developments of recent decades appear to us to be misguided, since the instruments at central banks' disposal dwindled progressively, until finally they were left with nothing more than interest rate policy. Central banks should once again be furnished with instruments with which they can actively combat domestic asset-market bubbles and unstable international capital flows. Such instruments should be part of the normal toolbox of central banks.

More equitable income distribution

In recent decades a marked inequality has increasingly arisen with regard to income distribution. This jeopardizes the social and political cohesion of societies. Apart from that, income distribution that is too unbalanced is economically destabilizing. If households consume primarily from their income, an increasing inequality in income distribution comes to have a detrimental effect on consumer demand, because those with high incomes have a higher savings rate. Germany and Japan are typical examples of substantial changes in distribution, with the growth in precarious living conditions further choking off consumer demand. In other countries – for example the United States and the United Kingdom – household consumption has been maintained, despite increasing inequality of incomes, by the increasing indebtedness of private households. These countries experienced higher growth from the 1990s until the outbreak of the subprime crisis, but this was accompanied by the build-up of financial instability. Such a model cannot be sustained in the long term, since it leads to the excessive indebtedness of sections of the population. Both the credit-driven consumption model of the US or UK and the exports-driven model of Germany or Japan came to an end with the subprime crisis; and they seem to be exhausted.[5]

A decent capitalist model must reverse the negative changes in income distribution and grant all population groups an adequate share in the wealth created in society. One secret of the success of regulated capitalism after the Second World War was the increasing mass purchasing power of workers on the basis of growing incomes and a relatively equal income distribution. It is now becoming clear that the old model has to be regenerated.

Income distribution has three important components: functional distribution of income in wages and profits; distribution within the national wage sum and the national profit sum; and state redistribution policy. A fall in the wage share is the result of a higher profit markup. The latter was possible, according to our analysis, on the basis of deregulation, in particular due to the increasing power of the financial sector and its willingness to take risks in pursuit of higher returns. The shareholder-value approach and the increasing role of institutional investors drove enterprises to pursue higher profit mark-ups. Correspondingly, the structures and rules of the game in the financial sector must be changed in such a way that the profit mark-up falls again.

The profit mark-up also depends on the level of monopolization and power structures in goods markets. The task of competition law is to prevent the monopolization of individual markets, because growing market power tends to go hand in hand with increasing monopolistic or oligopolistic profits, which in turn lead to more marked income inequalities and so to problems with steady demand growth in the economy as a whole. On the one hand, market radical globalization intensified competition on goods markets, and on the other hand multinational companies are becoming bigger all the time, due to growth, mergers or takeovers, so that the level of competition is decreasing. In many cases, natural monopolies – such as the energy and water supply, or the railways – were privatized without creating sufficient competition, as a result of which high profits have been made in these sectors. There is no need for privatization in these fields. If state organizations were to take over production and service provision in sectors characterized by a natural monopoly, this could also reduce the profit share.

Recent decades have been characterized by significant wage dispersion. In almost all countries in the world the low-wage sector, as well as that of precarious employment and informality, has increased, especially in the sector of goods and services that are not internationally tradable. Globalization trends, therefore, cannot directly explain the emergence of these sectors. They are the result of labour market deregulation. These unjustified income inequalities among wage earners must be dismantled by means of labour market reforms. The collective bargaining system must be strengthened, backed up by other labour market institutions to achieve the decent work conditions stressed by the International Labour Organization. Minimum wages and social security guaranteed by the state also play a crucial role in this. Such labour market regulations are not only important to reduce income inequality, they are also important to establish a nominal wage anchor against deflationary money wage cuts.

Even with strict regulation, markets do not lead to a politically acceptable income distribution. In addition to that, not everyone has equal chances in the market. The disadvantaged – whether on the basis of gender, childcare responsibilities, handicap, age, race and so on – can drop out of the market and be deprived of an income, or at best obtain only an inadequate one. Ultimately, by no means all incomes are obtained on the basis of personal achievements; consider, for example, large inheritances, which are an intrinsically alien element with regard to capitalism. Tax law and social systems must be deployed in order to organize income distribution in a socially acceptable manner. Tax law should therefore include a clear redistributive component, and this need becomes more pronounced the more evident it is that market outcomes alone will lead to growing inequality. Against this background, not only a markedly progressive tax system is important, but above all regulations that ensure that incomes from capital are adequately taxed. Tax evasion, for example, should be combated by the 'draining' of offshore centres and other measures. Public spending can also be used to reduce income inequalities, for example by providing public goods such as education, health care and public transport. This also applies to state transfer payments and social security systems, which can contain markedly redistributive components.

Robust financing of state budgets

We have already mentioned that economic sectors should not constantly register increasing debt ratios. This also applies to state budgets. A very high public debt stock, measured as a percentage of GDP, has a number of negative effects. First, a high level of public debt can lead to negative redistribution effects, for example if state interest income flows into higher income brackets and taxes are paid by medium or lower earners. Second, a period of high interest rates, coupled with a high public debt, can cause the budget deficit to escalate to such an extent that budgets face refinancing difficulties. Third, state budgets can also become excessively indebted and cut off from the credit market. This phenomenon typically occurs when the debt is in foreign currency, and it has afflicted numerous less developed countries that have experienced currency crises in recent decades. But the same can also happen when the debt is in the domestic currency. An example is the debt crisis of Greece and other counties in the European Monetary Union (EMU). A very high level of public debt ultimately limits governments' room to manoeuvre. In turn, it can cause legitimate demands for currency reform or other ways of alleviating public debt, which are hotly contested politically and can be destabilizing.

We are not calling here for the fixing of a particular debt ratio for public budgets, and certainly not for the fixing of a ratio for new borrowings. During sharp economic crises, such ratios cannot be maintained in the short term. Moreover, they could be harmful in the current economic circumstances, for example if the fiscal policy required by the economic situation is hindered by regulations on indebtedness of whatever kind. In addition, for public investment, public debt is justified, especially if measurable returns in the form of revenues from investments can be expected. However, in the long term a stable percentage of public debt to GDP should be achieved. In the short term, an active fiscal policy with sharply fluctuating budget balances is compatible with these norms.

At this point, the distinction between a capital budget and a current budget is helpful. The current budget includes state consumption expenditure and should be balanced in the medium term, while public investments are entered in the capital budget, which can be financed by long-term credit. In order to stabilize demand across the economy, first and foremost the capital budget should be deployed, bringing forward or putting off public investments in accordance with the economic situation. In the current budget, however, the automatic stabilizers that result from changes in tax revenues and public spending due to the economic cycle should be accepted, as only a medium-term balancing of the current budget is needed.

Levels of regulation

The fundamental problem of the globalization model of the past few decades lies in the asymmetry between economic globalization and the largely still national regulation. Existing structures for the regulation and governance of the world economy are too weak or have too little reach, although economic processes have long had a global dimension. This is not confined to the economy in the narrow sense, but also encompasses many other areas, such as that of environmental problems. The lack of global governance also manifests itself in the fact that the production of international public goods – for instance the prevention of further global warming, the coordination of global economic policies or the provision of a stable international reserve medium – is inadequate.[6] One function of global governance is to establish a more stable international exchange rate regime and a mechanism that prevents excessive current account imbalances. Without a certain degree of control of international capital flows, such a system is difficult to establish. To be sure, free capital flows are not a value in themselves, as has long been claimed by the protagonists of the Washington Consensus. In many cases they increased volatility, created shocks and currency crises and were definitely not promoting growth and efficiency.[7]

Not everything can or should be regulated and governed at supranational level. A great deal can remain at the national level. Which measures should be regulated at what political level should be decided on a case-by-case basis. In summary, what is needed is to furnish economic policy institutions with macro-economic governance mechanisms – either by introducing new ones or by restoring some that have been lost over the past few decades – in order to be better able to control and correct market developments that jeopardize the stability of the national and global economy, or even the future of humanity.

Insufficient progress so far

When we take a look at what has happened in terms of reform and regulation since the subprime crisis, overall progress is insufficient. Current and presently planned regulations of financial markets bring some improvements but are not sufficient to guarantee stability. In July 2010 US President Barack Obama signed the Dodd–Frank Wall Street Reform and Consumer Protection Act. In the US proprietary trading is now limited and ownership of hedge funds by commercial banks restricted. In Europe (planned) regulations go not that far, in spite of the fact that the De Larosière Report, which was established by the European Commission to develop proposals for financial market reform, recommended some delinking (Dullien and Herr, 2010). Both in the US and in Europe credit relationships between commercial banks and non-bank financial institutions, and thus the feeding of the financial ulcer, will not stop. A stricter separation between commercial banks and shadow banks would have been needed. The Basel Committee on Banking Supervision recommended a reform of Basel II, which in November 2010 was accepted by the G20. The new proposal to regulate banks, known as Basel III, goes in the right direction, as equity and liquidity holding of commercial banks should increase. However, Basel III does in no way sufficiently regulate the shadow banking system. The higher standards for commercial banks introduced by Basel III may even further stimulate the transfer of activities in the shadow banking system. Worst of all, the shadow banking system will not disappear. Not all financial institutions will be supervised sufficiently; hedge funds, for example, only have to register and can otherwise continue the business model they followed in the past; not all derivatives are standardized, checked and approved by a supervision agency; and there is no sufficient limitation of agents taking part in derivatives markets, for example in the derivatives markets for natural resources.

There are areas with almost no progress. First, the problem of international imbalances is not approached: there seems to be no willingness to cooperate in this field and to create a more stable international currency and financial system. Labour market institutions are likely to erode further; there is no serious attempt to stop this dangerous development. And, finally, it is frightening that steps towards a sustainable ecological development are stagnating.

The market is a good servant, but a bad master

In order to avoid misunderstanding, a decent capitalism does not provide a *carte blanche* for regulation and state intervention of all kinds – this is by no means one of the preconditions for building a good society. Not all forms of intervention by the state are capable of, or suited to, promoting stable economic growth, or the steady development of incomes and demand. Some of the forms of intervention are even harmful over the medium and the long term. Within a state-given framework that takes account of ecological needs, the liberalization of markets for products and services is the driver of innovations that increase productivity and living standards. The enormous impetus given to innovation by telecommunications in recent decades would not have been possible in a more heavily regulated market with higher entry barriers. The costs of state intervention must therefore always be weighed against their benefits. Since the notion of a good society is a dynamic and not a static one, it must above all be ensured that intervention does not nullify elements of the market economy which ensure that product and process innovations occur of the kind that brings about higher productivity, or simply higher living standards. As Joseph Schumpeter and Karl Marx showed, fair competition between enterprises and the possibility of achieving above average returns by means of innovation are drivers of the development of the economy's productive forces. The possibility of achieving success in the market, as well as of failing in the market, is a central element in economic dynamics. This is the mechanism that underlies the market economy's superiority over attempts at central economic planning.

Furthermore, despite their many negative elements, markets must be regarded as an emancipatory achievement, which increases the space for individuals to decide on how they prefer to work and consume (Sen, 1999). For example, from research into happiness, it is known that the self-employed tend to be more satisfied with their lives due to their largely self-determined daily work routine. As long as a move to self-employment is not the result of the economic pressure imposed by unemployment and does not lead to constantly deteriorating working conditions, the opportunity to start up a business must be considered a positive instance of freedom. Markets that are as open as possible without unnecessary red tape are important here, because they tend to allow more people to choose how they want to live.

Nor is there any question of transplanting the economic system back to the regulatory situation characteristic of, for example, the 1960s or

1970s. Instead, the general principle underlying the new framework and state intervention must be to retain the emancipatory elements of liberalization that have appeared over recent decades, while bringing the destabilizing elements of deregulation back under control.

Money, labour and nature are areas where markets fundamentally fail (Polanyi, 1944). Financial markets tend towards excesses. Because these markets – in contrast to, say, the market for shirt buttons – have an effect on the economic system as a whole, the state must set strict rules and must step in when correction is needed. Other markets, such as the labour market, also tend towards socially undesirable outcomes. Strong labour market institutions, strong trade unions and employer's associations with explicitly or implicitly nationwide coordinated wage negotiations and full employment are the best conditions for a labour market in a good society. And there cannot be any doubt that the market has been leading to a gigantic failure in the area of ecological problems. In a nutshell: the market is a good servant, but a bad master of any society. It must be given clear tasks, clear rules and clear limits in order to provide for the basis and frame for the project of a good society.

Notes

1. This contribution is based on the book *Decent Capitalism. A Blueprint for Reforming our Economies*, written by Sebastian Dullien, Hansjörg Herr and Christian Kellermann and published with Pluto Publishers in London in March 2011.
2. In a growing economy, this is entirely compatible with significant surpluses or deficits. With growth in nominal GDP of 5 per cent (3 per cent real and 2 per cent inflation), a sector can show a financing deficit of 3 per cent of GDP forever, without its net indebtedness ever rising above 60 per cent of GDP.
3. For a more detailed description of this and other functions of the financial system, see Priewe and Herr (2005, 140ff).
4. This was stressed by Keynes (1936).
5. For case studies dealing with these countries, see Herr and Kazandziska (2011).
6. The economic historian Charles Kindleberger (1986) provides a convincing account of this.
7. For an analysis of the inner life of the Washington Consensus, see Kellermann (2006).

5
As Much Market as Possible; as Much State as Necessary

Colin Crouch

A major symbol of German social democracy's rejection of state-centred socialism during the 1950s was the slogan: *So viel Markt wie möglich; so viel Staat wie nötig* ('As much market as possible; as much state as necessary'). Like all slogans, it begged important questions: what constitutes the possible, and what the necessary? And it is doubtful whether the majority of active social democrats, in Germany or anywhere else in Europe, ever fully accepted this a priori preference given to the market. The slogan does, however, provide far more food for thought than most other political ones, and it is well worth revisiting it today, after more or less three decades of dominance of the world by an ideology, neoliberalism, that seems to believe only in the first half of the statement. This has also been a dominance that culminated in one of history's biggest failures of the market, followed by the rush of states to its rescue, in the financial crisis of 2008–2009.

The following discussion of these issues will lead to doubts being expressed about the centrality of the market/state confrontation, which still dominates so much political debate. We shall question whether it really is the market, rather than the giant corporation, that represents the central force in today's economy; and whether states energized by modern political parties can be trusted to be civil society's representatives in their attempts to cope with this corporate power.

As much market as possible

First, it is important to remind social democrats why they should seek as much market as possible and not regard that institution as a natural enemy. To function perfectly, markets need to have five central characteristics:

I. All desired objects (material and immaterial) must be capable of being assigned prices within the market. If that can be achieved, prices would express our relative rankings of everything that was important to us. For this, it is necessary that prices connect *all* goods and services that are for sale. Although we often use the plural word 'markets', there is really only one market; in that way we can establish our relative preferences across a vast range of goods. Allocation by the state can never achieve that degree of finesse.

II. There must also be large numbers of producers and consumers who have easy access to and exit from the market. Only on this condition can we make the mathematical calculations needed to demonstrate that the prices that result from producers' costs and purchasers' preference are optimally efficient. In the market the price of a good rises if there is a rise in demand, because consumers compete for the existing supply by offering higher prices. If the market is perfect, this price rise acts as a signal, to other producers, that there are profits to be made; they enter the market, and their increased production brings prices, and profits, down again. For markets to function, therefore, what economists call the 'barriers to entry' must be low. So must barriers to exit: if a firm is producing inefficiently, it needs to leave the market, so that the resources of land, labour and capital it was using can be redistributed for more efficient uses. Or, if customers do not like the products on sale within a market, they need to be able to express their dissatisfaction by not making purchases, thereby requiring producers either to reduce their prices or to change the range of goods they are offering. The debate during the recent financial crisis over whether some banks were 'too big to fail' was a debate about exit barriers. If a firm is 'too big to fail' despite being inefficient, then high barriers are being erected to prevent it from exiting, and markets are prevented from doing their pruning work.

III. The market needs a high volume of activity in it if prices are to be set through the interplay of supply and demand. This is partly achieved by the criterion just discussed, but also through the willingness of players who have entered the market to keep making transactions. Without buyers and sellers there is no market.

IV. Markets depend for their efficiency on sellers and purchasers having high levels of information about prices and goods on offer across the full range of goods and services on offer. In fact, economic theory assumes that information is 'perfect' – that is, that participants in the market possess all the knowledge they need in order to allocate their resources efficiently.

V. Finally, in a true market economy, economy and polity need to be separated from each other. If this barrier is not in place, governments might use their power to distort prices or the allocation of resources. They might try to divert resources to the private benefit of political and government leaders, their families and friends; or they might interfere in order to have more money spent on health or education and less on alcohol. We may evaluate these two examples of intervention rather differently, but from the market perspective they both constitute distortions of the efficiency of the market. But the interference might happen the other way round: forces in the economy may interfere in the polity. From the point of view of classical market theory, this is just as bad. Individuals and firms in the business world might use the wealth they accumulate in their market activities to buy political influence. They can then use that influence to win contracts or other favours from governments. This, again, distorts the market. It is therefore essential for the functioning of pure markets that strong barriers are in place to prevent *either* the political world from intervening in the economy *or* businesspeople from intervening in politics.

If it were possible to achieve such pure markets, social democrats would have little to complain about. Valuable social goals would be achieved, because (particularly if condition (I) were operative) people would be able to demand them through the market. There would be inequalities of income and wealth, resulting from differential market success, but these would be limited if, particularly through condition (II), high incomes and profits acted as a signal to new entrants to enter a market and bring down prices, and therefore rewards, and if, thanks to condition (V), the rich could not transfer wealth into political influence.

As much market as possible would therefore in principle be a good thing. Unfortunately the amount of market that is possible is very frequently inadequate for social democratic purposes. We can review these limitations briefly under each of the conditions discussed above.

I Everything has its price

The attempt to allocate a price to all goods and services within a single market encounters three problems, well recognized in the economics literature: those associated with externalities; those associated with public goods; and those associated with merit goods. The market can be used to alter incentives, so that we do take account of externalities and pursue public and merit goods, but only after some intervention to restructure the market, usually from government. Similar to, but going beyond, these is the general human tendency to insist that some things simply should not have a price put on them. Should people be permitted to sell their bodily organs if someone needing a transplant is willing to pay for them? Should a young woman be permitted to claim unemployment benefit if she refuses to try to earn a living as a prostitute? Should mountain rescue activities devote costly resources to saving the life of a stranded climber without making an estimate of whether the individual's life is worth the cost? Economists can point to the opportunity costs involved in refusals to enter the market in all such cases – that is, what is lost by taking one path rather than another. However, they have no means of dealing with arguments that establish moral priorities over the market. Economics can tell us that we 'ought' to do certain things if we wish to maximize efficiency, and it has good reasons for encouraging us to do this, since inefficiency implies the wasteful use of resources. But the assertion of moral criteria that we believe trump the market does not regard the opportunities foregone as waste, but as the pursuit of concepts of the good that lie beyond the reach of economic argument.

II Entry and exit barriers

The market's requirement for low entry and exit barriers is simply difficult to fulfil in many sectors of the market. There is often simply no space for multiple producers: for example, there seems to be room in the world for only two manufacturers of large aircraft, Boeing and Airbus. One firm, Microsoft, is completely dominant in computer software systems. It seems technically impossible to have more than one firm managing water supplies from any one river basin. Whenever there are monopolies or very small numbers of producers, with serious technical or organizational barriers to the market entry of further competitors, prices and the quality of goods cannot be set by the process assumed in the mathematical models of economic theory. While technical change has eased these problems in some cases, in some other important instances modern high-tech economies have greater problems in making pure markets than classic industrial ones. This is particularly the case where there are network externalities: it is a characteristic of certain kinds of network that they are more useful the larger the number of people connected to them. This gives enormous advantages to a first mover, the first firm to develop a network in a particular field. Even if other firms develop superior products, they will have difficulty selling them, as the first firm has developed a network that must be larger and therefore more useful than that of the newcomer. Wherever competitive advantages accrue to the owners of networks, entry barriers are erected against competitors. The greatest single example of a network, the Internet, has provided many opportunities for first-mover advantage in establishing monopoly products like search engines that everyone uses, creating large barriers against potential competitors.

A major reason why this is happening is related to the implications for product standards of high rates of technical change. When a standard is needed for something that moves slowly, it can be set on the basis of long usage, or widespread discussion and agreement, and applied by national or international authorities. Such is the case, for example, with standard weights and measures, the design of electric plugs and sockets, or the alphabet. Such standards are public goods. Individual firms cannot own them and exclude others from designing products around them. But where a need for new standards develops rapidly and is subject to frequent change through technical development, there is no time for processes of widespread acceptance or formal public processes. If a large number of firms offer different standards in the market place, but the need for interchangeability is strong, so that there cannot be continuing choice among many options, then one option will be preferred for its superior qualities, and the market rather than public authority will provide the standard. However, in many cases the 'superior quality' is merely the power of one dominant firm to assert its practices as the industry standard, not through competition but through first-mover advantage and the establishment of network externalities. No one can make us change the alphabet we use, but a dominant computer software firm is capable of preventing the alphabet we type on our computers from triggering a set of electronic symbols that can be read by others, because it has changed the standards that govern those electronic symbols, which it owns and controls. Only giant corporations are in a position to impose standards of their own, and they can do so in order to prevent competitors from entering the market with products that consumers might well want to buy.

A consequence of high barriers is that the market cannot do its work in keeping inequalities within certain bounds. It is notable that the shift during the past three decades towards an economy dominated by giant global corporations, with growing network externalities and corporate standards, has seen a rise in overall inequalities of wealth and income in advanced societies, reversing a longer-term trend in market economies towards reduced inequalities.

III An adequate volume of transactions

The vitality of a market economy will not be very much hindered if occasional commodities are not traded; but if there is a widespread collapse in confidence, such that buyers in general withdraw from markets, discouraging producers from producing for fear of having stock left on their hands, the market as a whole will fail. Such collapses in confidence can occur if consumers fear that they are facing a major decline in their income or a major increase in the need for a certain kind of spending, which will have to be at the expense of others. Economic theory recognizes failures of this kind as being consequent on what it calls exogenous shocks: a natural disaster, a war or an economic crisis originating in a part of the world outside the economy concerned. It has more difficulty accepting that purely economic shocks can happen within a market economy, as the pure model assumes that buyers and sellers have perfect information. It is therefore expected that they will take anticipatory action against looming difficulties, thus avoiding sudden shocks. There are two problems with this. First, our starting point is never a pure market economy; we might be able to reduce economic shocks if we could establish one, but first we have to get there through an economic environment that throws up many shocks. Second, as we shall see immediately below, it is very difficult to have perfect information. An economy that is highly competitive, but in which information flows very imperfectly, and that is therefore vulnerable to shocks will create unstable economic circumstances for people who have to earn their living. In the absence of any countervailing factors they may become highly cautious and unwilling to spend money in order to save against an uncertain future. If they do this on a wide scale, markets may collapse. This is what happens in major economic recessions; and government intervention is usually needed to alleviate them.

IV The need for perfect information

In practice the requirement that market participants are perfectly informed is hard to meet. The central problem is that, in a market economy, most information itself has a price; acquiring information is in fact a major transaction cost. It is a problem that seems to grow in importance the more complex an economy becomes – for example, through the technical sophistication of products or of financial instruments – and it is therefore likely that it has greater importance today than in earlier periods. The issue for consumers is whether it is worth their while paying to acquire the information that would enable them to make fully informed choices; but, in advance of having the information, they can rarely decide whether it would be worthwhile or not. In practice, therefore, the acquisition of information depends, not on whether it would turn out to be value for money, but on whether we can afford it in an absolute sense. In other words, we are likely to acquire more information the wealthier we are; as a result, the wealthy are likely to make more efficient decisions and therefore to become even wealthier.

This further helps us to understand why the present period is seeing a reversal of the decline in inequalities that characterized the first few decades of democratic history. The problem is particularly severe in financial markets, where the wealthy can afford highly skilled professional advice to help them in their decisions, enabling their incomes to grow much faster than those of small investors. Similarly, organizations are in a better position to acquire information than are individuals. This means that producers are likely to be better informed than customers (unless the customers are other firms), employers better informed than employees, and large firms better than small ones.

V The separation of economy and polity

For three principal reasons, the segregation of economy and polity that the market model requires is rarely present. First, government is one of the likeliest sources of remedies for the market failures we are discussing. Second, the market itself needs law to function: at a very minimum, recognition of the right to own private property, the maintenance of a currency and guarantees against forgery, the provision of remedies for breach of contract and protection of patents and copyright. Third, there are, however, more negative entanglements between government and market. In a free economy it is very difficult to prevent economic wealth from being converted into political influence. The wealthy can use their resources to finance politicians and parties who agree with them, or to persuade those who disagree to change their minds. They can also run campaigns to influence public opinion, even by owning and controlling newspapers and telecommunications channels in order to make these help them. Sadly, democracy and the market economy, far from inhibiting the political power of the rich, as each of them aspires in its different ways to do, make the problem highly intractable. Mass democracy requires enormous resources to mobilize opinion; the opinions may be those of the many, but the resources to mobilize them belong mainly to the wealthy few. The market system may depend on the separation of economy and polity, but it can do nothing to prevent the rewards earned in the former from being deployed in the latter – partly in order to secure, in turn, privileges in the economy. Political power and economic wealth are mutually convertible currencies. This becomes a further means by which inequalities can be enhanced in market societies. Concentrations of wealth – the origins of which we have already seen in other market failures – bring a small number of individuals and corporations to the point where they can buy political influence; this influence can then be used to make them richer still; and this wealth can in turn be used to secure more influence – and so on.

Of all the market failures, therefore, those that tend to favour massive concentrations of wealth are the most worrying, as in the end they can be used to undermine the market itself and the reality of democracy. And at several points such concentrations are encouraged by several distinctive features of the contemporary economy.

As much state as necessary

As the above discussion has shown, many of these failures of the market to fulfil its promise have provided the premise for government intervention in the economy, and these have been the classic stamping ground for social democracy, the forces that have made the state 'necessary'. Weaknesses emerged in these state interventions, providing the basis for the neoliberal critique of the social democratic state. Government actions and public services were characterized as being unresponsive to consumers, dominated by producer interests, centralized and remote. If services were not inadequate, then they were excessive, offering things that people would not have chosen to have if offered a market choice and doing so with inadequate cost effectiveness, leading to high taxes. To remedy these defects, neoliberals advocated privatization, the use of internal markets within public services and competition against publicly provided services from private providers and sub-contractors, but within a publicly funded system. Public services were also accused of being out of touch with how services were being improved in private business, because their providers were out of touch with businesspeople. Here neoliberal reformers offered two strategies: the adoption of business criteria in how government conducted its own services, and, partly to facilitate this, the encouragement of intensive interaction with, and learning from, the private sector by public servants.

There is no space here to pursue the implications of all these themes, but to draw attention to a line running through several: the privatization and sub-contracting of services, with government remaining virtually a monopoly purchaser – which often entailed fixing long-term contracts with small numbers of producing firms, which developed cosy relations with politicians and public officials. More generally, there has been interaction between politicians and officials on the one hand and businesspeople and consultants on the other, and this has intensified. These central tendencies of neoliberal reform, carried out in the name of the market, all breached a fundamental principle of the pure market ideal: the separation of polity and economy. Neoliberalism might have limited major forms of government intervention in the economy, but it opened the path to greatly increased intervention of the economy – or, rather, of firms and highly wealthy corporate individuals – in the polity.

As much a giant corporation as necessary?

These tendencies need to be set against some of the failures of the pure market discussed earlier: the growth of conditions, in many markets, that make it impossible for large numbers of producers to enter – which produces markets dominated by very small numbers of firms; and the consequent growth of inequalities in income and wealth, which leads in turn to a concentration of economic resources that can be used to gain political influence. To these factors we can add certain other characteristics of the early twenty-first century economy: the ability of some global firms to propose to governments conditions that they want met if they are to invest in the country concerned; and the emergence, especially in the financial sector, of some firms so large that governments cannot risk their failure: governments must either give them virtually whatever they need in order to survive or take the risk of enormous economic damage, for which voters will blame government.

Political debate that concentrates on the confrontation between market and state completely misses this dimension of contemporary politics. We have a triangle of forces: state, market, giant corporation. Often indeed state and giant corporation conspire together to weaken markets. Further, there is no thoroughgoing way out from the power of the corporation by reasserting the power of market and/or state. The fate of the Soviet economies told us what happens to economies dominated by the state. At the same time, the economy of small- and medium-sized enterprises necessary for a pure market economy, as envisaged in the ideals of the German *Ordoliberalen* and American Jeffersonians, is not possible given the reality of the global economy and today's monopoly-prone – or at least oligopoly-prone – industries.

The Chicago school of law and economy grasped this fact over 30 years ago, and fashioned a theoretical justification of oligopolistic markets on the grounds that they maximized 'consumer welfare' – which was more important than consumer choice, or even than keen prices. Assuming axiomatically that firms would not seek to grow beyond a size that was maximally efficient, they argued the following points: that large firms would almost always be more efficient than smaller ones; that greater efficiency would create increased wealth somewhere in the economy; and that consumers would always gain from being in a wealthier economy than in a poorer one. Their arguments were mainly directed against US anti-trust law, which maintained an increasingly unrealistic, historical American ideal of a market economy that led it in practice, paradoxically, to advocate increasing government intervention.

The naïvety of the Chicago school's arguments about size and efficiency, and its inability to deal with problems of network externalities characteristic of advanced economies prevented it from triumphing completely in its war with anti-trust. These shortcomings did, however, demonstrate the impossibility of Jeffersonism and of *Ordoliberalismus* – and therefore of the search for pure market economies. Also, although tacitly, it entered deep into the philosophy of neoliberalism. While this is seen, by its advocates and opponents alike, as being 'pro-market', the above brief discussion of the neoliberal response to the perceived failings of the social democratic state has shown that neoliberals have no qualms at all about strengthening either the economic or the political power of giant corporations. It is the rather paternalist concept of 'consumer welfare', more than the liberal idea of consumer choice, that has determined their policies.

Whatever justification there might be for the Chicago approach to the market economy, there can be no justification for its political implications: that corporate wealth should dominate politics and reduce the scope of democracy. Such corporate political influence breaks all rules, both of the free market and of democracy, and no neoliberal even tries to produce a set of rules that will legitimate it. Instead neoliberals assert that only neoliberalism is compatible with the market and democracy, and they completely ignore the damage that politicized giant corporations do to both.

Here, one might have thought, is the basis of a social democratic critique of neoliberalism, especially after the financial crisis has shown us the damage done to both markets and democracy by banks being 'too big to fail'. But, in practice, social democrats in government have been completely ensnared by the logic of the corporation-dominated polity. It is possible to point the finger at individual social democratic politicians who found great rewards in the snare – going off to lucrative careers advising US private health firms or Russian gas corporations. But the problem goes far deeper. As argued above, today it is not possible to envisage an economy that is not dominated by global corporations. There is therefore no possibility of 'breaking them up', except in isolated cases of unjustifiable monopoly power. They can be regulated, but their power to use their wealth to lobby parliaments and ministers, and their threats to move to the lowest regulated parts of the world place severe limitations on that route. In the special case of the mass media, primarily owned by giant corporations, there is a further double weapon against governments seeking to tame corporate power: direct persuasion of public opinion and voting intentions, and the blackmail threat of exposure of any scandals in the private lives of the politicians who create difficulties.

Through our dependence on giant corporations for our standard of living and our vulnerability to media persuasion, we turn democracy into a weapon against itself and we inhibit any capacity of governments, parties or electorates to confront the main source of the inequalities of wealth and power in our societies. Governments rarely believe that they can flourish economically other than in a close relationship with major corporations. Challenging this has proved too much for any major social democratic party, particularly after the decline of the manual working class removed social democracy's fundamental power base. The 'third way' forms of social democracy (new Labour, *die neue Mitte*) recognized – as those further to the left did not – that this base had declined, but they believed that it was possible, even preferable, to do without a core constituency of this kind. As a result, they had only weak resources for resisting the political power of corporate wealth, and they usually made concessions to it. In the absence of any successful movement to unite major new social categories to social democratic parties, it is difficult to see how this particular political form can contribute more than marginally to a confrontation with the challenge that this wealth and power present. The corporations are necessary to us; who is in a position to ask what are the limits of that necessity, and how far they can be challenged?

As much civil society as possible?

We need 'civil society' – a phrase that, today, usually denotes those organizations and informal groupings that concern themselves with public affairs but operate outside the power of both state and firm. Significantly, they have become known in English by the nonsensical name 'non-governmental organizations' (NGOs). Better is the German term *Bürgerinitiativen*, 'citizens' initiatives'. Whether civil society includes religious organizations is often left ambiguous – they are usually included when they have lost their power, which reinforces the idea of civil society as 'the power of the powerless'. This phrase itself was coined in the 1980s by the Czech writer, civil activist and sometime president of his country Vaclav Havel (1985), to refer to the civil society outside the party-state, which then existed in central and eastern Europe. Civil society includes, though it extends further than, the voluntary sector. It defines all those extensions of the scope of human action beyond the private that lack recourse to the primary contemporary means of exercising power, the state and the firm.

This approach to civil society was captured and developed in a project organized by Jürgen Kocka at the *Wissenschaftszentrum* Berlin in the early years of this century, and it is well synthesized in his article 'Civil Society in Historical Perspective' (2004). Pointing out that at different historical periods the phrase has had different meanings, he stresses that today it identifies a sphere connected to, but separate from, economy, state and private life. It is oriented towards public conflict, discourse, compromise and understanding, recognizing plurality, difference and tension as legitimate forms operating non-violently. This is the space in which a value-oriented critique of market, state and corporation can be conducted in contemporary democracies. States and firms do dominate our societies, but there is a lively field of contention. Challenges to domination can be made and concepts of public goals explored and turned into practical projects, against the state's claim to monopoly of the legitimate interpretation of collective values and against the firm's claim that the conversion of values into the maximization of shareholders' interests is as good as life can get.

Battle can be joined in the field of values, because that it is where corporate power and the state are vulnerable: the former because it often claims exemption from ethical criteria on the grounds of the absolute priority of the bottom line; the latter for the opposite reasons, that it has taken on the mantle of standing for society's collective values. Values are weak weapons in a conflict with money and power, but they are not meaningless. On occasion, the causes of the powerless can also deploy more substantive resources – such as demonstrations, strikes, boycotts, even moments of disorder.

Corporate dominance has some paradoxical consequences for the corporation itself. Far too obviously and publicly prominent, giant corporations can less and less escape with the argument that they just exist in the market and cannot be expected to take account of anything wider than their immediate financial interests. Whether they like it or not, whether it can be justified by economic theory or not, firms are increasingly being seen as politically and socially responsible actors. There is a whole new politics around corporations, as campaigners expose their undesirable actions and try to influence customers, and sometimes investors and employees. This can, given the right pressures from activists and regulators, turn corporate social responsibility from being an aspect of corporate public relations into the major object of a sharp and penetrating demand for corporate social accountability. There is growing recognition among political scientists that both the firms and the campaigns that criticize them now form part of the global polity. Ironically, this is, in turn, yet another means by which corporations become the dominant organizations in society. It is through their internal, undemocratic and non-transparent decision-making procedure that some causes are adopted and publicized, others ignored. In so many different ways, all the routes through the neoliberal agenda, including attempts to oppose it, lead, not to the market as such, but to the corporation.

Some civil society groups can also span national boundaries, while political parties remain overwhelmingly tied to the nation state, defining interests in national terms. In an increasingly global economy this is not only unrealistic, but it encourages an irrational nationalism. From here it is an easy slip to arguments in favour of the public realm becoming the territory of defence of a particular national population against 'foreigners', especially immigrants and ethnic minorities. As formal competition among the main established parties in many countries is drained of content – partly because all parties are essentially following a corporate agenda – xenophobic movements emerge as the only sources of real choice and novelty. And all they are doing is taking to an extreme the exaltation of competitive national identity, which is being used by nearly all shades of political opinion.

In this context, transnational corporations appear as refreshingly cosmopolitan forces, responding flexibly to the post-national geography appropriate to a globalized economy. Paradoxically, they also help to construct a post-national civil society. Operating across the globe just by themselves, they enable campaigning groups to recognize some shared interests, which such groups would rarely discover if they limited themselves to formal politics and its national confines. If asserting the democratic state against global corporations becomes a matter of nationalistic protection, it will be a step backwards. As we know from past protectionist periods, the consequences would be not only shrinking trade and overall decline in wealth, but also an increase in tension and hostility between people from different ethnic and national backgrounds. There is, then, a major problem, if the assertion of national citizenship rights becomes our only defence against the power of giant firms to disrupt our lives. There are particularly important issues here in labour law, where the protection of employee rights against corporations that play off groups of workers in wealthier countries against workers in countries with low wages and bad working conditions can only be waged at national level. Parties – even in Europe, where there is at least a continent-wide parliament – can rarely rise above the national level in a way that can be achieved by citizens' initiatives, precisely because the latter are not defining themselves in relation to national parliaments.

Arguments about the importance of civil society beyond formal politics are not new. Back in the 1950s the late US economist J. K. Galbraith (1952) wrote about the need for groups of 'employees, consumers, savers and shareholders' to exert a balancing power against corporate might. In the late 1990s Giuliano Amato (1997) ended his study of anti-trust law by explicitly recalling Galbraith's words and commending them to our own day. Slightly later the British political scientist David Marquand (2004) wrote of the 'need to redress the balance between the commercial invasion of government and a top-down state by reasserting civic muscle' through the moral commitments of an engaged citizenry. It is a remarkable fact that all three of these men have been political insiders, at different periods and in different countries. Galbraith was a central member of the group around the US presidency of J. F. Kennedy in the early 1960s; Amato has in recent years held the posts of prime minister and other senior offices in the Italian state; Marquand was a British member of parliament in the 1970s and subsequently played an important role in the European Commission. Yet none of them suggests that we try to resolve the issues at stake through the formal political process. They direct us to that wider concept of civil society.

This is both bad and good news. It is bad, because it amounts to pitting, against the might of both corporate and government institutions, the 'power of the powerless'. Also, in the end, much civil action has to find a response at the level of government if it is to get anywhere. This is the sobering message of a recent book by Debra Spini (2006) on post-national civil society (*La società postnazionale*). Having opened to us an exciting vista of citizens' actions extending across national boundaries, she reminds us of the continued presence of the indispensible gatekeeper: the solidly national democratic state. And the political party, manipulated though that institution has become, remains a major gatekeeper *en route* to that primary gatekeeper.

But the news is good, because it shows us that there are things that ordinary citizens can do. Citizens' initiatives do score victories. Governments do intervene to protect citizens from corporate abuse, as official campaigns against smoking and unhealthy foods, which (if anything) have been strengthened in recent years, demonstrate. Such cases give us hope. These government actions can usually be traced back to small groups of poorly funded but passionately committed professionals and people of good will. Firms that boast of their green or fair trade credentials did not dream up these ideas in their marketing departments; they were responding to serious customer pressure, which was in turn responding to campaigning by small numbers of concerned activists in ecological groups and trade unions. There is no need to be defeatist. Rarely before in human history has there been so little deference shown to authority, so much demand for openness, so many organizations, journalists, and academics dedicated to a cause, devoting themselves to criticizing those who hold the power and to putting their actions to scrutiny. New electronic forms of communication are enabling more and more causes to express themselves in highly public ways.

Civil society action can embrace the political role of the corporation in a way that political parties, even where they have not become dependent on corporate funds, have little incentive to do. The main incentive for a political party in an electoral democracy is to throw the blame on the rival parties. If firms misbehave, there are few rewards for an opposition party in criticizing them; it is better to blame the government for not having controlled the firms' behaviour. Corporate perpetrators slink away out of the spotlight. A good deal of that happened during the financial crisis. There were even attempts to blame President Obama for the Gulf of Mexico oil disaster, even though he had a record of criticising off-share oil drilling – while his opponents supported it.

If, as we have seen above, firms are active and powerful in shaping the rules of the market and the general political framework within which they operate, this party politicization becomes totally inadequate. Civil society campaigning groups do not have the same incentive as parties do to turn all criticism towards government alone, and in this way, too, they are in a better position than political parties to shape a debate appropriate to our times. They can create spaces of political opinion that parties then find it safe to enter. It is hard for parties to do the pioneering, entrepreneurial work of creating new areas of political opinion themselves, as they have to win elections in the context of existing and established values.

Of course, movements dedicated to a cause can themselves be corrupted. On the one hand, they are tempted to exaggerate their case in order to attract publicity. On the other, in desperate need for resources as they always are, they are easily compromised through being susceptible to political or corporate blandishments, whether for the sake of their organizational funds or for that of the individual careers of their leaders. Fighting for a cause is tough, unremitting work. It goes on unceasingly, in permanent watchfulness, and one is never able to say: 'We have achieved our goals; we can rest now.'

Part IV
Re-Framing Social Democracy

6
The New Language of Social Democracy

Elisabeth Wehling and George Lakoff

Introduction

Political language and reasoning are inseparable. No tie between parties and voters is more intimate and holds more potential for political empowerment through generating majorities in a democracy than the one that is established – from brain to brain – through language.

Recent work in cognitive science and in the neurosciences has shown that an estimated 98 per cent of what happens in the human brain as one 'understands' ideas happens as a matter of automatic, reflexive thought processes along neural blueprints such as conceptual metaphors and frames. Such blueprints are acquired and strengthened in our brains through world experience, including the socially shared experience of public language use.

Using examples from the 2010 UK election campaigns, this chapter illustrates the linkage between the brain, political thought and language, and it exemplifies common linguistic pitfalls of political campaigning. By way of concluding, advice will be given as to how the European social democratic movement may establish cognitive transparency through effective and honest linguistic framing: a new language of social democracy.

Words matter, in the short run: How language evokes ideas in our minds; Words matter, because they create meaning in our minds

But how so? By evoking what is known to cognitive scientists and to neuroscientists as 'conceptual frames'. Frames are neural structures in our brains that organize complex world knowledge and enable us to process the meaning of ideas, including linguistically expressed ideas. Every frame that is evoked through language leads to a vast amount of inferences about the nature of a thing or situation, inferences that go far beyond what we usually think of as 'being present in the word itself'.

This happens in the brain, inevitably, every time we hear a word. Take the word 'child' as an example. It activates a frame that infers concepts such as 'mother' and 'father' as well as prototypical notions about genetic, biological and social relationships between the three. The word 'child' has no meaning outside of such a frame. Frame inferences are evoked, or activated, as a matter of reflex. They are part of our automatic, unconscious reasoning. Take another example – the phrase 'tax oases', which is commonly used by parties across Europe to refer to places with low taxation, such as Liechtenstein or Switzerland. The term 'oases' implies that places with low taxation are places of refuge within an existentially threatening environment. Via frame inferential structure, taxes are interpreted as an existential threat. Words matter. They determine our interpretation of social and political realities day after day.

Words come with a worldview: Political language and moral values

There is something crucial to notice about the frame 'tax oases', and it has to do with the fact that public political language commonly mirrors and evokes value-based political reasoning. 'Taxation' is an abstract idea. You cannot touch, smell or see taxation. Therefore no single, commonly shared interpretation of what taxation is exists. Our understanding of taxation relies on how we morally reason about our nation and its social institutions. In the above frame, taxes are construed as something negative and threatening. This is a notion commonly based on the understanding of taxation as an immoral punishment of the economically successful self-reliant individual. Many conservative and libertarian parties across Europe seem to share this ideology. Phrases they use when talking about taxes – such as 'tax burden', 'tax relief' and 'tax refugees' – reflect this moral reasoning, and more: they evoke it in the listener's mind.

Taxation may be understood quite differently, namely as a system for sharing the common wealth for the common good: a system that benefits the individual and secures freedom, empowerment and protection for all. Notice that, on the basis of this different moral interpretation of taxation, a phrase like 'tax oases' would become meaningless straight out. It would equal the notion of relief from freedom, empowerment and protection.

The negation problem: How Social Democratic Parties promote conservative values

We have outlined above two moral interpretations of taxation – interpretations that correlate roughly with conservative and social democratic worldviews across Europe. But, astonishingly, phrases like 'tax relief' are used not only by conservative but also, quite commonly, by social democratic politicians across Europe – politicians who oppose certain forms of tax cuts and propose a fair taxation. Clearly, a conservative politician who argues for 'tax relief' stays true to his or her moral worldview. A social democratic politician, on the other hand, who uses the same phrase is promoting a conservative understanding of taxation and, even worse, fails to communicate an alternative moral understanding of the matter to the public.

The general lack of value-based framings from liberal movements and parties is probably one of the major reasons for the defeat of social democratic ideology in Europe over the past years.

But why are liberal politicians and parties so apt at using and promoting their opponents' frames? At least one answer to this question lies in the fact that they often negate political ideas put forth by the opponent. Linguistic negation is problematic: in order for our brain to negate a concept, it first has to represent for itself that very concept. Therefore, every time a social democratic politician, journalist or activist says, 'I am against tax relief', a conservative interpretation of taxes is activated in the public's mind.

Words matter, in the long run: How language changes our minds

We might ask ourselves: does it really matter whether we refer to lower taxation as 'tax relief' or, say, 'tax cuts', and that the frame 'tax relief' is being used by the European media and parties across the ideological spectrum? It does. It matters a great deal. This is because, every time two ideas are associated within a conceptual frame, their connection grows stronger. Political language changes our brain.

Brain cells function in clusters. Every neuron has between 1,000 and 10,000 inputs and outputs to connect to other neurons in order to form extended neural circuits that are used to compute complex ideas. Those circuits are not given by nature and they do not develop randomly. When we are born, our brain has a vast amount of neural connections that are not yet organized in circuits. Linking circuits are strengthened through recruitment learning: the strengthening of synaptic connections that happens each time neurons are activated simultaneously as we experience things in the world. This is how our brains 'learn' ideas, including political ideas and notions of socio-political realities. They are shaped and strengthened – word by word and day after day – through public language use. Words matter in the long run. They literally change our minds by strengthening neural structures in our brains.

Immigration is... : The power of metaphorical framing

Political frames often rely on conceptual metaphors, which structure most of our everyday reasoning (Lakoff and Johnson, 1981). These arise, like frames, through recruitment learning and are coined in our neural structure. Take the metaphor 'affection is closeness'. Circuits are strengthened between the brain region that computes spatial relations and the emotional centre of our brains every time we are physically close to our parents and simultaneously experiencing affection as a child. On the strength of this metaphor, we speak of 'growing closer' or 'more distant' with friends. Experiments show how, due to this neural mapping, spatial distance creates emotional distance: subjects who are primed with high spatial distance cues are less affected by emotionally distressing media reports and report less attachment to their families and home towns (Williams and Bargh, 2010).

Conceptual metaphor determines language, reasoning and decision-making in politics too. In a recent study subjects were primed to think of health-threatening viruses and then they read texts that implied the metaphor 'nation as person' (think of the expression 'neighbour states'), other metaphors for the nation or no metaphors whatsoever. Subjects who read the text using the 'nation as person' metaphor took a stronger stand against immigration in a subsequent poll. Their opinion was influenced by the conceptual metaphor that had been evoked through language. Metaphors are a powerful tool in political discourse. They structure a great part of our everyday unconscious political reasoning.

The self-interest myth: What people really vote

Studies in the social and psychological sciences have long shown that self-interest is at best a marginal indicator for voting behaviour (Kinder,

1998; Miller, 1999; Sears und Funk, 1991). People vote on the basis of their identity and of their moral values, as part of their identity. But values are not universal. Support for political action and identification with political parties correlate with different morality models – that is, with different assumptions about what is the *right* and what is the *wrong* thing to do in the face of sociopolitical facts (Lakoff, 1996).

But what are, prototypically, conservative and social democratic values? While their clustering and distribution in correlation to political identity seem to differ somewhat across nations, there appears to be a set of values that generally correlate with cross-cultural conservative and social democratic ideology. Conservatives tend to use the values of self-reliance through competition, moral strength through reward and punishment systems ('tough love') and authority (*strict father morality*: Lakoff, 1996). Social democrats are apt to reason about morality in terms of shared responsibility for the individual's well being (for example through protection via government regulations and social support systems, or through empowerment via access to education independently of individual social advantage), cooperation and open two-way communication instead of hierarchical decision-making (*nurturant parent morality*: Lakoff, 1996).

However, morality is not always clear-cut. People may use both moral worldviews in different parts of their lives (*biconceptualism*: Lakoff, 1996). The question is: Which one will they apply to politics? The answer is, the one that is evoked through public political language use.

Take, as a graphic example, the Reagan democrats, blue-collar workers that were apt to reason either in a conservative value system (for example when it came to family interaction) or in a liberal value system (when it came to their interaction in labour unions). In the 1981 US presidential election campaigns, Ronald Reagan talked about his authoritarian values and how they led to his issue positions. Jimmy Carter did not talk about liberal values at all; he stated issue positions and talked facts and self-interest. The Reagan democrats voted for Reagan, against their material self-interest, because he offered them a morality-based identification. Ever since the Reagan elections, republican candidates in the US have run their campaigns on the basis of values. Democrats, for the longest time, have not. As a result, conservative ideology became commonsense among the US American population. Barack Obama was the first democratic candidate to talk overtly about issue positions embedded in progressive values during the 2008 presidential election campaigns. He talked about empathy, cooperation and two-way communication. After years of progressive ideological vacuum in the US American public mind, he offered the electorate a moral alternative to the conservative value-system and showed how it had everything to do with politics.

So is it all just values? Are issue positions and political facts obsolete as long as a politician uses enough value-laden buzzwords like 'empathy' or 'self-reliance'? Not at all. Not even close. Issues matter. Facts matter. But the interpretation of both relies on values. Parties' different issue positions have their roots in different moral assumptions. If there were one single shared morality in politics, then everyone would agree on issues and we could all go home. Political plurality is, at its core, moral plurality. Moral assumptions govern issue positions and the interpretation of sociopolitical facts. And so the latter have to be communicated in terms of the first. Recall that linguistic frames in the public debate structure a huge part of our unconscious reasoning. A framing bias towards one of many morality systems in the public debate – take again the very graphic example of the 'tax relief'-frame – makes a truly democratic conceptual plurality impossible.

But most European Social Democratic Parties have not yet caught up with this reality. Instead of making their issue positions understandable as embedded within a moral worldview, they list them one by one and talk facts and figures, in an attempt to address the electorate's self-interest. Conservative and libertarian parties have recently been much more effective in communicating their moral visions – and as a result have left Social Democratic Parties in the dust across Europe. A recent example of this, to which we shall pay closer attention in the remainder of this chapter, was the 2010 United Kingdom general election, in which the Labour Party lost 91 seats (minus 6.2 per cent), while the liberal democrats lost 6 seats (plus 1 per cent) and the Conservative Party won 97 seats (plus 3.7 per cent). So what went wrong?

The big conceptual defeat: Brown's four campaigning mistakes

Throughout his campaign, former Prime Minister and Leader of the Labour Party Gordon Brown repeatedly made four mistakes.

First, Brown talked issues, not values. His three main issues were police, the national health service (NHS) and schooling. He ran his campaign almost exclusively on those issues. Take the following excerpt from his opening statement during the first prime ministerial TV debate on 15 April 2010: 'we will protect your police, your National Health

Service, and we will protect your schools'. What Brown failed to do – in this statement as throughout his campaign – was to communicate the moral foundation of the Labour Party's positions on those very important issues. Instead of arguing within an overarching social democratic vision, he discussed the issues one by one.

Second, Brown talked self-interest. In his opening statement he went on to say: 'we can have everybody better off'. The error lies in what Brown does *not* say. Namely, he does not talk about why a common effort to have everybody 'well off' is a moral obligation from his ideological perspective. He, again, fails to address the moral imperatives his party's policy is based on.

Third, Brown's language detached him from his addressees, the electorate, and repeatedly evoked a frame in which he took on the role as a policy expert. Consider again the following sentence from his opening statement: 'we will protect your police, your national health service, and we will protect your schools'. He drew a distinction between himself and the Labour Party – referred to through *we* – and the electorate – referred to through *you*. He failed to evoke a frame of inclusion and shared responsibility in which both the goals of his policy proposals and the efforts of putting them into place are shared by his party and the electorate. Simply put, Brown evoked a frame of top-down politics rather than political two-way communication and decision-making. He remained within that frame as he went on to state: 'I know what this job involves, I look forward to putting my plan to you this evening'. Brown defined his role as a political leader as a *job* – not a moral mission – and he talked about '*my* plan' rather than a common plan. This overall frame of Brown's was especially harmful to his case since social democratic values have everything to do with non-hierarchical, common decision-making and bottom-up communication.

Fourth, Brown used frames from his political opponents that reflected a conservative worldview rather than framing the issues at hand in a social democratic worldview, for example when talking about class room interaction – 'I too want discipline' – and deregulation – 'I too want freedom for schools'.

Brown talked issues and self-interest instead of values. Brown used language that detached him from the electorate in a way that is out of synchronization with some of the most crucial social democratic values. Brown used frames that interpreted issues in terms of a conservative worldview instead of framing them on the basis of a social democratic vision of governance.

Talking values: How Cameron gained support across the ideological spectrum

While Brown didn't communicate his moral visions sufficiently, David Cameron, former leader of the opposition and leader of the Conservative Party, integrated in his argumentation traditional social democratic values, which would resonate with many people across the ideological spectrum, with conservative values. However, he did so without abandoning the main values of conservatism (such as self-reliance, competition and authority), which ultimately remained at the core of his major arguments and issue positions, and even governed his interpretation of traditional social democratic ideals such as togetherness and cooperation.

Here is an excerpt from Cameron's closing remark during the ITV-debate:

> You heard a lot about policy tonight, but I think as important as policy is your values. Let me tell you mine: If you work hard, I'll be behind you. If you want to raise a family, I will support you. If you're old and you become ill, we'll always be there for you. This is an amazing country; we've done incredible things. [...] We need two things: A government with the right values and also an understanding that we are all in this together. And real change comes when we come together and work together. That is the sort of change and that is the sort of leadership that I would bring to our great country.

Cameron explicitly talks about the shaping of society – in the past and future – as a common effort. He evokes a frame of cooperation and empathy. Contrast this with Brown's closing remarks during the same debate: 'We have to make sure we are fair to the NHS, fair to policing, fair to our schools. [...] We have to protect our NHS, schools and police.' Once more, Brown talked issues, not values.

The 'big society' frame: An easy conceptual steal

One of Cameron's core frames during the election campaigns was that of a 'big society'. Consider this statement of his during the ITV-debate: 'We can build a bigger society. But we can only do that if we recognize we need to join together, we need to come together, we need to recognize we are all in this together.' Again, Cameron evoked a frame that infers a shared societal effort, entailing the notions of togetherness and cooperation.

But notice that the policies Cameron had in mind were nothing like the ones social democrats would derive from the notions of togetherness and cooperation. At the basis of Cameron's 'big society' frame were straightforward conservative ideals such as self-reliance, less governmental protection through regulations and slimmed-down governmental support systems. By saying 'we need to recognize we are all in this together', Cameron meant that everyone ought to take on more self-responsibility and rely less on governmental protection and empowerment. But he didn't just say it. He meant it. He interpreted the concepts inferred from the 'big society' frame in terms of classic conservative values.

The conservative electorate shared Cameron's interpretation of a 'big society' in which everyone 'joins together' by increasingly relying on him- or herself when it comes to issues such as schooling and childcare; a society in which every citizen contributes to the well being of the nation by increasingly managing his or her own fate.

A social democrat's interpretation of what 'joining together' means would be quite different. That interpretation would infer a society in which shared responsibility and empathy for others guide the actions of both government and citizens, in a common effort to secure the well being of all. It would infer governmental protection and empowerment through regulations and support systems. How is it possible that one idea – 'togetherness' – elicits such utterly different interpretations? It is an *essentially contested concept* (Gallie, 1956). Essentially contested concepts are concepts such as those of democracy, freedom and equality, which do not have one commonly shared meaning. Rather, the interpretation of the concept depends on the value-based frames that structure one's worldview. One word can have utterly different meanings, depending on what political morality one uses to interpret them. By contesting the idea of a 'big society' repeatedly throughout his campaign in terms of conservative values, Cameron evoked one of many possible interpretations of the concept and strengthened that interpretation in people's minds.

Furthermore, there were plenty of cases in which Cameron used the 'big society' frame without overtly interpreting the moral entailments and policy proposals behind his vision. In all those cases, the electorate was likely to interpret the notions on the basis of its understanding of what 'joining together' morally entails. Brown didn't address this issue. What could he have done? A lot! He could have talked about the fact that behind Cameron's 'big society' frame stood the idea of leaving citizens increasingly to face life on their own; that Cameron's understanding of 'togetherness' implied the notions of self-reliance and decreased governmental protection and empowerment; and that Brown and his party stood for a 'true togetherness', governed by the ideal of shared responsibility for the common well being, achieved through government protection and empowerment. Brown didn't. Cameron gave the concept a conservative interpretation. It was an easy conceptual steal for Cameron.

Inclusion and care: Where Clegg got it right, in speech and gesture

The popularity of Nick Clegg, leader of the liberal democrats during the general election campaigns, came as a surprise to many. At first sight, Clegg ran his campaign on two credos: honesty; and change from 'the same old politics' to something new. Those credos were the overt cornerstones of his campaign slogans and speeches. But a third matter, which received relatively little attention, was bound to contribute greatly to his success and popularity.

Clegg embodied the values of inclusion and care. Clegg talked *we* instead of *I* – also during the 15 April 2010 debate: 'Don't let anyone tell you that the only choice is old politics. We can do something new, we can do something different this time.' He evoked a frame in which he and the people were one, *we* – while Brown and Cameron ('the others') stood for 'old politics'. Clegg further showed that he cared about people's opinions, and most effectively so during the televised prime ministerial debates, which for the first time in the history of general election campaigns in the United Kingdom allowed a mass audience to witness the three candidates' direct interactions with each other and a live audience – an interaction that metonymically stood for the candidates' style of interaction with the population as a political leader. Clegg outmatched Brown and Cameron in the way he interacted with the audience in three ways.

First, Clegg addressed by name audience members who asked questions, and he summarized their concerns and opinions during his answers as well as during his argumentation later in the debate. He showed that he listened and understood, and he created the impression that the audience's concerns were the concerns to be debated, even if his answers did not always refer directly to the questions posed. This form of interaction had a further side effect: it caused a higher number of camera shots to go back and forth between Clegg and the audience while he was speaking. People at home witnessed a two-way communication between the audience and Clegg, in terms of both linguistic and visual input. Brown and Cameron were more apt to give lengthy, monological answers.

Second, Clegg made people's concerns his own concerns – and most graphically so in his closing remark during the 15 April 2010 debate. Recall that Brown talked issues and Cameron talked values. Clegg didn't talk values. Rather, he embodied the values of inclusion and care first by thanking the audience for its input, and then by giving his closing remark in the form of a summary of all the audience's concerns, once more referring to everyone by name. He showed that he had listened and that he cared.

Third, Clegg embodied involvement with the audience in his gestures. He used a high number of *interactive gestures* (Bavelas et al., 1992), gestures that function to keep interlocutors involved in the discourse while one is in the speaker role – for example by referring to the other through pointing gestures and hand reaches. Clegg also frequently stepped aside from his podium and towards the audience – a gesture that signals involvement with the audience and breaks up the stereotypically monological 'lecturing' frame that a podium commonly evokes. Gestures embody a crucial part of the political discourse. Studies in multimodal communication show that people – both consciously and unconsciously – derive great amounts of information from the gestures that their interlocutor produces (Kendon, 2004; McNeill, 1992; Sweetser, 1998; Wehling, 2010).

Clegg got his interactive speech right, and Clegg got his interactive gestures right. Both are powerful tools in embodying values, and what Clegg embodied were the notions of inclusion and care. Whether those govern the liberal democrats' agenda or not, they were implied by and inferred from the discourse frame, and they were bound to resonate with audiences that hold those values. Brown and Cameron performed significantly fewer interactive gestures and had a higher number of *beats* – that is, rhythmic gestures that accompany speech segments and do not relate to the interlocutor. As a result, they evoked a monological frame that metaphorically implied discursive detachment from the electorate.

The hypocognition problem: Conservative and social democratic value systems and issue framings

Both David Cameron and Nick Clegg primarily used, throughout the general election campaigns, issue frames that imply traditional conservative values. As a brief example of this, take Cameron, who applies the conservative notion of moral strength through punishment – a classic notion of *strict father morality* (Lakoff, 1996) – when discussing both the judicial system ('put them [the criminals] in prison and keep them there for a long time') and the schooling system (in which he wanted to see 'more discipline').

In addition, both Cameron and Clegg evoked frames of togetherness, cooperation and inclusion when interacting with the electorate or talking about general societal goals. But, importantly, when it came down to the specific issue framings, they contested those notions primarily in terms of traditional conservative values. Where they didn't, one must assume that certain values that are, traditionally, strongly associated with left-wing ideologies also govern (to some extent) the issue framings of some European conservative parties. But, even so, values such as empathy, cooperation and non-hierarchical communication remain at the core of the social democratic worldview in Europe. Gordon Brown did not claim those values. He did not establish issue frames that entailed them. He did not offer a coherent social democratic worldview to the electorate.

The most central value of social democratic morality remains empathy. The notion of empathy refers to understanding others and caring about them. It implies recognizing oneself in others. In recent years we have learned a lot about how empathy works – in terms of body and brain. Social cognition (understanding the other's actions and emotions) seems to be based on *mirror neurons* (Gallese et al., 1996; see Gallese, 2003 and Iacoboni, 2008 for a review). Those neurons fire in our brain every time we see someone else perform an action. The same neurons fire when we perform the action ourselves, only they do it more strongly. This means: our brain processes what the other is doing by neurally simulating the same action. When we see someone in pain, our brain simulates pain. When we see sadness in others, our brain simulates sadness. Our brains and bodies are wired for empathy. It is a powerful mechanism. And it lies at the core of social democratic policy, issue after issue. But someone needs to say it and to introduce accordant frames to the public discourse.

The new language of social democracy: Towards cognitive transparency

Getting your frames right is imminent if you want to create cognitive transparency, in other words if you want to enable others to understand what moral assumptions and ideals your issue positions and policy proposals are based on. There is no true democracy as long as biased public frames govern people's minds. Conceptual plurality is imminent for democratic ideals, and it is your job to bring about conceptual plurality by understanding how your own values relate to your political worldview and by using the right language to go with it. If you want to communicate effectively and contribute to a fair and honest political argumentation, just keep in mind that framing is where it all starts. Below is a summary of the ten most important things to remember when it comes to cognitive transparency. And it all starts with knowing your own values.

A ten-step guide towards cognitive transparency:

i. Think about how your issue positions relate to values. Don't stop to ask yourself: 'What do I want for this society' (the answer will be your issue positions), ask yourself instead: 'Why do I care about this issue, what is the moral imperative behind my position'?
ii. Don't assume that language doesn't matter. Every word evokes a frame, and frames in the political debate always imply some form of moral argumentation, whether overtly or covertly.
iii. Talk values. Issue positions are not values in themselves; they are derived from them. Every argumentation for issue positions should start with a moral premise.
iv. Use this moral premise across all issues (your positions on many issues are likely to be based on the same general values) and repeatedly over time. The more often people hear a frame, the stronger it will become in their minds and the more likely they will be to understand where you are coming from as you talk about new issues.
v. Talk about essentially contested concepts like togetherness, fairness and justice in terms of your moral worldview. Stating that your support a 'fair' society will not be enough, people will apply their contestation of fairness to the issue if you do not make yours transparent. Don't leave the contestation of important political ideas to your opponents. You risk that an idea like 'togetherness' gets a whole new interpretation (for example in terms of self-reliance instead of empathy-based shared responsibility) and that this interpretation of the concept becomes public common sense.
vi. Don't reduce framing to election campaigns. The everyday public discourse is based on moral frames, so you need to get your frames out there day after day. It will be much easier to find good slogans

during election campaigns, when people are already used to (also) thinking about politics in term of your moral frames.
vii. Don't use your opponent's frames. Those frames will interpret the issue at hand from his/her moral perspective, will promote your opponent's worldview and will hide facts that you may find crucial.
viii. Don't negate your opponent's frames. Negating an idea means to evoke it.
ix. Be proactive, not reactive. In a debate or interview, establish your own frame on the issue and then argue within it. Don't just accept the frames your opponent or an interviewer uses. You can never win a debate by arguing within a moral worldview that is not yours. If necessary, discuss the worldview that underlies your interlocutor's frame and show how your worldview changes the matter of what the issue at hand is about (for example, empathy instead of self-reliance).
x. Get your interactive gesture right. Very likely, the gestures you naturally use when you are in a conversation or argument with friends and family mirror your way of morally interacting with others. The way you gesture is part of your social identity. Do not try to change your gesturing artificially in political speech and debate. Trust that the values you hold will come through in your gestures. If your worldview is about empathy, cooperation and tolerance for other's opinions, then you are unlikely to produce gestures that evoke frames of competition, hierarchy and disrespect.

7
Social Democracy and Trade Unions

Dimitris Tsarouhas

Introduction

Are trade unions still relevant for social democracy? Not so long ago such a question would have sounded very odd indeed. Social democracy was the natural habitat of the trade union movement, the political space where union aspirations for better living conditions and the quest for solidarity found a sympathetic hearing and, more often than not, materialized in progressive legislation. The relationship was reciprocal, too: Social Democratic Parties enjoyed the benefits of close union ties in the electoral arena, directly through union political support and indirectly through funding campaigns, sponsoring and political propaganda. Perhaps more importantly, social democratic activists and politicians cultivated strong union ties to get a foothold in workplaces and thus to experience firsthand the fears and needs of working people. Social democracy and trade unions cultivated intimate ties at many different levels.

Not any more. To be sure, some bonds between Social Democratic Parties and trade unions remain. However, even in Scandinavia, where large and encompassing trade union confederations maintain strong links with Social Democratic Parties through personnel, campaigning and organizational structure, support for Social Democratic Parties is in free fall and future prospects look very bleak indeed.[1] In some parts of Europe the unions have turned their back on mainstream social democracy and increasingly support variants of left-wing populist parties (such as Die Linke in Germany). More often, the bonds between the two sides have been severed without any kind of 'replacement'. The politics of the new era, it seems, has made the party–union link something of an aberration, a historical relic underpinned by the interest-based congruent action that brought politicians and union people together, in support of workers' rights and collective emancipation, in the now-forgotten golden age of welfare capitalism.

But does the party–union story need to end this way? In fact, is there a reason for it to end at all? In what follows I will argue that, far from being obsolete, strong organizational and political links with trade unions ought to be at the heart of social democracy's attempt to resuscitate its political fortunes. I will argue that the collective nature of the trade union movement and the bonds of solidarity it can cultivate among the working people, social democracy's natural support base, offer a promising way back for the future of social democracy: that of a mass movement rather than just an electoral machine; that of a conscious political object, driven by the aspirations of real people rather than by the 24-hour media culture and instant opinion polls tracking every utterance of the 'leader'. The unions can be vital partners in the big challenge to social democracy of our time: to rebuild a broad coalition of progressives in support of traditional social democratic objectives, as well as against the new anxieties of late modernity, fuelled as they are by individualism, rampant consumerism and the loss of the 'we' factor crucial in collective action.

The chapter begins with some necessary definitions surrounding the nature of social democracy, its relationship to trade unions and the achievements of the labour movement in the twentieth century. The next section draws on the most recent attempt to redefine social democracy for the new era: the Third Way. Focusing on the UK paradigm, it asserts that the vague communitarianism of the Blair–Giddens mantra could have done better than dismiss the unions as relics of the past. Yet in the next section I argue that a revitalization of the link between social democrats and trade unionists cannot simply be an attempt to repeat the past. Too much has changed in recent times, from cultural mutations to labour market upheaval, for it to make sense merely to resuscitate a partnership of old. To that end, the conclusion seeks to propose an optimistic way forward. Concretely, it points to the need for a new progressive majority, which would incorporate trade unions, through a genuinely broad appeal, into a progressive social pact encompassing the anxieties as well as the aspirations of a redefined, rejuvenated cross-class coalition. After all, as the conclusion section shows, there is every reason to work towards that goal. Social democracy remains as timely as ever, with economic insecurity and uncertainty about the future now touching deeply into its middle-class heartlands.

Social democracy and the trade unions: the struggle for democracy and beyond

In its long history, social democracy has put to use different policy instruments to achieve its ultimate aims of ameliorating the unjust effects of capitalism on working people and of creating conditions that will lead to their liberation, at least to an extent, from capitalism's commodifying and dehumanizing effects. Three goals were concretely set: first, to democratize capitalist society through the ballot box; second, to regulate the labour market in the interests of its labourers; and, third, to socialize the costs of labour's reproduction, creating what later became the welfare state (Sassoon, 2006, 19). The working class, in its institutionalized expression through the trade unions, was a default ally in the struggle to achieve these aims.

Even before its electoral and political apogee in the post-1945 period, social democracy was a broad church. The battle for universal suffrage was conducted in close cooperation with the liberal segments of the political spectrum. Often enough, the welfare state was first put in place by religiously minded conservatives fearful of social unrest. Indeed, looking at the different goals of social democracy in isolation, it is hard to escape the conclusion that its agenda has, more often than not, been shared by other parties too (Baldwin, 1990). The phenomenon has not gone away in the contemporary era, when liberals and conservatives alike praise, for instance, universal healthcare – which the social democrats have put in place (the NHS in Britain, for example).

Whilst social democrats struggled to distinguish themselves from other political forces in the interwar years, the Great Depression offered a viable platform for reform based on the principle of state intervention. Proof was now offered aplenty that the unregulated market does not work, and the lessons learned were put in practice after 1945. The result was the golden age of welfare capitalism. The political dominance of social democracy translated into policies regulating the labour market in favour of a viable work–life balance and the development of comprehensive welfare arrangements that ameliorated the effects of the market to an important degree.

This 'social democratic image of society' (Castles, 1976) was made possible through the trade unions. As Moschonas argues, trade unions fulfilled two vital functions: first, they helped to institutionalize a compromise with capital, trading moderate wage increases and a rare use of the strike weapon for stable rates of productivity growth and for predictability in the labour market. On those occasions where their presence was of a comprehensive, encompassing sort, their influence on the labour market rose all the more. Second, and more significantly for the purposes of this chapter, the unions worked in close cooperation with the social democratic party in order to get it into office, so as to secure a favourable stance with the government and to benefit directly from the compromise achieved with capital (Moschonas, 2002, 67).

The partnership between social democrats and trade unions was thus based not only on their common historical roots; it also resulted from a win–win game in conditions of Keynesian economic management, regulated capital flows and stable employment. It also allowed social democrats to combine the goals of efficiency in economic management with a high degree of social justice. Social democrats were the 'people's party' of the working class, through their close union ties and policy programmes, whilst also defending the general interest in a way that proved appealing to the expanding middle class too (Moschonas, 2002, 68). 'Respectable' mass party and the authentic voice of the working class: social democrats never had it that good. The international post-1945 *Zeitgeist* offered social democracy a great opportunity to put its mark on socio-economic and political events. More often than not (and emphatically in Scandinavia) it succeeded in doing so.

Reflecting the trend away from industrialized capitalism and having to rely ever more on the middle classes and on public sector employees to maintain its position, social democracy diluted its earlier, more radical politics aims. The 1959 Bad Godesberg programme of the German social democrats (SPD) is a symbol of that process, as social democracy became increasingly preoccupied with the preservation of status quo achievements. Soon, however, capitalism would prove the accuracy of Marx's insight regarding its volatile, dynamic and ever-changing nature. As Sassoon succinctly put it,

> Social democrats [...] remained wedded to a nationalist conception of politics and reinforced it constantly, ring-fencing their achievements [...] within the territorial boundaries of the state, while capitalism set out to stride the globe. (Sassoon, 2006, 32)

What is more, the rise of the 'affluent society' (Galbraith, 1959) meant that intimate ties of communal living that had sustained generations of working-class people and trade unionists started giving rise to individualism and a newfound sense of privacy that was, until then, restricted to the middle and upper classes (see Favretto, 2006, 166).

By the 1970s social democracy was in crisis. Economic crisis, lower rates of growth, rising unemployment and the collapse of Bretton

Woods shook the foundations of the post-war compromise, challenged its effectiveness to deliver efficiency with justice and forced social democrats to a defensive stance they have yet to recover from. Social democrats were confronted with the realization that national Keynesianism had reached its limits, and Mitterrand's U-turn in 1983 in France was a catalyst. Its electoral appeal waning and its distinguished character questioned, social democracy proved unable to resist the forces of neoliberal economics unleashed first in the United States and then progressively throughout the world. Despite the fact that it gained new electoral footholds in newly democratized states in southern Europe and its power in north-western Europe remained on the whole intact, social democracy was suffering from a *structural* problem of self-identification in a rapidly changing world.

As deregulation, privatization and welfare cuts spread, the trade unions became a favourite target of the new consensus-makers, who described them as 'anachronistic', 'wasteful' and 'spendthrift'. New dividing lines among working people emerged, as a division between the competition-exposed, tradable sector of the economy (and its unions) and the allegedly 'sheltered' and inflation-driven domestic sector was identified. More generally, unions were significantly weakened as globalization offered new exit opportunities to capital and diminished its returns regarding centralized collective bargaining (Swank, 2002, 27). In Europe, the project of European integration took the form of market integration and accommodated the demands of supply-side macroeconomic policies that favoured capital's volatility. The era of globalization also witnessed massive population movements resulting in flows of immigration towards the western world, which often transformed the social fabric and further contributed to a frantic search for identity among the working people.

The best articulated response to those changes was the Third Way project, which originated in the US and the Clinton-led Democrat Party but found its most elaborate expression in the 'New' Labour Party in the UK. Its recipe for social democratic renewal soon found imitators throughout Europe and beyond. In its 1990s heyday, the Third Way appeared as the *only* available strategy for progressives in coping with our complex reality.

The Third Way and its vision of social democracy

It is slightly unfair to add to the barrage of criticism that the Third Way (Blair, 1998; Giddens, 1994, 1998) has received over the years (but see Hall, 1998). This is not only because this particular approach to social democracy is by now pretty much obsolete, or because it assumed different characteristics in different countries (save for an inbuilt reluctance to assess critically the wisdom of following market principles in all spheres of life), which led to a loose usage of the term (Faux, 1999).[2] It is mostly because the Third Way rarely addressed the question of the relationship between the trade union movement and social democracy, save for a few isolated references. In those, the link to the unions was portrayed as old-fashioned, a relic of the past that hardly fit the expectations of the electorate from new social democracy (Ludlam, 2005, 104).

Still, the Third Way was for long the reformist left's main ideological and political mantra. Its prescriptions and analysis of contemporary society fundamentally affected the ability of social democracy to formulate its vision of the good society. In that crucial sense, its overall approach had a lot to do with how social democrats should relate to this crucial link with their political and ideological roots.

One of the most interesting aspects of the Third Way approach, as espoused by Tony Giddens and implemented in office by Tony Blair, was its embrace of community-oriented policies and programmes to 'reclaim' the right-wing agenda on issues such as crime or policing. As Giddens put it, 'the traditional left's indifference to issues such as crime and family breakdown damaged its credibility in other areas where its policies were strong' (Giddens, 2000, 50). The tough approach to 'crime and the causes of crime', as well as the attempt to build a new social contract, consisting of 'no rights without responsibilities', were concerned with enabling Third Way sympathizers to appear connected to everyday people and to address the issues they cared about. The 'old left's' elitism was out and community politics was in (though not all: see Giddens, 2000, 63–65). Moreover, the social nature of human beings was promoted by 'new' social democracy as evidence of its anti-Thatcherite orientation and of its recognition of the important community bonds that hold society together. Full community participation led not only to the avoidance of social ills like crime and drug abuse; it also enabled individuals to maximize their potential and participate fully in social activities. If globalization had rendered equality a utopia, community-based policies founded on fairness could perhaps lead to acceptable forms of accommodation with inequality.

The Third Way project, in the UK and elsewhere, proved unable to connect with voters despite its tough rhetoric and occasional policies (something it may come to regret in the face of a rising pan-European far-right movement). Its community-oriented recipes neglected the salience of the union movement in making such a community real and vibrant. That is to say, 'new' social democracy appeared to believe that disengagement with the roots of the labour movement was a hallmark of its modernist credentials, and that this would make Social Democratic Parties electable in the long run. It was a mistake committed earlier by US Democrats, who decided to distance themselves from traditional constituencies in order to champion a more appealing, 'centrist' agenda. Over time, this led to a widening gap between party preferences and the everyday politics of working people. Ordinary citizens felt disempowered and the Democrats lost their natural support base (Skocpol and Greenberg, 1997).

This was not a coincidence or a misunderstanding of Third Way intentions. As Eric Shaw has argued, 'the New Labour concept of community is quite distinct from that familiar to traditional social democrats for whom it was inextricably bound with ideas of social solidarity and equality' (Shaw, 2005, 202–203). The community-based understanding of the Third Way was permeated by the logic of rights alongside obligations, of taking something back after offering something in return. A *quid pro quo* in welfare was required, along with an agenda for reform that became increasingly reliant on the private sector to deliver public services. This approach affected the relationship with the unions at two levels: first, in terms of policy content through public–private partnerships, labour law and so on.[3] Second, and more centrally to this contribution, this approach produced an indifferent and often hostile attitude to the union movement and its alleged 'complacency' to the major challenges that globalization *inevitably* introduced. The unions were not part of the Third Way's brave new world and were useful only insofar as electoral support was concerned regarding financing the party and assisting its candidates' (re)election.

Quite simply, the whole logic was flawed. The partnership with the unions certainly needed, and still needs, rethinking. Wherever union bosses assume functions befitting those of political leaders, they lead to confusion, internal wrangling and ultimately electoral defeat. Trade unions have a big responsibility to give voice to the excluded and the marginalized combining practical politics with an open-minded, progressive approach to legislation and social partnership. The ranks of the newly excluded, those on low incomes, precarious jobs and no social security, have swelled. The unions have generally failed to address their concerns and often give the impression of an aloof grouping interested in preserving the rights obtained for its members before addressing the concerns of non-members.

Yet the Third Way fallacy of excluding the unions from the attempt to build a progressive alliance betrays a dangerous neglect of the labour movement's foundations, as well as a disregard for the practical realities of the labour market. If, in the famous words of Tony Blair, 'what matters is what works', excluding your natural allies from the social democratic project is bound to make the new coalition more shallow and less value-driven than it ought to be. When the crisis hit home in 2008–2009, this is exactly the picture that emerged. Social democracy had ceased, in most countries across Europe, to be a movement. It had carelessly abandoned its mass character in favour of individually oriented policy packages appealing almost exclusively to metropolitan tastes and middle-class concerns. When the time came to stand up for an alternative political and economic project that would free productive forces from the asphyxiating constraints of the market, social democracy's natural constituents either remained silent or, worse yet, turned their back to their former allies. At any rate, trade unions in the UK and across most of Europe are by now as 'moderate' in their demands as they have ever been.

This is a relationship that needs urgent repair at a time when, across the continent, budget cuts and harsh austerity measures threaten to undermine welfare achievements for millions of employees and their dependants. Social democrats and trade unionists cannot afford a moment of complacency any more. But the road to renewal goes through an honest assessment of the status quo and of the socio-economic transformation of our time.

Social democrats and trade unions in the new era

The shortcomings of the Third Way with regard to its approach towards the trade unions should not blind us to the fact that real changes in the party-union linkage have indeed occurred. Contemporary changes in society, economics and politics are profound, facilitated by technological innovation and spearheaded by the communications revolution (Held et al., 1999). Both social democrats and trade unions face a set of dramatic challenges, which call into question their ability to retain their mass character and to inspire a progressive way out of the current conundrum.

Social democracy is a somewhat paradoxical political animal. It is a radical movement in the sense that it envisions a socio-economic reality freed from the impositions of market fundamentalism, calling for a cross-border solidarity that reaches beyond the confines of the nation state. However, its major achievements took place in the post-war conservative era of cultural certainties and economic stability underpinned by the Bretton Woods settlement. Today it has to battle with a historic challenge, as it seeks to accommodate the cultural demands of late modernity whilst addressing traditional socio-economic grievances caused by deregulated markets. The challenge becomes even greater when one considers one of the central paradoxes of our time: we face global problems regarding terrorism, climate change, energy security and so on, yet our mode of operation, way of thinking and institutional armoury remain geared to an ineffective national framework. Even the European Union (EU), the regional project geared towards circumventing the dominance of nation-mindedness in the aftermath of the Second World War catastrophe, is showing signs of exhaustion and a dangerous lack of political initiative as the Eurozone crisis threatens to undo decades of progress in supranational norm-creation.

Surveys conducted over decades confirm that a shift towards post-materialist values and the rise of identity politics have occurred (Inglehart, 1987). The result has been the breakup of the social democratic constituency and its internal division on a number of different issues. A capable leadership and deep bonds of loyalty to the party and its history can address the problem, at least up to a point. More often than not, however, new generations of social democrats lack the charisma of the war generation, and their approach to politics is driven more by the requirements of 24-hour media scrutiny than by broader considerations of the movement's political direction.

In party political terms, this fragmentation is usually expressed through the creation of influential parties to the left of social democracy, as well as of powerful green parties. Left parties style themselves on the model of 'traditional' social democracy, adopting earlier slogans centred on national economic and political sovereignty. They enhance their appeal by adopting popular causes (for instance a legally binding minimum wage) and usually side with conservatives on questions of identity politics, multiculturalism, immigration and so on. Should the electoral system favour smaller parties, their influence on national politics could be decisive and their rhetoric very harmful for social democrats.

The green movement and its party political expression reflect the split in social democratic constituents and go beyond it at the same time. Their political platform often runs parallel to social democratic concerns regarding environmental sustainability and the need for balanced growth, but their often post-ideological approach to socio-economic issues of concern to social democratic constituents makes an alliance with green parties a precarious choice.[4] At the heart of social democracy's dilemma in the modern era stands therefore the question of how to combine its left-wing credentials with the new agenda brought forward by new social movements and by the rise of identity politics (Kitschelt, 1994). Furthermore, 'modern' conservatives and liberals alike have been quick to try and claim the 'green' agenda for themselves in a number of countries.

> The unions too face a world much less accommodating to their traditional agenda. Their source of strength has been industrial labour, preferably with a strong class identity cultivated through union work, industrial activism and ideological leadership. But conditions have changed in a number of fronts, and some of these changes are irreversible. Workers have become a heterogeneous body and their common interests have been affected by the rise of the affluent society and the individualization of lifestyle choices. This has led to a fragmentation of the union movement and an increase in intra-union conflicts as to the strategies to be pursued and the goals to be fulfilled. (Locke and Thelen, 1995)

Clearly, this has marked a decline in union power, both with regard to its influence in the post-Keynesian world and in terms of numerical strength and declining membership (Tsarouhas, 2008; Visser, 2006). What is more, the formerly encompassing union confederations have come under attack by employers favouring flexibility and the decentralization of collective bargaining at branch, local, or even individual employee level (Golden et al., 2008, 174). Although interpretations about the precise nature of union decline differ, increased capital mobility is coupled with structural constraints in macroeconomic policy making. In the case of Europe, the process of European integration has added a further impediment to the influence of unions, to the extent that demand-led policies have been institutionally ruled out since Maastricht, and this fact has made unions less significant partners for governments.

The loosening of ties between social democrats and trade unions is therefore the result of factors that sometimes reach beyond the ability of both actors to control their environment. To take but one example, collective bargaining decentralization and its negative effect on union influence are unlikely to be reversed in the near future, and the same holds true for the fragmentation of the social democratic constituency. What is required therefore is a new strategy befitting our times.

The importance of social democracy and the trade unions today

The task ahead for social democrats willing to rebuild their movement and to offer a fresh impetus to their mission is undoubtedly difficult. Yet there are grounds to be optimistic, even in this complex policy environment, regarding both the relevance of social democracy and the positive role that trade unions can play in this process.

To start with, social democracy's commitment to encompassing, generously funded welfare states is in tune with contemporary economic reality. Evidence suggests that the shift in state revenues derived from taxation in favour of a lessened burden on income tax is a political choice rather than one necessitated by economic globalization. The challenge, therefore, is to be able to make the *political* argument in favour of a shift towards higher income taxes for those who can afford them, so as to back up a universalist model of welfare (see Pontusson, 2005, 216). Moreover, the (potential) social democratic constituency on the issue has risen in recent decades, as economic insecurity has spread to include ever larger parts of the middle class (Pontusson, 2005, 201).

The argument regarding welfare and social democracy holds true in more general terms too. Duane Swank has persuasively argued that institutional features approximating social democratic objectives, such as social corporatist interest representation and universal welfare programmes, mitigate the impact of globalization and need not lead to welfare state retrenchment (Swank, 2002). While global capital and financial markets constrain governments everywhere, social democratic policies are not necessarily doomed, considering that investors hardly ever follow the singular logic of lower taxes before deciding on investment sites (Mosley, 2003).

Trade unions need not despair either. They have been weakened everywhere and have suffered great losses in influence. Yet, at least in Europe, they have managed to retain their institutional significance in terms of public policy reform, and they remain decisive players in resisting the politics of austerity. Furthermore, the evidence of an inevitable clash between the trade union movement, conceived in traditional terms, and the new social movements remains flimsy at best. Callaghan, for instance, has used examples from trade union politics in the UK, Denmark and Germany to argue that, far from categorically objecting to the 'greening' of Social Democratic Parties, unions occupy a more complex position and are willing to embrace the agenda of ecological sustainability to the extent that wages, employment and working conditions are not undermined (Callaghan, 2006, 187). Finally, encompassing unions have a positive effect on economic performance, since coordinated wage bargaining can still deliver a good macroeconomic performance in the medium term. What is more, unionization correlates positively with relatively higher levels of wage compression. Deunionization, on the other hand, contributes to the rise in wage inequality.

The evidence summarized above indicates that social democracy is relevant. It is also more necessary than ever, in light of the recent economic crisis, which highlights the unsustainable nature of unregulated capitalism. The project of social democratic renewal goes through the rebuilding of strong institutional ties with the trade union movement and the formation of a broad progressive political platform. This broad coalition, including NGOs and other social movements, can only be built if social democracy succeeds in combining its message of materialist restoration of welfare and social compensation with a positive response to the anxieties of late modernity. Social democracy needs to articulate a new vision of the good society as the secure society, one in which solidarity and a sense of community offer individuals the chance for collective self-expression. In building such a coalition, the support of representative, innovative and forward-looking trade unions can prove very valuable.

Notes

1. In the 2010 Swedish general election, the Social Democratic Party (SAP) recorded its worst election outcome since the First World War, gathering only 30 per cent of the votes and thus allowing the incumbent centre-right coalition to remain in office. A factor in the defeat was that only 50 per cent of the votes cast by members of the social democratic Trade Union Confederation (LO) went to SAP. Meanwhile some surveys suggest that LO members are increasingly of the opinion that LO ought to cease its financial and political support of SAP (Kronlid, 2010).
2. Some of the criticism exerted against the Third Way claimed that this agenda had nothing to do with social democracy. To the extent that Labour Party policies were representative of the Third Way, this is an unfair criticism. Labour funded public services generously, introduced the minimum wage and moved (albeit timidly) towards a mild redistribution by stealth.

Hugh Collins (2001, 205) has argued that the British Third Way was an interesting mix with regard to labour law. While endorsing the freedom of association principle held dear by social democrats (albeit subject to criticism if used to hinder partnership-based solutions with employers), it was suspicious of free collective bargaining to set the price for labour. The Third Way

preferred instead to promote alternative channels of employee representation, so as not to compel employers to enter collective bargaining agreements. Clearly its endorsement of collective bargaining was a qualified one – a very different stance from the practice of social democrats in Scandinavia.
3. While in Germany the SPD and the Greens worked together in relative harmony in the past at federal level and there are signs that this may be repeated in the future, Sweden tells a different story altogether. There the decision by the SAP leader to enter a formal coalition with the Green party a year and a half prior to the 2010 election led to loud intra-party protests and calls for an inclusion of the Left Party into the coalition, so as to balance out the 'bourgeois' credentials of the Greens on issues regarding social insurance reform, the unemployment benefit system and so on. The clear defeat of the 'red-red-green' coalition and the sharp decline in SAP's popularity following the announcement of the pact testify to the difficulty of combining the often clashing demands of left and green parties in a common platform.
4. That percentage is roughly 20 per cent and holds true for the rise in wage inequality in the US from the 1970s to the late 1980s. See (Pontusson, 2005, 61).

8
The Greatest Happiness Principle: An Imperative for Social Democracy?

Christian Kroll

Regaining discourse sovereignty

European social democracy is in crisis – both in terms of popularity and in terms of visionary thinking. While the Third Way politics of the late 1990s and early 2000s seemed to yield a seemingly endless era of social democratic hegemony, today the number of centre-left governments has declined significantly. More importantly, the catastrophic results of centre-left parties over the past years in, for example, Germany, France and the UK illustrate a deeper problem: social democracy has lost its *Deutungshoheit* – its analytical sovereignty – in many of the important societal discourses of our time. The most important and basic of those discourses is probably the one about 'what makes the good society'. While this question has usually been approached in the past through theoretical and ideological reasoning, new approaches are currently developed on the basis of findings from an emerging academic discipline, which analyses the levels and determinants of human well-being: the science of happiness. This research field gives us clues as to what the ingredients of the good society are – clues derived not from armchair philosophy but from empirical grassroots evidence, by asking people themselves how they evaluate the quality of their lives and by analysing the socio-economic correlates. These approaches are increasingly catching the attention of national and international policymakers and organizations that are in the process of redefining what progress means today.

This development comes at a time when the strong link between class affiliation and voting behaviour is dissolving in favour of a market logic in the political sphere. People no longer vote for the same party over and over again, out of loyalty, but have become consumers of political ideas who feel free to decide anew, before each election, who deserves their vote. Consequently, a more complex level of political competition is emerging on the basis of our improved ability to monitor well-being. As a result, the leading political force of the future is likely to be the one that facilitates the *greatest happiness for the greatest number*, similarly to what the British economist Jeremy Bentham envisioned 200 years ago, through his utilitarian principle of the *greatest happiness* (see also Layard, 2009; Veenhoven, 2004). Back then, the idea quickly disappeared into the bookshelves of economic history, because policymakers did not have the social indicators at hand to measure happiness on a large societal level. By contrast, we now do.

The following chapter shall therefore present the recent discourses on measuring progress, happiness and quality of life in more detail; and it will ultimately show how all these factors matter for the renewal of social democracy. The key take-away is this: not only is social democracy capable of becoming a strong voice in these discourses, but engaging in them in order to formulate a convincing social democratic narrative of how we want to live together in the future is also imperative to ensuring the relevance of social democracy as a dominant political force in the twenty-first century.

A new paradigm for policymaking

Just like seafarers, politicians need an accurate compass to steer them through the unknown waters. They – and everyone else – only know how well they are doing if there is a precise way of assessing their performance. In fact, the path to the good society begins with the question of how we define and measure it before thinking about how to achieve it. Hence, this is not just a debate in the ivory towers of academia, but one that is relevant to all of us in deciding towards what goals society should develop.

So – what has guided public policy in the past century? First and foremost, politicians have been busy trying to encourage economic growth, and all of us in the industrialized world have enjoyed tremendous advancements in our standards of living since the Second World War. The main parameter in this endeavour, ever since its invention in the 1930s, has been the gross domestic product (GDP): a measure of all goods and services produced in an economy within a year. This measure indeed has a range of important advantages. It captures entities with different units of measure and summarizes them in one single monetary figure. Furthermore, it can easily be compared across nations once it has been adjusted for power purchasing parity. Finally, the assumption behind using this metric is that the higher the GDP, the better people are able to satisfy their needs.

Despite the fact that its inventors after the Great Depression never meant GDP to be anything but an indicator of economic production, over the past decades GDP has increasingly been treated as a measure of progress or – even worse – of well-being in our nations. This has to be viewed in the context of the Cold War and of the two superpowers flexing their muscles in a contest for world hegemony. Moreover, the fixation on GDP mirrors the materialistic value orientations prevalent in the war and among immediately post-war generations (Inglehart, 1990). Until today, though, the smallest fluctuations in GDP are meticulously observed and the latest figures are announced in a solemn tone in the evening news, as the number appears to signal whether a government is doing a good job or failing at its core mission of raising the levels of production.

But 'the times they are a-changing': society and policymakers are becoming more and more aware of problems around using GDP as a compass for the good society. The latest summary of long-standing criticisms around the metric was given by the Stiglitz Commission, a blue-chip roundtable of experts, including five Nobel Laureates; it was commissioned by President Sarkozy to establish how well-being should be measured. The experts reiterated that GDP, among other things, does not take into account the distribution of income, whether the money is spent on actually improving people's living conditions, and that no reference is made to sustainability and informal labour (Stiglitz et al., 2009). Moreover, the metric may actively promote the making of wrong decisions, as in the case of the recent global financial crisis, which was partly brought about by chasing short-term profit. Furthermore, the discourse on climate change and the experience of the social limits to growth (as formulated back in the 1970s by Hirsch) have left their mark on the public consciousness. Thus an international consensus is building that the *quality of life* within a nation must become the central aim of government policy. This approach does not mean underestimating the importance of a prosperous economy for societal well-being; but, instead of treating it as an aim in itself, it rather regards it as one means among others for reaching this societal well-being.

How can we measure quality of life?

If a higher quality of life for the population and the good society are our aims, then what should be our compass? Although GDP suffers from a range of shortcomings in this regard, politicians, the media and thus most voters have their eyes firmly fixed on this dominant benchmark. This comes as no surprise, given that academics and statisticians have failed to come up with a viable alternative. But what could such an alternative be? This question is both complicated and overdue for an answer, as the sheer number of institutions currently investigating it, from the Organisation of Economic Co-operation and Development (OECD) to the European Union (EU) Commission, illustrates.[1]

Stiglitz himself uses the analogues of a doctor who would never assess a patient on the basis of one indicator alone, or of a driver who will want to know not only how fast his car is going but also how much fuel he has left, what gear he is in and so on (Gertner, 2010). As a matter of fact we have a range of such metrics already on our national dashboards – which is in part overlooked even by the Stiglitz Commission (Maggino and Ruviglioni, 2010; Noll, 2010). Although the debate seems to have not reached beyond the ivory tower until very recently, quality of life is in fact a well-known and researched concept in the social sciences.

In academia, quality of life is usually understood to comprise 'objective descriptors and subjective evaluations of physical, material, social and emotional well-being' (Felce and Perry, 1993, 13). In other words quality of life contains outer descriptions of people's living conditions – that is, indicators of objective well-being such as income, the number of doctors per 1,000 inhabitants, education levels – as well as statements about how people perceive these conditions and how they evaluate the quality of their lives – that is, indicators of subjective well-being such as reported life satisfaction and happiness.

Particularly the first group, that of (objective) indicators, is fairly well developed across Europe's statistical offices. These indicators are widespread due to their advantage of being easily compared across observations and of not suffering from potential biases of social desirability or from ordering effects (as social surveys do). A prominent example of a combination of objective indicators to formulate policy aims is the United Nations Development Programmes (UNDP) Human Development Index (HDI), which incorporates education, income and life expectancy measures into a single country score (see Table 8.1). For the developed world, however, indexes such as the Canadian Index of Well-Being or the Stiglitz Commission's list of dimensions may be more informative, due to the narrowing of gaps at the top end in the HDI.

Objective measures of the quality of life are based on the premise that certain societal traits are desirable. Thus such measures contain a normative approach to the good society. Researchers and politicians formulate goals and measure the extent to which societies conform to them. There

Table 8.1 Comparison of prominent approaches to quality of life

Canadian index of well-being	Stiglitz commission	Human development index
1. Democratic engagement 2. Community vitality 3. Education 4. Environment 5. Living standards 6. Healthy populations 7. Time use 8. Leisure and culture	1. Material living standards 2. Health 3. Education 4. Personal activities including work 5. Political voice and governance 6. Social connections and relationships 7. Environment 8. Insecurity (economic and physical)	1. Income 2. Education 3. Life expectancy

are some major problems with such an approach, though. First of all, it is unclear precisely what and how many elements should be part of such an index (or should even form just a loose collection of single indicators) for the good society. This problem is complicated particularly (though not exclusively) in relation to politically sensitive areas: Should inequality or divorce rates be among the criteria? Even if one has reached an agreement over the different dimensions of the quality of life index, the next question is how to weigh them. In other words, how many years of education are equivalent in worth to good health, or how important is it to have green areas in one's neighbourhood, by comparison with the level of job security? Finally, the figures, no matter how accurate they are, contain no information about how people themselves actually perceive these living conditions. That is to say, it is unclear, just from looking at the numbers, how far what these figures represent actually makes them *happy*.

Happiness as a new guide to the good society

Advantages

Such shortcomings may be overcome by using happiness as the guide to the good society. This idea is rooted in a new 'science of happiness', which has been established over the past few years at the intersection between psychology, economics, sociology and political science. The number of publications is rising exponentially, and the research field is on its way to forming a mainstream discipline, complete with research centres, doctoral dissertations, debates in major academic journals and its own *Journal of Happiness Studies*. Seminal introductions to this research area, with particular focus on the policy context, were written by Layard (2005), Diener et al. (2009), and Bok (2010).

Knowledge is gathered by asking people in a range of global and national surveys how satisfied they are with their lives and certain life domains, which then allows researchers to establish the statistical determinants of happiness. In the academic literature, the concept has gained prominence under the description 'subjective well-being', which is defined as 'people's evaluations of their lives, and includes variables such as life satisfaction, the frequent experience of pleasant emotions, the infrequent experience of unpleasant emotions, satisfaction with domains such as marriage and work, and feelings of fulfilment and meaning' (Diener and Oishi, 2004, 1). Thus there is a range of ways to assess somebody's subjective well-being. While more complex scales, such as the 'Satisfaction with Life Scale' (Diener et al., 1985), or the General Health Questionnaire (GHQ; Goldberg and Williams, 1988) cover several different aspects, the most widespread survey question is about generalized life satisfaction: 'All things considered, how satisfied are you with your life as a whole these days?'. Respondents can then rate themselves on a scale going for instance from 0 (completely dissatisfied) to 10 (completely satisfied). Alternatively, many surveys ask: 'Taken all things together, how happy would you say you are? Very happy, quite happy, not very happy, or not at all happy?' While the latter is taken to represent the affective side of well-being, the former is usually known to capture a more reflective, cognitive statement and therefore is better suited as a basis for designing and evaluating policy.

Either way, a large amount of research undertaken by psychologists is devoted to testing and assuring the quality of those well-being indicators. In sum, it has been shown that such a measure is capable of adequately capturing a person's state of happiness (see Diener et al., 1999; Kahneman and Krueger, 2006; Kahneman et al., 1999). More precisely, these indicators have proven valid and reliable on the basis of correlations with neurological functioning and many other related quality-of-life measures – such as the rating of one's happiness by friends, colleagues, and family; health; the frequency of smiling during an interview; or the frequent verbal expression of positive emotions during experiments. Furthermore, the answers are interpersonally and to a large extent even cross-culturally comparable. Even critics agree that, while the current indicators are not perfect and ought to be refined further, in their current state they are no less accurate than dominant indicators of economic activity (such as the GDP).

Starting in the 1960s, the social indicators movement has been supported for the first time in modern academia through the pioneer studies by Wilson (1967), Andrews and Withey (1976), and Campbell et al. (1976). However, it is only since the beginning of the twenty-first century that the science moved into the mainstream and caught serious attention from policymakers. This process was in part fuelled by the fact that the psychologist and happiness researcher Daniel Kahneman was awarded the Nobel Prize in 2002 for his contributions to behavioural economics.

Today empirical evidence and the database are ever increasing, which allows us to put together the puzzle of human well-being piece by piece. Surveys such as the German Socio-Economic Panel look at thousands of people over time and allow for the examination of well-being fluctuations by following the same person, over decades, through unemployment, marriage and divorce. At the same time, the Gallup World Poll and the World Values Survey include representative samples of countries that cover almost 85 per cent of the world's population. Yet more remains unknown than is known in this research field; but we are at the beginning of an exciting evolution, with an average of one new academic publication on this topic every week[2] (Clark et al., 2008).

A key strength of subjective indicators of well-being, in particular as opposed to the more traditional objective ones, is that they do not contain a normative judgement about what a good society should be. Instead this approach asks people directly about how they actually perceive their living conditions, thus allowing for a subsequent statistical analysis of what factors correlate with (or even causally precede) high well-being. By not imposing an outside ideal of the good life, such a procedure is bottom-up more than top-down. In fact, although this school of thought is only now gaining prominence, its roots go back to Aristotle, who maintained that, rather than theorizing about the good life, one should assess human well-being by asking people directly how they are doing.[3] Moreover, the procedure is ideologically neutral and inherently democratic, as it gives each respondent a voice.

Subjective indicators of well-being therefore overcome the missing variable and the weighting problem of objective indexes described earlier by allowing each respondent to decide and weigh for him- or herself what is important to his or her well-being. At the end of this cognitive process, respondents express their life satisfaction in one single figure, by implicitly comparing their ideal living conditions with their actual living conditions. Objective indexes, by contrast, assume a certain weighting, which comes from the outside; furthermore, they do not allow for different weights for different individuals, despite the fact that we can assume that preferences and the relevance of certain factors for well-being vary between individuals and nations at least to a certain extent (Diener et al., 2009).

Last but not least, the method of identifying the correlates of happiness powerfully prevents a repeated error that respondents make when asked directly about what they *think* would make them happy. People usually 'mispredict utility' by overestimating the effect of monetary factors (a higher income, winning the lottery) and underestimate other important aspects, which – when looking at the subjective well-being distributions – will actually make or keep them happy, such as the quality of human relationships (Frey, 2008).

Evidence

What are the main findings from this research field so far? It is impossible to summarize a whole body of literature in only a few paragraphs,[4] but, in short, it turns out that the biggest drivers of well-being are close interpersonal relationships at the micro-level and cohesive communities at the macro-level. Especially in richer countries, where basic economic needs are met, social capital – that is, the quality of human relationships illustrated for instance by the ability to trust others – is more important to well-being than material factors (Helliwell and Putnam, 2004; Helliwell et al., 2010; Kroll, 2008).[5] In fact, the biggest added value of the literature on happiness so far has been to point out the imminent role of non-material aspects, in particular social relations: this has caused a shake-up in the mainstream economic world view that some have called 'a revolution in economics' (Frey, 2008, 4).

Material wealth is important, too, but it seems to be so especially at the lower end of the scale. A debate is going on about whether the marginal utility of income is decreasing, and whether relative income is more important than absolute income; some support these ideas (Inglehart and Klingemann, 2000; Layard, 2005; Layard et al., 2010), some dispute them (Deaton, 2008; Stevenson and Wolfers, 2008),[6] and others find mixed evidence, depending on the indicators used (Kahneman and Deaton, 2010). The most widely discussed phenomenon in this regard is the Easterlin paradox, which mainly holds that although richer countries are generally happier than poorer countries, increases in GDP over time have not led to significant increases in average national subjective well-being in the industrialized world. It has been attempted to explain this finding by the fact that we adapt to material gains (hedonic treadmill), and that we assess our wealth in relation to other people, who have also become richer at the same time (positional treadmill, 'keeping up with the Joneses'; see, for example, Layard, 2006).[7]

Another important finding from the existing studies concerns the detrimental effect of unemployment: losing one's job reduces life satisfaction as much as bereavement or marital break-up, even when the income remains constant. This is proof that the harmful effects of unemployment go way beyond the financial loss, to include reduced self-esteem, perceived lack of a purpose in life and social isolation (see Clark and Oswald, 1994). What is clear, however, is that our biggest priority so far, economic growth per se, is less important for people's subjective well-being in view of other factors. Happiness research implies that it is more important to allow people to have fulfilling and dignifying jobs and to be active than to let them accumulate as much wealth as possible, or to foster growth for its own sake. In other words, *the sport of employment*[8] is more important for happiness.

What about macroeconomic and social conditions? With regard to the national averages in life satisfaction, Figure 8.1 displays the latest available data from the European Social Survey for 24 EU countries. Denmark comes out at the top, with 8.52, followed by Switzerland and several other Nordic countries. Hungary and Bulgaria are at the bottom, with 5.29 and 4.41 respectively. Although it would be tempting, especially for social democrats, to declare from these figures that equality and a bigger welfare state correlate to higher life satisfaction, such conclusions would (yet) be premature. While some strongly support such a view (following Radcliff, 2001), others have disputed a correlation between social security and life satisfaction at a global level (following Veenhoven, 2000). What seems certain at this point is that cultural differences moderate the effect of equality on subjective well-being, and that, as a side effect of (at least perceived) higher social mobility, there is a stronger tolerance for inequality in the US than in Europe (Alesina et al., 2004).

In this regard, interesting findings in the form of a huge macroeconomic field experiment can be observed in the East European countries, which have undergone dramatic socio-economic changes after 1990. As the Romanian example shows (Figure 8.2), capitalism has brought about a significant diversification of subjective well-being. While in 1990 all income groups were more or less equally (dis)satisfied with their lives, the gap between rich and poor has now widened enormously. While the left-wing interpretation of such a finding would

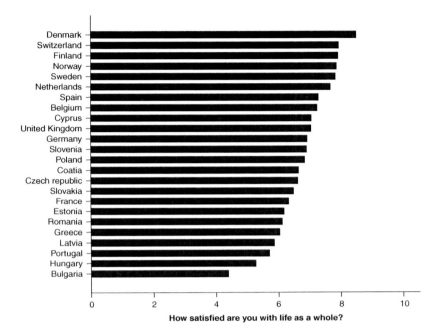

Figure 8.1 Life satisfaction across Europe (European Social Survey data)

probably be related to the deterioration of society in relation to a bumpy transition to capitalism, the right-wing conclusion would be that a meritocracy took hold in which the rich are rewarded through higher happiness. In any case, it has to be noted that the richest decile (number 10) was most successful at improving the well-being of members of this groups after 1990, while well-being declined for many other people, and especially for the poorest (decile number 1). While these figures in no way should lead us to advocate a return to the terrors of the communist regime, they do give us an indication of how well we are doing in building a fair democratic capitalist society.

Critiques

Despite the accumulating evidence, the idea of using happiness as a guide for public policy may be criticized by those who suggest that happiness is a private matter and that attempts to bring in the state would end in an Orwell-like nanny state. However, although no proponent of subjective well-being would actually come close to making

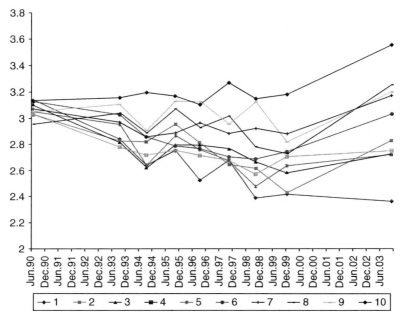

Figure 8.2 Subjective well-being after 1990 in Romania by income decile (1 = poorest, 10 = richest)
Source: Bălțătescu (2007).

the case for a 'happiness police', the research itself shows that people in free democratic societies are much happier than those under repressive regimes. Furthermore, individuals have very little control over their surroundings, such as crime levels in their neighbourhood or the way the economy is organized. These factors, however, have a huge impact on our well-being and call for collective action. Hence communities, society and the state do have a duty to create the most favourable conditions for citizens in this regard, in a concerted effort. An individual's happiness is to a very large degree socially determined, which means that, whenever there are externalities involved, the state has a responsibility to do its best using all available evidence on quality of life.

Another important and long-standing criticism originally comes from Amartya Sen, who argued that, if 'a starving wreck, ravished by famine, buffeted by disease, is made happy through some mental conditioning (say, via the "opium" of religion), the person will be seen as doing well on this mental-state perspective, but that would be quite scandalous'

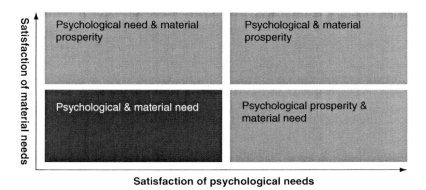

Figure 8.3 Objective well-being (material need) and subjective well-being (psychological need)
Source: Young Foundation (2010).

(Sen, 1985, 188). In other words, if happiness is our goal, then the reduction of existing material inequalities could lose priority, as depressed millionaires would get more attention from policymakers than jolly slum-dwellers. Hence those off-diagonal cases in which subjective indicators could add most information (that is, cases where these indicators diverge from objective assessments, as in the upper left and lower right corner of Figure 8.3) would ironically also be the most critical, especially for social democrats keen on eradicating material poverty. Recent research, however, shows that the 'happy poor' in fact do not seem to exist. Instead, people who live in an environment with a worse objective quality of life also report lower life satisfaction (Oswald and Wu, 2010). The authors compared objective quality of life scores of US states with the average reported life satisfaction in them and found a strong correlation.

Implications for the renewal of social democracy

The main challenge for social democracy, at this time in its history, is to regain a convincing narrative, and the discourse on happiness could be a powerful base for this. More precisely, it follows from our improving ability to measure well-being and Bentham's *greatest happiness principle* that the one political party that stands for improvement in the quality of life of most people will gain power in the democratic process. In this sense, it is of secondary importance just now if we measure quality of life by objective or by subjective measures.[9] What is an imperative, however, is that we measure it *at all* and allow it to take a central place in the evaluation of government's performance through the media, statistical offices and, most importantly, electoral decisions by ordinary citizens. A wide societal debate about which precise social indicators make the good society is necessary, with social democracy formulating its own distinct vision.

Furthermore, a large amount of data[10] is already at hand, but they do not play a big enough role in public debates at the moment. They must be collected more centrally and published in a more accessible manner, in order to take their well-deserved place. Perhaps the national roundtables which Stiglitz et al. (2009) call for could find agreements over how this idea can be implemented in the respective countries, so as to replace GDP with a more rounded well-being index or a collection of single figures designed to constitute a national dashboard of progress. Several countries have made initial efforts in this direction (see Kroll, 2010).

So, will social democracy make us all happier? Arguably, such a conclusion sounds naïve. Also, if anything, it will most probably make some people less happy whilst making other people happier. However, with a more relevant, accurate and extensive system of quality-of-life indicators in place to hold politicians accountable for their actions, social democracy could prove whether it has the better vision of the future and whether it delivers the better outcomes for the majority of people. Of course, it is a gamble for any government or party to commit itself to a more binding system of social monitoring, which measures its performance more closely. Shortcomings in its policies would be laid bare more easily for the electorate to see. However, there are huge potential gains for social democracy: its core mission is one of empowerment and of increasing the quality of life of a large majority of (less well-off) segments of the population – a mission rooted in the workers' movements of the nineteenth century. Thus a firm commitment of the political class to being monitored in this way would give a far more accurate picture of which party is able to improve the lives of the electorate by following the greatest happiness principle.

In fact, such a framework would force all parties to formulate clearly and communicate their vision of a good society indicator by indicator. This way, differences between parties would become more visible again, and the election campaigns would most likely be more focused on actual policy outcomes. In addition, this would allow voters to have a much better basis for their decision and to enhance our democracy crucially. The result would therefore be a democratic process strengthened by the giving of more accurate information for well-reflected decisions.

Moreover, beyond everyday politics, engaging in the debate about how to measure and foster progress would give social democrats a chance to reinstate their longer-term vision of a better society. Policy overlaps with well-being research, and examples abound: strengthen the society's social capital, foster solidarity, empower people through education, create an economy that serves humanity and not vice versa. All these aims are both social democratic and compatible with a focus on quality of life, especially if a decrease in misery at the lower end of the distribution can be prioritized over an increase in average happiness. There is in fact a long tradition, in social democratic thinking, of emphasizing a well-rounded approach to progress, as exemplified in the German SPD's 1972 election manifesto, which stated: 'More production, profit and consumption do not automatically equal more satisfaction, happiness and capabilities for the individual.' The centre-left across Europe ought to reconnect with these ideas, as they are even more relevant in the twenty-first century. It is from here that the party should begin its search for a new narrative.

Finally, it has to be said, though, that no party should, and in fact can, claim entire concepts like 'quality of life' as theirs. More precisely, an impartial field such as academia is not to be exploited by any one particular political movement. This is especially true for research on well-being. In fact, there is strong support from the subjective well-being data for the conclusion that typical issues of the political right, such as marriage and religiosity, are positively correlated with life satisfaction outcomes. Furthermore, it is needless to emphasize that moral values, human rights and the protection of minorities form the foundation of any dignified society, and these would of course be untouchable by any happiness principle.

It emerges as clearly, however, that any democratic discussion about how to build the good society and how to improve the quality of life of a population should start from the question: Which party will facilitate the greatest happiness for the greatest number? Taking on this challenge is a crucial opportunity for social democracy across Europe, as chances are that it would do quite well in such a contest; or would it not? The debate is open.

Notes

1. To name but a few: the OECD Global Project on Measuring the Progress of Societies, the EU's Beyond GDP Initiative, the State of the USA Project, the Canadian Index of Well-Being, the Australian Unity Wellbeing Index, Bhutan's Gross National Happiness, the Legatum Institute's Prosperity Index,

or the German Parliamentary Commission on Growth, Wealth, and Quality of Life.
2. As opposed to only 300 studies in the first phase of research, between 1960 and 2000 (Diener and Suh, 1999).
3. As Aristotle put it: 'We must therefore survey what we have already said [about what 'the good life' objectively consists of], bringing it to the test of the facts of life, and if it harmonizes with the facts we must accept it, but if it clashes with them we must suppose it to be mere theory' (*The Nicomachean Ethics*, Oxford World's Classics, translated by David Ross, 2009, Book 10, 1179^{a}23, in Helliwell, 2003, 333).
4. The interested reader may consult one of the recently dedicated reviews on the state of the knowledge, such as Dolan et al. (2008).
5. Even Ben Bernanke (2010), chairman of the United States Federal Reserve, notes the importance of social capital by acknowledging that 'economic policymakers should pay attention to family and community cohesion. All else equal, good economic policies should encourage and support stable families and promote civic engagement.'
6. Time series data for richer countries indeed show that relative income matters more than absolute income (Layard et al., 2010).
7. In addition, it has been argued that Subjective Wellbeing (SWB) has not increased due to the upper ceiling of the life satisfaction measure (i.e. you cannot score 11 out of 10). However, while this explains why life satisfaction has not increased to an average of 11 on a 10-point scale, it does not offer an explanation for why the average has not risen to 8, 9 or 10.
8. I owe this fitting formulation to Ruut Veenhoven.
9. In fact, the author would conclude that a comprehensive assessment of a nation's or individual's quality of life should always combine subjective *and* objective indicators. The former group of indicators has caught policymakers' and the public's attention only more recently, though, which is partly why this book chapter laid more emphasis on presenting subjective indicators. The point of the conclusion is a larger one, though.
10. For instance, the French *Données sociales*, or German *Datenreport*.

Part V
Political Futures

9
Dispossession
Jonathan Rutherford

Outside my house the street is quiet, the children are in school. Mrs A walks past with her shopping bag. She is in her seventies and lives with her husband in the flats next door. They were the first tenants and have lived here most of their lives. Her husband worked in a family-run hardware store down the road, which has now been turned into a betting shop. Her familiar neighbourhood has disappeared over the years as friends, family and acquaintances have died or left and strangers have moved in. Today her neighbours are from Poland, Africa, Turkey, Ireland, the Caribbean, the United States, Malta, Scotland, Mauritius and India.

Mrs P is a devout Muslim who came to this street with her husband from Indonesia. The two women used to walk together regularly to the shops. But Mrs P's husband died and she fell victim to heart disease. Immobile and confined to her tiny flat, with her son looked after by relatives, she has been left 'entirely alone in the world'.

A few people walk through the gates with their dogs into the small park opposite. The trees have grown, and it is no longer possible to see the distant, pyramid-shaped roof and blinking light of the Canary Wharf Tower. With its financial, legal and media industries, it is a monument to the 30 years of globalization that brought Mrs P across the world to this street and has dispersed Mrs A's old neighbourhood.

The street may not be typical of the rest of England, but in its ethnic diversity, in its mix of housing tenure and in its class differences it has been a microcosm of the social and economic changes of three decades of globalization. The contradictory trends of deindustrialization, cosmopolitan modernity and a financialized capitalism have been played out here with great intensity. They have created a more transient and insecure society, which has weakened the ties of kinship and locality.

People are more prone to isolation and loneliness. Young new mothers lack the steadying presence of an older female relative, older people have lost the domestic support of sons and daughters. It is a neighbourhood of weak associations, where households can be separated by a chasm of unshared history and cultural meaning. Ties to kin stretch to Africa and India, or go no further than the front door. Taken together, our individual lives do not add up to something more than their sum. There is a freedom without belonging, which emphasizes a person's rights over his or her obligations to others. It leaves an intangible sense of dispossession; we are like strangers who do not quite feel at home; uncertain of who we are and of our relationship to the past we come from.

What do we hold in common with each other, and what do we hold in common with you, reader, wherever in Europe you might live? What do we share that will allow us to lay claim to a common end, which we might call the good society? How we answer the question will define the future of the left. It will not be found in the abstract idea of 'European social democracy'. A new set of policies will not be enough; nor some technocratic fixing of European Union (EU) procedures, nor simply refining our political principles. Something more is at stake.

Social democracy is losing its place in the world. It has no home in the lives of people. It does not speak for a common life or a common good, but has become an administered politics associated with technocratic elites and a centralized state. Its origins in the vast body of collectivist voluntary activity, in the societies for mutual improvement, in the friendly societies and self-governing institutes of the nineteenth century have faded into history. Its roots in local life and in the workplace have either disappeared or been grievously weakened. It represents everyone and no-one in particular. What does 'European social democracy' stand for? It believes in multiculturalism, but it suspects the iconography of working-class patriotism. It believes in fairness, but fairness has been colonized across the political spectrum to the point of meaninglessness. It is for solidarity; but, when in office, Social Democratic Parties embraced liberal market policies that destroyed solidarity. The neoclassical economics adopted by many national parties has been discredited, leaving them without a distinctive alternative political economy. Social democracy has lost its meaning in Europe and it is foundering and disoriented.

It is time to return to the local, re-engage with the everyday lives of people and rebuild a political movement of ethical life, of community and of workplace organizing. There will be no European movement without strong national movements, and there will be no strong national movements without powerful local organization. We begin where our forefathers and foremothers began: from home, with a love of home, in defence of home and for a better future home.

It's time for social democracy to get personal and to get militant – to rebuild its foundations amongst local people, in local places, around local issues. In each country across Europe it must, in a literal sense, go out to the people and once again become an organizing force in the life of its country, from the cities to the market towns and villages. In this chapter I focus on the experience of England. Each country has different histories and traditions, but we can learn from one another and build alliances this way.

The local in Europe

Here in England, Labour shares similar predicaments with its sister parties across Europe. New Labour was in government for 13 years, from 1997 to 2010. Following the general election result in May, it had lost 5 million voters. The election defeat fell short of a catastrophe; New Labour was profoundly beaten in the prosperous south of England. It is at risk of losing touch with a generation of younger voters. Since then it has gained 50,000 new members; but hundreds of thousands of party members, embittered, disillusioned and ignored, have left. Many people no longer trust that the party is on their side. What is Labour's historical purpose? The answer is unclear. Something fundamental has been lost, and this is a Labour language and culture that belonged to the society it grew out of and enabled its immersion in the life of the people. Labour has lost the ability to renew its political hegemony within the class that created it.

This hegemony was historically about community, work, country and a sense of honour. It was also about men in particular. In the last three decades the meaning of all of these has been thrown into question and irrevocably changed. Labour's patrimony, the party loyalty and culture of work that fathers handed down to sons – and daughters too, but Labour has been a deeply patriarchal movement – is dying out. To renew itself, Labour along with its sister Social Democratic Parties needs to develop a new kind of inclusive culture and a politics of belonging that draws on the traditions of the common good and the common life.

Without the shared meanings of a common life there is no basis for living a life of one's own. Without society there is no individual; the two are inseparable. First there is 'we', then 'I'. We are born to our parents, and in our birth we transform their lives and identities. We become individual social beings in our relationships, in the associations we join and through the civil society institutions we identify with. Our values are shaped by them, and our corporate identities are formed in the imagined communities of class and place. Our learning and the work we do is our reciprocal engagement with society and, if we are fortunate, a source of self-development. And there is something more to each of us that cannot easily be defined, it remains unfinished and open to the world. We can name it love, hope, optimism, desire, faith. It is inextinguishable, and its impact on us is transformational. As individuals we can never be reduced entirely to sociological context and explanation. We know things that we cannot always think.

This, broadly speaking, is our individual 'life world'. Culture gives meaning to this life world. It makes us intelligible to ourselves and to each other through the shared symbols of a common life, which both relates us to one another and separates us. Without it, as Hannah Arendt says, we become imprisoned in our own singular experience (Arendt, 1998). Culture provides a society with its collective idiom: out of the traditions of the past and on the basis of the experience of present time, we shape a future and we project ourselves into it. Culture tells us the story of who we are.

It is a story that Labour, like many other European Social Democratic Parties, lost during the last decade. The achievements of Labour in government were considerable; but, for all the good it did, it presided over the leaching away of the common meanings and social ties that bind people together in society. It was its apparent indifference to 'what really matters' that incited such rage and contempt amongst constituencies that had been traditional bastions of support. When a common life fragments, a culture becomes disoriented and individuals no longer know who 'we' are, they succumb to a state of bare life. In such a state life continues, but the symbols that give it meaning and hold individuals in a common life die. Its institutions, rituals and customs lose their vitality and fade into shadow. Its leaders and its most capable persons find themselves ill equipped to deal with the new. In the meaninglessness of a disoriented culture, hope fades and people experience a sense of dispossession.

The American anthropologist Ruth Benedict describes this dispossession as a 'loss of something that had value equal to that of life itself, the whole fabric of a people's standards and beliefs' (Benedict, 1968, 16). The loss is irreparable. Benedict is describing the cultural death of highly integrated societies of indigenous people. But in the diverse societies of Europe a similar, less extreme form of cultural devastation is a consequence of transformations in modes of production and consumption. Ways of life associated with redundant industries and forms of work are destroyed. Here too, the future collapses because the concepts for understanding it have disappeared. People are left impotent, redundant and defeated. Some become enraged and others become sick, or debilitated by depression and addictions. Despair and rage find their nemesis in cultural difference and in the figure of the immigrant, who becomes the harbinger of disruption and of the loss of a familiar life. The common capacity for kindness, reciprocity and generosity is undermined and overshadowed by a victim culture of sentimental nostalgia, intolerance and hatred. A populist politics of blame and resentment takes root in which the stranger becomes a scapegoat, and the poor are accused of being the cause of their own misfortune.

This story of dispossession lies in the shadow of the bright lights of consumer culture and of the glamour of celebrity and money. In England, the experience of dispossession is most evident in former industrial towns and amongst members of the working class, who have either lost their economic role or feel it threatened. Men who were the agents of the culture of work and solidarity of this class have lost their standing and authority. The Labour Party, which grew out of this culture, has suffered a similar fate. More widely, a sense of loss extends across class and society to those who have made material gain and climbed the meritocratic ladder. Professional occupations have experienced a diminishing of their autonomy. The state and commodification, between them, have eroded these people's sense of vocation and public service. Over the last three decades a culture of capitalism has come to dominate our society. Its logic is to disentangle people from their social ties in order to establish market relations and a language of exchange value. What it brings in terms of choice and in the form of a greater abundance of things it takes away in terms of non-monetized social value and relations.

In government, the influence of Third Way politics meant that Labour stopped valuing settled ways of life. It did not speak about identification with, and pleasure in, local place and belonging. It said nothing about the desire for home and rootedness, nor did it defend the continuity of relationships at work and in neighbourhoods. It abandoned people to the market, in the name of a spurious entrepreneurialism. Estranged from people's lives and communities, lacking the institutional memory of campaigning and organizing, and denuded of internal democracy, it leavened an increasingly dour politics with abstract principles and policy jargon. In its impotence as a social movement it tended to idealize the dynamism of the market, and in doing so it ended up dispersing its own historical purpose and meaning to the four corners of the earth.

Benedict argues that 'our civilization must deal with cultural standards that go down before our eyes and new ones that arise from a shadow upon the horizon' (Benedict, 1968, 195). In England, and similarly across Europe, Social Democratic Parties must once again become the shadow on their nation's horizon. Their historic task is to organize so as to conserve the good in society, to speak of it when it is silenced, to defend it when it is threatened by the market and the state, and to nurture it back into existence when, like today, it has been reduced to piecemeal.

Social democracy in Europe is the product of almost 200 years of a counter-movement against capitalism. Karl Polanyi describes the double movement of capitalism, whereby capital sought to establish self-regulating markets through free trade and *laissez-faire* principles. The logic of the new forms of capitalism was to commodify land, money and human labour. And in reaction to this a counter-movement grew up to defend and conserve individuals, society and nature against commodification (Polanyi, 1957, 132). In England the counter-movement suffered an historic defeat in the 1970s. Even at the height of its post-war collectivist power, the working class had begun to change. The Miners' Strike of 1984 marked the final moment of the old mass industrial unionism. The ways of life of an industrial working class that shaped England are passing into history. The decades since have belonged to capital unbound. The counter-movement has been significantly weakened. The consequences of this diminishing of political power vary in different countries, but in England there has been a new wave of dispossession, which has profoundly reshaped the economy, family life and culture.

Economy

In the park across the road the boys hang out on the benches. Throughout the day and long into the night, when the call comes in, one will cycle off up the road and return with the small wrap. It's a just-in-time, overheads free, networked, post-post-fordist economy of primitive accumulation. A life of selling crack or heroin is a quick but dangerous route up the status-seeking ladder of peer respect and a short-cut, for the excluded, to the capitalist good life. Demand is inelastic and insatiable. Drug-taking is driven by the two impulses that propel modern consumer capitalism: (1) desire freed from obligation to others and

(2) the never-to-be-satisfied pursuit of pleasure. The drugs trade is its purest expression. At its centre lies the absence of law and morality. It is an economy without ethics, and what holds together its relations of exchange is the exercise of power and the threat of violence. In this respect it exemplifies, *in extremis*, the financialized capitalism that has transformed the social order in Britain over the last three decades.

Marx argued that there are different epochs, characterized by their mode of production. Simon Kuznets, in his 1971 Nobel Prize lecture, identified economic epochs defined by technological innovation (Kuznets, 1971). Each epoch transforms the mode of production and the relations of production; this in turn destroys old forms of social life and gives rise to new ones. Kuznets describes economic growth as a 'controlled revolution'. Joseph Schumpeter describes it as 'a method of economic change' that can never be stationary, constantly revolutionizing itself from within, in a process of 'creative destruction' (Schumpeter, 1976, 82). Marx would disagree with both men's evolutionary economics and with the primacy they give to technology as a determining force; but they nevertheless echo his description of capitalist modernity as a world in which 'all that is solid melts into air'.

The economic historian Carlota Perez, following Kuznets and Schumpeter, describes how successive technological revolutions have created distinct stages of capitalism (Perez, 2003). She identifies these stages as the Age of Steam and Railways, the Age of Steel, the Age of Electricity and Heavy Engineering, the Age of Oil, the Automobile and Mass Production, and the Age of Information and Telecommunications. These stages are surges of economic development that progressively extend capitalism into people's lives and facilitate its expansion across the planet. In the process, social relations are commodified, and institutions of governance, cultures and ideologies are transformed. Capitalism in its pursuit of profit undermines the conditions necessary for its own existence. Schumpeter describes a capitalist order that 'derives its energy from extra-capitalist patterns of behaviour which at the same time it is bound to destroy' (Schumpeter, 1976, 162). His comment echoes Rosa Luxemburg, who argued that capital accumulation requires the expropriation of non-capitalist, extra-economic modes of production and relations (Luxemburg, 2002).

There is a risk, in the *longue durée* analysis, of producing a history to fit the theory. But Perez is aware of this and offers an heuristic method that allows us to explore the long durations of economic history. We can argue that, in Britain since the 1970s, we have been experiencing what Perez describes as the transition from the Age of Mass

Production to the Age of Information. The main phase of the transformation came to an end in the financial crash. She argues that the economic conditions now exist to bring capital under more democratic control by regulating finance, rebuilding institutions of social cohesion and redistributing wealth. There are no laws that make this inevitable. Politics, contingencies and the balance of social forces will determine the prospects.

Following the failure of Britain's old model of industrial production and the election of the conservatives in 1979, low-profit, traditional manufacturing was shut down and deindustrialization was allowed to accelerate. Capital controls were abolished. Mass unemployment was used to drive down labour costs and to undermine the influence of the trade unions. New information and communications technologies began to revolutionize the generation, processing and transmission of information, turning information itself into a fundamental source of productivity. Radical innovations, backed by financial capital, penetrated the old order and began to modernize the whole productive structure. Following the deregulation of the City of London in 1986, the financial sector began to play an increasingly dominant role in the economy. As the economy had opened up to global flows of foreign investment, trade and finance, the business model of the financial sector became the paradigm of capitalist revival.

This economic transformation was facilitated by new cultural sensibilities. During the 1960s, under conditions of growing and sustained affluence, the imperatives of economic security gave way to a 'postmaterialist' set of values. Amongst fractions of the young middle classes, these created a powerful cultural trend towards a 'liberation ethic' of individual self-expression and creativity, anti-establishment sentiment, emotional attunement to the world and personal pursuit of pleasure. 'There is a revolution going on – in the direction of more fully human people' announced the psychologist Abraham Maslow, from its centre in California (Maslow, 1971). Ironically, the personal growth movement became a key resource in the revolution of capital. Its individualist language of informality, intimacy and pleasure-seeking helped to create new regimes of accumulation that transformed capitalism into an economy of gratification and consumer choice.

A financialized capitalism has transformed the social order in Britain over the last three decades. The new model of capitalism was underpinned by a popular 'neo-liberal' compact between the individual and the market. Chancellor Geoffrey Howe's 1981 'austerity budget' of public spending cuts and tax increases brought the post-war consensus of welfare capitalism to an end. But it was the 'right to buy' of the 1980 Housing Act and the privatization of the utilities that broke its collectivist ethos and secured the 30-year hegemony of neo-liberalism. Both promoted a market compact that provided the foundational structure for a market society of consumers. Economic growth depended upon this compact and the housing market became its epicentre, turning homes into assets for leveraging ever-increasing levels of borrowing.

The financial sector began to play an increasingly dominant role in the economy. Millions became entangled in the global financial markets as their savings, pensions and personal and mortgage-backed debts were appropriated for the profit-seeking of the banks. David Harvey has described this appropriation as capitalist accumulation by dispossession (Harvey, 2005). This accumulation through dispossession created an indentured form of consumption, as the financial markets laid claim to great tranches of individual future earnings. The phenomenon has led to unprecedented levels of private debt, which in September 2008, at the beginning of the financial crash, stood at £1.4 trillion, of which £223billion was unsecured (Credit Action, 2010).

Financial capital did not create wealth so much as redistribute it on a massive scale, from the country to the City, from the public sector to the private and from individuals and households to a rich plutocracy. In 1976 the bottom 50 per cent of the population owned 8 per cent of the nation's wealth; by 2001, despite a near threefold increase in GDP, this figure had fallen to 5 per cent (National Statistics, 2010). The bank bail outcapped this transfer of wealth with one gigantic bonanza. The neo-liberal compact promised freedom through individual market choice and cheap credit. It provided rising living standards and new avenues for many, but its housing market consumer axis was a dysfunctional model of economic development. It was unsustainable, and it is now redundant. The compact evolved into a central facet of the economy not by design, but because of a larger failure of macro-economic policy, which encouraged the global imbalances in production and sustained the over-consumption of goods produced in foreign, low-wage economies.

In government, Labour did not address the larger macro-economic problem of an unbalanced economy. It allowed City excess and redistributed the tax revenue, via health and education expenditure, to the Midlands and to the north. Tax credits boosting low wages helped to disguise an anaemic private sector, unable and unwilling to pay a living wage. The financial crash ended public confidence in the neo-liberal compact and exposed the transfer of risk from the state and business to the individual. It brought to an end Labour's state distributionist strategy. At this point in time Labour has still to develop macro-economic policies for deficit reduction and for productive and ecologically sustainable wealth creation.

Social democratic policies for the coming decade will have to address a number of significant problems. How will finance be brought back to its proper role of serving business entrepreneurs and productive wealth creation? What kind of state can combine a new strategic authority for investment in economic development with a network of partnerships with civil society institutions? The state needs to be a guiding hand for the green economic revolution and the development of a learning society. The old nation state welfare contract is discredited and in tatters. A national system of apprenticeships and technical training, and affordable access to higher education, all remain out of reach. At the heart of political renewal is the question of a new model of social and democratic economy.

Family life

Deindustrialization and the growth of a market society have accelerated the long historical decline of the puritan moral economy that underpinned British capitalism. Individual self-control, hard work and a willingness to delay or forego reward and gratification provided a social glue and the purposefulness of a national, imperial destiny. These values were an essential element of the culture of the dominant class, which was passed down from father to son. The narrative of a patriarchal social order that they sustained ensured the reproduction of a normative family and social relations, status hierarchies and moral values. All these transmitted a common life down through the generations – mankind, fraternity, masterful, sons of free men, faith of our fathers. This patrimony has now been fragmented and disrupted by changing cultural attitudes, new patterns of work and the growing independence of women. An inter-generational rupture was most evident in the emergence of the youth and counter-cultures of the 1960s and in the growth of social movements around gay and lesbian liberation, women's liberation and black emancipation. Francis Fukuyama declared the 1970s to be the period of the 'Great Disruption' – such was the rate of change in earlier patterns of life (Fukuyama, 1997). Uneven changes in patrimony have continued ever since, at different rates within different classes and around different causes.

Women have born the brunt of the changes with the strains placed on their labour and time, which made ordinary family life difficult for many to sustain. Economic participation has brought with it scarcity of time and work-related stress. Research shows very high levels of mental ill health amongst girls and women (Platform 51, 2011). While the pressures on women as employees, carers and housekeepers have intensified, it is men who have been identified as the gender disoriented by the changes. Men's incomes have stagnated, the old 'family wage' has disappeared and, for increasing numbers, the traditional role of family breadwinner and head of household is unattainable. The loss of patrimony, the rise of single-parent households and the challenge to men's traditional roles have led to recurring moral panics about a crisis in masculinity, family and fatherhood. The 1990s witnessed a growing consensus of opinion, in the media and popular literature, that men were emotionally inarticulate, socially and personally disoriented and demoralized.

In the historical past paternity was never enough to qualify men for fatherhood. There were plenty of biological fathers who lived without families, not due to any moral failing on their part, but to the economic structures that ordered their lives. Have the changes in the jobs market, in the law and in gender relations returned us to an age when paternity once again does not automatically mean fatherhood? There is no consensus of opinion, but the kind of democratic, involved fatherhood that many men and women aspire to is not compatible with an economic system which leaves men with either too little or too much work. With the decline of patriarchal authority, policy development will need to address the way normative social relations are reproduced from one generation to the next. For example, what are the sources of non-official, non-state authority that hold together families and communities, and how shall we define them? In our pluralistic society there is a degree of ambiguity about what provides the ethical basis of civic virtue and decency. What moral authority, apart from the state, will hold in check the anti-social behaviour of young men? The question has been around for centuries, but it is one that always needs re-asking. The values and behaviours that mark out youth from adulthood have become less distinct. When does one become an adult, and what does it mean to be an adult man or woman? To a greater or lesser degree, these questions apply to countries across Europe, and social democracy will need to develop a sexual and personal politics and ethics to address them.

Culture

Globalization has brought with it the expansion of cosmopolitan modernity. New Labour, following Anthony Giddens, accepted the argument that 'detraditionalization' and 'self-reflexive individualization' have replaced the valency of class as a social and political category (Giddens, 1991). Cultural difference, novel experience, the optimizing of individual choice are all unquestioned social goods that enrich life and enlarge freedom. But this is a point of view that ignores the need for social stability and continuity of relationships for human flourishing. And, while it is true that there has been great individualization, its development is uneven, not only across consumption and work, but also within the psyches and cultural identities of individuals. Class has not vanished but is being reconfigured around new modes of production and consumption, and the cultural changes and threats have become sites of conflict.

In contrast to the impact of worklessness and precarious work on family life and individual well-being, there has been an expansion of cosmopolitan modernity. In England's larger cities, and particularly amongst the elite, economic modernization has led to a celebration of cultural difference, novel experience and the expansiveness of individual choice. These have been part and parcel of the neo-liberal era and have been considered unquestionable social goods that enrich life and enlarge freedom. But across the rest of the classes and country a more conservative culture holds sway, which values identity and belonging in the local and the familiar. Economic modernization, 'the new' and difference are often viewed more sceptically and as potential threats to social stability and to the continuity of community. These two cultural sensibilities of cosmopolitanism and conservatism need not be mutually exclusive. They can divide along differences in age and region, and they constitute the contradictory desires, within each of us, for freedom and security, difference and familiarity. However, the neo-liberal model of capitalism and its market society have created a more insecure, fragmented and divided country. Conflicts around class and life chances have been played out in a cultural politics of belonging and dispossession. Cosmopolitanism is viewed by many as a symptom of a wider loss of control over one's working and daily life, over immigration, and over the cultural integrity of the nation.

Across Europe, the decline of social democracy has been accompanied by the rise of cultural movements of the racist right. The English Defence League is the new symptom of cultural dislocations and economic crises.

It is a street militia dominated by men who came of age in the 1990s – the sons of the 'defeated' and 'absent fathers' – and who are willing to fight to 'defend England' against the 'civilizational threat' of Islam. Its language of belonging and cultural dispossession speaks for much larger, politically disenfranchised forces, which have been unleashed by the transformations in capitalism and in society. It promotes a 'civilizational politics' that matches its Islamist enemy. 'Tommy Robinson', a former British National Party (BNP) member and one of the founders of the English Defence League (EDL), has described it as a 'community' and has framed its politics not around race but around democracy: 'While our troops are fighting for democracy in foreign fields, we're losing it here' (Lowles and Painter, 2011). Unlike other European countries, Britain has never produced a mass fascist party; however, camped outside the political centre ground is a large element of the electorate, waiting for an English kingmaker to appear.

The EDL is powered by resentment and hatred for a metropolitan elite who, it believes, has heaped humiliation upon people and robbed them of their English identity and culture. In 1970 the conservative politician Enoch Powell similarly accused a liberal intelligentsia of being an 'enemy within' and of destroying the moral fabric of the English nation with its promotion of cultural difference and 'race' (Powell, 1971). Powell and his politics of racial difference laid the groundwork for neo-liberalism, its political transformation of class and new modes of capitalist accumulation. Margaret Thatcher followed his example, laying the blame for moral decline on the counter-cultures and permissive values of the 1960s. Tony Blair mimicked her, in an opportunist attack on the 'swinging sixties' and their 'freedom without responsibility' (Blair, 2004). Most recently, 'Red Tory' Phillip Blond has accused 'a self hating cultural elite' and 'a newly decadent middle class addicted to its own pleasure' of breeding contempt for tradition and virtue (Blond, 2009).

It was Powell, with his politics of cultural difference, who was the prophet of the Thatcher revolution. He gave it words and a language. Powell as much as Thatcher championed market liberalism and transformed our country. In 1997 New Labour both accommodated itself to the revolution and blunted its impact. In England, the experience has come close to destroying it as a national political force. The era that Powell began is now coming to an end with the financial crash of 2008. Labour must renew itself in order to establish a new hegemony. It must confront what Enoch Powell began; it must do it by seizing and transforming the political terrain of identity and belonging, which

Powell established as his own and which has been held by the right ever since. It must ask the question: What, in our differences, do we hold in common? And it must find answers capable of holding together broad alliances across classes and cultures. Only by speaking for a common life can Labour – and Social Democratic Parties across Europe – build the political power to resolve the disenfranchisement of large swathes of their national population.

Across Europe there is a feeling 'in the air' that a shared moral and cultural national life has been eroded. It is manifest in hostility towards the European Union, in a nostalgia for older ways of life and in a more insidious search for scapegoats to blame. The controversies over immigration and Islam are about a politics of belonging – a reaction to the dispossession of particularly men from the sources of their authority and entitlement, to the loss of their capacities to determine their own ends and to the loss of an identifiable and coherent, collective national culture. These conditions raise the question: What is the ethical relationship of individuals to one another? Social democracy needs to build and strengthen institutions that create synergies between people's individual aspiration and the common good. Cultural struggles around economic freedom, race, sexual morality and fatherhood play a significant role in establishing new hegemonic political formations. Social democracy needs an authentic cultural politics, which connects with the everyday life experiences of the people.

Conclusion

I have concentrated on the experience in England. England has been the locus of a virulent form of liberal market capitalism. Its open economy and powerful financial sector have always distinguished it from other European economies. During the 1990s British politicians had an unfortunate habit of lecturing fellow Europeans on the wonders of their Anglo-Saxon model. The crash of 2008 has been a salutary lesson – still unlearned by the right – about the weaknesses of this model. The country is left with considerable problems, from significant levels of inequality and household indebtedness, to a chronic housing crisis and structural worklessness.

The future of Labour in England will be conservative, because our time requires a reparative politics of the local and a re-affirmation of our human need for interdependency. Society needs to be defended against the destructive incursions of capital. The state needs democratic reform. The neo-liberal model of capitalism has been a form of permanent revolution and the architect of its own downfall. No counter-movement brought it down. Labour and social democracy on the continent certainly did not. Social democracy possesses no collective agents of social change ready with an alternative model of the economy. What will come next? The answer is ours for the making.

10
The Challenge of European Social Democracy: Communitarianism and Cosmopolitanism United

Henning Meyer

Social democracy has been – yet again – searching for a new political direction in recent years following a series of crashing electoral defeats all over Europe. And it was not just the poor showings at Europe's ballot boxes who revealed the problems of social democracy. The fact that, in the wake of the economic and financial crisis, the widely anticipated 'social democratic moment' never happened was further evidence of the social democratic malaise.

On platforms such as the *Social Europe Journal* there has been a vivid debate on what the reasons for this predicament are and what possible political reforms could be implemented in order to change the fortunes of European social democracy once more. Informed by these debates, this chapter provides in the first part an overview of what I consider to be structural weaknesses of social democracy, which have to be addressed by moving forward. Many of them are linked to the 'Third Way' renewal of social democracy that took place in the 1990s and early 2000s.

Next I will briefly examine the re-emergence of communitarianism in the social democratic debate, and I will relate it to the cosmopolitan strand of social democracy before tentatively trying to set out a path that combines the advantages of both approaches and attempts to minimize its weaknesses.

The arguments in this chapter are pointed, and sometimes sharpened, for the sake of clearly revealing some of the general faults that I think have been too concealed so far. In reality there are, of course, many shades of grey. But the purpose of this chapter is to teach lessons for social democracy to move forward, which also means that much of the analysis of the past has to be sketchy rather than detailed.

Structural problems of social democracy

Political programme

The key reason why Third Way reforms of political programmes, and in many cases also organizations, were powered through in the 1990s was that social democrats became tired of losing elections at the highest level of national politics (although they still reported electoral successes at lower levels). Proponents of the Third Way deduced from this situation that the political programme of social democracy was out of date and not aligned with what people wanted. Social democrats therefore had to change their political offerings in order to become electable again. In terms of political content, the resulting reforms clearly represented a political approximation to the neoliberal mainstream.

From a purely electoral point of view it is perfectly understandable why such social democratic reform was pursued. This victory of power politics over programmatic politics, however, had long-term consequences. One consequence certainly was that social democrats more and more gave up the development of clear political alternatives, as Third Way politics meant assimilation to the political mainstream. It is true that in the heyday of neoliberal orthodoxy it was hard to win elections with political alternatives. But joining the Neoliberal Party – as long as it was in full swing – also led to social democrats being accused for the hangover once it set in. When the question of how to move towards a new politics was asked in the wake of the financial and economic crisis, social democrats had no answer. And this was no surprise, as, by design, they had increasingly neglected the development of an alternative politics for the world we live in, a politics clearly distinct from that of the neoliberal mainstream. When crisis hit, social democrats were at best perceived as politically clueless and at worst as collaborators in a failing project.

In political practice, the Third Way also introduced a reversal of the very reason for politics. Do social democrats develop a political identity and a programme, and do they seek to implement this programme by competing for votes in elections? Or do social democrats first and foremost want to run governments while remaining flexible in adjusting their identity and political programme to achieve this aim? If the latter is true, what is the benefit of having social democrats in government?

Of course, in many respects the social democratic governments of the 1990s and 2000s were more social and humane in their politics than the conservative or liberal alternatives – as can be observed now that the latter are back in power. But there is nevertheless a fundamental problem with the social democratic formulation of politics. Is its first purpose to develop a political programme based on values, an analysis of the world we live in and a vision of the world we would like to live in? Or is its primary purpose to run governments and manage societies being a bit more socially minded than their political competitors, but still within a rather narrow corridor of 'pragmatic' politics? How one answers these questions has profound consequences.

The manner in which the Third Way debate was conducted was also part of the reason why there were many intellectual blind spots that did not get the attention they deserved. Nothing epitomizes this better than the misleading dichotomy of New Labour versus Old Labour. Whereas New Labour stood for an approximation to the neoliberal mainstream, everything else had to be Old Labour, and thus hopelessly outdated and backward. It did not help social democracy at all to proclaim that there is only one future and many misguided pasts; that only one way is progressive and the others are by definition outdated and backward. There is never just a single way forward; politics is always evolving. But the intellectual over-confidence of claiming to know the only viable way out for the future further stifled programmatic thinking and caused many social democrats to be branded as stubborn Neanderthals, when in reality there were valuable lessons to be learned from them.

Electoral strategy

Unsurprisingly, the Third Way shift of social democratic politics, which had electoral concerns at its heart, also focussed on specific electoral strategies in order to engineer success at the ballot boxes. Triangulation, a concept adopted from Bill Clinton's new democrats, was one of the key words in this context, meaning that specific policies were designed with a view to satisfy the perceived interests of certain key voter groups (in the case of New Labour, for instance – middle England).

There is evidence to suggest that voter interests are not always clear (and sometimes are inconsistent, depending on the level of identity they refer to). And voter interest itself is not self-evidently a good guide to winning elections (see Wehling and Lakoff's chapter in this volume). Furthermore, in most cases the triangulated combination of policies does not fit well into a broader political programme. And, by pursuing this kind of strategy, social democrats implicitly gave up much of the political power in order to shape societies. Why is this?

To exaggerate slightly: if all you do is chase and try to satisfy the perceived interests of specific segments of the electorate, as identified by focus groups and opinion polls, then you are practising a very reactive brand of politics, and you are surrendering much of its transformative character and potential. This politics was called 'pragmatic', but it was just a politics of managing the status quo at the expense of real efforts to transform societies for the better.

Undoubtedly helped by the first-past-the-post electoral system, New Labour's electoral strategy focussed on the middle-class swing voters and neglected traditional working-class concerns. Given that the electoral system did not provide a viable political alternative for many traditional voters – although the rise of right-wing protest votes has also been evident in Britain – it is certainly true that not enough attention was devoted to the concerns of traditional Labour voters. This electoral strategy was partially to blame for the erosion of Labour's traditional electorate, most of whose members could be ignored because they lived in 'safe' constituencies. Even though this approach was often also referred to as a 'big tent' strategy, in reality the tent did not provide cover for many traditional labour supporters.

Movement and party organization

Even though Third Way reforms in many cases also meant the further centralization of political power in party headquarters, partly because the reforms were rather unpopular with what was left of grassroots members, 1990s-style reformism is not exclusively to blame for what can only be called the demise of social democracy as a movement and as a party.

What happened? Social democracy in many respects has lost its roots in society and its character as a movement. And this happened over decades. Comparing today's situation with the origins of social democracy exemplifies this rather well. When you look at the origins of the first social democratic party, the German SPD, you notice that, in the nineteenth century, when the movement evolved and organized, being a social democrat was not merely about membership in an organization; it was a way of life. There were educational leagues that looked after workers' education. There were a whole variety of sports clubs and social democratic newspapers – two name just two institutions – that added a strong cultural dimension to the movement. It was this character of a movement with its distinctive culture that created the social glue amongst members and made sure that social democracy was strongly rooted in society – and thus receptive to the economic and social problems on the ground.

Fast forward 150 years, and Social Democratic Parties have a dwindling membership across the board, the cultural aspects and the movement character are largely gone, the parties are organized as electoral professional parties – machines designed to run elections – and they are often perceived as being out of touch with the sorrows and concerns of ordinary citizens. If the movement character of social democracy and its strong roots in communities were a source of strength, it is not hard to see why much of the lifeblood of social democracy has been lost as these roots have withered.

Cosmopolitan and communitarian social democracy

In reaction to the liberal nature of the Third Way brand of social democracy (and its end in government), an interesting intellectual current of new communitarian social democracy has developed in the United Kingdom. Below I briefly set out the core assumptions of communitarian social democracy and explain why it needs to be complemented by a cosmopolitan social democracy if it is to form a comprehensive new approach.

Key proponents of this communitarian approach, which is often referred to as Blue Labour, offer an alternative and more complex interpretation of Labour's political tradition. As its founder Maurice Glasman says:

> Labour is a paradoxical tradition, far richer than its present impoverished mix of economic utilitarianism and political liberalism. [...]
>
> Labour values are not abstract universal values such as 'freedom' or 'equality'. Distinctive labour values are rooted in relationships, in practices that strengthen an ethical life. Practices like reciprocity, which gives substantive form to freedom and equality in an active relationship of give and take; or mutuality, where we share the benefits and burdens of association. And then, if trust is established, solidarity, where we actively share our fate with other people. These are the forms of the labour movement, the mutual societies, the co-operatives and the unions. The movement was built on relationships of trust and mutual improvement that were forged between people through common action. They were transformative of the life and conditions of working people. The Labour tradition was rooted in a politics of the Common Good; it was a democratic movement that sought its rightful place in the life of the nation. The Labour tradition has never been straightforwardly progressive – and that is not a defect which we are on the verge of overcoming, but a tremendous strength that will offer the basis of renewal. (Glasman, 2011)

The strong focus on the personal relationship aspects of the social democratic tradition is accompanied by a very sceptical view of the state. In the same way as the market, it is argued, the state has helped to undermine local solidarity, communities and their institutions. The solution, the proponents of communitarian social democracy argue, is to rediscover the socially 'conservative' roots of the labour movement and to reclaim issues such as family, religion, nation, mutualism, reciprocal obligation and community from the political right, where those issues have been largely located ever since social democracy became liberalized. In terms of the organization of the (national and local) economy, Germany's social market model is often quoted as an example to learn lessons from.

Blue Labour certainly addresses some of the pressing issues I mentioned before – especially the lack of societal roots and the loss of the movement character and cultural identity. But why are communities under such pressure, particularly in the UK? At the heart of the crisis of local communities are deliberate socio-economic choices introduced by the Thatcher government and further pursued by the Labour governments of Tony Blair and Gordon Brown, as well as a particularly neoliberal conception of globalization. The comparison with Germany is again insightful in this context.

An important reason for the erosion of local community life in the UK has been its exposure to major – and in the grand scheme of things relatively sudden – shifts in the British economy. To put it starkly, the economic, social and cultural devaluation of industries and the too one-sided concentration on the service sector have led to major restructuring dislocations in many parts of the UK, which had a whole series of negative consequences for local communities.

The underlying neoliberal economic philosophy was one clearly shared by New Labour. It was argued (simplistically) that in a globalized world we will necessarily see an international division of labour. Manufacturing will be uncompetitive in rich countries and should thus be abandoned and left to the emerging economies. The best bet for rich countries was to focus on high value-added service jobs – especially in finance.

This understanding of economic globalization was wrong for several reasons. First of all, the history of development economics shows that countries do not stop their development once they have mastered one sector (for instance manufacturing). And why should emerging economies not be able to compete successfully in banking and insurance, if they were capable of doing it in the knowledge-intensive manufacturing sectors? The argument that the historic location of banking and insurance in the City of London is a competitive asset is true, but this is also true of places with an industrial history.

The story according to which Britain (or Europe) will be the service provider and emerging economies will be and remain the workbench has always been more a fairy tale than a reality. True, there was more job creation in the service sector. But this had not only to do with the outsourcing of low-skilled work, but also with productivity increases in manufacturing processes. To infer from this that the service sector alone is the way forward was the wrong conclusion, especially given the reliance of service sector demand on industry jobs.

In Germany, this philosophy has never dominated the political mainstream. Germany has a traditionally strong industrial sector and has chosen to compete internationally rather than wind the sector down. This choice has led to less economic restructuring and related conflict in local communities and has kept Germany's character as a mixed economy intact. This is not to say that there was no restructuring pressure on production and wages – there was; but there was never a politically sponsored funeral of the industrial sector. On the contrary, from today's perspective the focus on support for green technologies seems to be one of the best policies of the red–green government (1998 – 2005) under Gerhard Schroeder.

Only now, after the prevailing economic model has revealed its flaws, does Britain start to talk again about a new industrial policy. During the years that saw the winding down of British industries, a lot of skills and knowledge has been irrecoverably lost, and it will be very hard to catch up and regain a competitive position in world markets.

Because of the political choices I described above, there were more dislocations in British communities than in Germany. Not everything, as was often argued, was due to creative destruction and to the natural force of progress, but – as even this very superficial comparison reveals – much was due to conscious political decisions. This is not to argue that in Germany everything goes well. That is certainly not the case. But it gives, nevertheless, an insightful comparison of political economies.

It is also interesting how the language about the same economic system has changed. When Germany recovered reasonably well from the economic crisis – after having suffered severely – and interest in the German political economy resurfaced, there was talk about the resilient and solid nature of the German mixed economy, talk that was based on a social market philosophy and on strong stakeholder institutions. A few years back, neoliberal language described the same model as a reform-resistant, overregulated and sclerotic continental European economy that was uncompetitive and too reliant on industries bound to decline. It is truly remarkable how points of view can change.

The specific economic path followed by the United Kingdom also had severe consequences for the education sector. More and more young people had to attend university to hope for a decent career. By definition, everybody else was implicitly confined to less rewarding and socially less well-regarded work. The core idea of Richard Sennett's concept of craftsmanship – that people work hard, try to be good at what they do and take pride in their profession no matter what this profession is (Sennett, 2008a) – seems to be applicable much more to the higher education route than to alternative paths. And this has more to do with how society views such jobs rather than with any lack of craftsmanship on the part of people working in these alternative areas. In private conversations, key New Labour figures admitted that the downside of their policy to get 50 per cent of young people into universities was that they had no real idea about what to do with the other 50 per cent. So the key policy itself illustrates the problem vividly.

Again, there is a contrast here with the German case. Many jobs – especially manual labour – that are perfectly respectable in Germany are much less socially valued in the UK. Reinforced by economic choices, I think what this has done was to create a culture in which only a relatively narrow choice of professional paths is seen as desirable. And this narrow choice corresponds neither with the needs nor with the talents of society. This narrow path is, for one thing, a driver of immigration, as the demand for non-academic professions is still there (think of Polish plumbers) and it is likely to leave many British dissatisfied, as not everybody's talents – thank God – lie in academic subjects.

To support a balanced society, it is important to create and encourage a wide range of meaningful professions, as Richard Sennett observed:

> The carpenter, lab technician, and conductor are all craftsmen because they are dedicated to good work for its own sake. Theirs is practical activity, but their labour is not simply a means to another end. [...]
>
> Most men and women today spend the largest chunk of their waking hours in getting to work, working, and socialising with people they know at work. The desire to do a good job is one way to make these hours matter. Competence and engagement – the craftsman's ethos – appear to be the most solid source of adult self-respect, according to many studies conducted in Britain and the US. (Sennett, 2008b)

Sennett's argument touches on a key point, which is particularly important for social democrats: most of us take pride in what we do and try to do it well. We spend a large part of our time working, and we take not just self-respect but also identity from our professional life. A mixed economy provides more opportunities for people to realize their potential, especially if there is no social discrimination attached to professional choices. If this is achieved, empowering people in the workplace can institutionally help craftsmanship to flourish (more on this in the last part of this chapter).

So my core argument here is that much of what communitarian social democrats in Britain rightly criticize has its roots in particular political choices and could at least partially be addressed by shifting economic priorities. The weakness of communitarian social democracy, nevertheless, is its lack of clear concepts for the wider globalized world we live in. To compensate for this social democracy also needs a cosmopolitan approach. What is the bedrock of cosmopolitanism? As David Held has argued:

> Cosmopolitan values can be expressed formally in terms of a set of principles. These are principles which can be universally shared, and can form the basis for the protection and nurturing of each person's equal significance in the 'moral realm' of humanity. Eight principles are paramount. They are the principles of: (i) equal worth and dignity; (ii) active agency, (iii) personal responsibility and accountability; (iv) consent; (v) collective decision-making about public matters through voting procedures; (vi) inclusiveness and subsidiarity; (vii) avoidance of serious harm; and (viii) sustainability. (Held, 2011)

No brand of social democracy could disagree with any of these principles and their application at the national and international levels. It is a simple truth that many of today's pressing problems – from climate change and physical security to financial regulation – are international, and that globalization, in its many forms – including power shifts from West to East – is having a decisive impact on all of our lives. As David Held further argued in his book on global social democracy:

> Globalization is not, and has never been, a one-dimensional phenomenon. While there has been a massive expansion of global markets which has altered the political terrain, the story of globalization is far from simply economic. Since 1945 there has been

a reconnection of international law and morality, as sovereignty is no longer cast merely as effective power but increasingly defined in terms of the maintenance of human rights and democratic values; a significant entrenchment of universal values concerned with the equal dignity and worth of all human beings in international rules and regulations; the establishment of complex governance systems, regional and global; and the growing recognition that the public good – whether conceived as financial stability, environmental protection or global egalitarianism – requires coordinated multilateral action if it is to be achieved in the long term. (Held, 2004)

Held refers to a key aspect that Third Way social democracy in practice fundamentally neglected: this new global context requires a political understanding of regional and global spaces, because the pursuit and provision of the public good – no matter how you define it – require binding rules and regulations as well as governance mechanisms.

This is in stark contrast with the understanding of globalization as an unstoppable force of nature, which was widespread in Third Way governments. Too often, the economic logic of globalization was not questioned but simply taken for granted. Social policy served an economic purpose and was designed to make citizens fit to compete in professions that were still seen as viable in the given economic circumstances (see above). There was no serious attempt to question and to shape what has unfolded in the name of globalization.

For instance, there has been much discussion about the nature of European welfare states, about their focus (on caring for citizens or on enabling people to compete?) and about whether such states were still affordable, given the price pressure resulting from competition with countries that not only had wage cost advantages but also did not incur costs related to comprehensive welfare states and other social achievements. For quite some time I have believed that it was a fundamentally flawed manner of thinking to talk only about the reform of the European social model, without rigorously questioning and trying to reform the external source of pressure at the same time (Meyer, 2007).

Is it really necessary for Social Democratic Parties to sacrifice social achievements that generations of workers have fought for, in order to compete with lower paid workforces that do not receive these levels of protection? Or should social democratic politics be about understanding regional and global spaces as political entities and about using them to push for higher social standards, both in Europe and elsewhere? For me, the answer can only be in favour of the latter. I have for instance always thought that a social tariff, a charge that adds the costs of social externalities at the point of sale if they are not incurred at the place of production, was a legitimate way to incentivize trading partners to implement higher social standards.

Questioning the current form of globalization is not the same as trying to turn back the clock. The former is in essence about understanding the complex globalization process as something political and not as something merely inevitable. It is not about rolling back progress and technological advancements, but about creating a political framework that channels these processes and constructs a reformed system in which benefits are more widely shared and negative consequences are much better mediated. What we need – and not just at the global level – is a new *Ordnungspolitik* that establishes a political framework around spaces that have not been seen as political. Creating these frameworks must be one of the key aims of social democracy, as nobody else is likely to do it.

To conclude, I think that Maurice Glasman is absolutely right when he argues as follows:

> Labour is robustly national and international, conservative and reforming, christian and secular, republican and monarchical, democratic and elitist, radical and traditional; and it is most transformative and effective when it defies the status quo in the name of ancient as well as modern values. (Glasman, 2011)

This also means that social democracy can be communitarian and cosmopolitan and can have a values-based politics for local communities, but also policies and programmes to put these values into practice beyond the nation state. I would argue that the future of social democracy lies in the marriage of communitarianism and cosmopolitanism. People are rooted in their local communities, but they are also necessarily part of globalization and exposed to global political problems. What social democracy needs now is a new combination of both approaches.

More social and more democratic – The new social democracy

Even though the intellectual discourses and examples I have used are from the British–German context, I nevertheless believe there are some wider lessons for European social democracy to learn. The many debates and conferences that were held all over Europe over the last years clearly revealed that there are similar problems in many European countries.

The previous part of this chapter explained some of the more fundamental connections that I think are necessary. I will now try to funnel this into some more concrete proposals. Let me start by sketching out a new approach, which addresses the structural problems of social democracy I referred to earlier.

As Elisabeth Wehling and George Lakoff also argue in this book, we need to move away from an electioneering based on rational choice models. It does not seem to work, and forever chasing specific segments of the electorate is almost certain to be a dead end. If it is true that society is increasingly diversifying and that socio-economic interests are becoming more and more distinct, sticking to the current strategy would also mean that Social Democratic Parties are chasing smaller and smaller groups of society in their election campaigns. Not even socio-economic groups such as 'employees' are monolithic, and there is potential for significant conflict of interest within such groups.

Also, the mood of the electorate can swing wildly and, when you are caught on the wrong side, you find little sympathy. The early 2011 state election results in Germany are a good example. Following the nuclear meltdown in Fukushima, the already much debated (and partially reversed) end of nuclear power in Germany became a hot topic again. The vast majority of Germans have turned against nuclear power and the governing parties were caught on the wrong side of history. The beneficiaries of this situation were the Greens – they brought their first ever state prime minister into office – who had argued for the end of nuclear power long before this position became popular. Similarly, social democracy could have been in a position to benefit from the financial crisis if it had been clearly associated with a plausible political alternative.

What else, if not rational choice electioneering? I think it is time to reclaim the transformative power of social democracy and to construct a politics based again on values, on the analysis of the world we live in and on a vision of where we would like to go in the future. It was a joke of the times of pragmatic politics that, if you have visions, you should go and see a doctor. But, without new visions and a distinct programmatic identity, no doctor will be able to stop the maybe incurable decline of social democracy. In formulating such a new social democratic programme, social democrats would be well advised to take on board how to frame a new political message correctly and how to use new insights from emerging social sciences, such as happiness and well-being.

It is also important to re-root social democracy firmly in society and to reinvigorate its movement and cultural character. This can be done by rejuvenating the link with trade unions once more, as Dimitris Tsarouhas has convincingly argued in this book, by strengthening the local institutions and relationships that communitarian social democrats talk about, but also by using new technologies to organize and create channels for exchange and for discussing matters in new ways.

Furthermore, it is essential for social democrats to develop new concepts of justice, equality and sustainability. Recent research has shown how, in more egalitarian societies, everybody is better off (Wilkinson and Pickett, 2010). But under the watch of social democratic governments inequality increased further across Europe. It is time to live up to the challenge that social policy is about more than just poverty reduction and enabling people to participate in the market, and to realize that we need a rebalanced political economy, which not only avoids putting all eggs into one basket but makes sure that the primary and secondary allocation of economic proceeds are much more just and that more people can realize their ambitions and talents. This rebalanced economy must also be socially and ecologically sustainable, to make sure we are not destroying the future of our children.

One key way to make a new political economy socially more sustainable and supportive of craftsmanship is to empower stakeholders in decision-making procedures. The German system of co-determination and similar forms of economic democracy are a source of economic strength and help to create ownership and identity at the workplace. As argued before, the workplace is much more to people than just a place where employees trade their labour for payment from employers. It is important for a reformed political economy to acknowledge and incorporate this truth.

In contrast to many communitarian and liberal social democrats, I think that the state is a very useful institution, and much better than its reputation. The relationship between state, civil society and markets is symbiotic and should not be dominated by one dimension. At its best, the state is the expression – not the antagonist – of civil society, as it is guided by democratically elected representatives. Civil society has not played the role it should have played in the past, but a further democratization of the economy, of local and national government and, hopefully, also of supranational spaces will help to rectify this problem.

To conclude, I think that social democracy needs to become a transformative political force again. This does not mean becoming unrealistic! But it should not be too difficult to imagine a better world than the one we live in. Social democrats need to fashion a concept of the good society and then compete in elections to put it into practice.

Social democracy also needs to become more social and more democratic in its policies and organization. Apart from becoming again a transformative rather than a reactive political force, it needs to re-establish its societal roots by creating new alliances as well as new forms of communication and organization. The challenges in economic, environmental and social policy are well known, as are the systemic reforms that are needed at the local, national, regional and global level. Not being able to implement every aspect of a programme in the short term cannot be an excuse for not articulating it in the first place.

Social democracy is in crisis. But it is also a truism that you should never waste a 'good' crisis, as crises provide the opportunity for major reform. And there is an opportunity for European social democracy: if it addresses today's pressing issues and finds convincing political answers, then there is hope that the future will be brighter than the recent past.

11
Not without a Future
Jenny Andersson

What is the 'good' in 'society'?

What is the good society? At the moment this is a question that is being asked by political actors all over the political spectrum, and not only by social democracy. The very word 'society', at least in the UK, has become a rather troublesome one, as New Labour's active state was transplanted by Cameron's big society, made up as this was of social conservatism and rather disturbing continuations of New Labour policy – such as the behavioural Nudge Unit. The latter is charged with making people behave in ways deemed better for their own and society's good. It is not only the paternalism and the social engineering latent in this conception that are troubling; troubling is also the way in which 'good' has come to be understood in its economic sense, as determined by sociotechnical parameters of efficiency. Is this the enduring legacy of New Labour? The conservatives did not come up with this themselves; on the contrary, this is a notion of the good that social democracy has actively promoted, not only in its Fabian past, but specifically in the last decades, as the welfare state was reinvented from a moral and ethical argument to a form of socioeconomic investment. With such heavy legacies from past and recent history, it would seem that neither the element of 'good' nor that of 'society' is particularly useful in terms of rethinking social democracy and a possibly better world to live in. At least at the moment, both elements are tainted by political discourses emanating from a central field that seems to have become a kind of intellectual prison.

This centre is not, and never was, a neutral compromise or middle ground, but it is a political field dominated by a pervasive ideology, the importance of which I think we have only really begun to understand.

It is clear, in the present, that this central ground is giving birth not only to a new and vibrant modern right, not that different from watered-down versions of social democracy, but also to a much more radical and dangerous neofascism emanating from populist and extremist fractions. We cannot see this as a matter of random elements – it is the direct result of an appeal to a centre that ends up leaving a sentiment of abandon for a great mass of people, a sentiment of abandon that goes, I would suggest, beyond obviously salient economic factors and has also to do with an existential and moral sense of disorientation and lack of future.

Politics, in the last decades, has become a movement for the strong people, as if it were only the strong that make up society. Those who are not strong, self-sufficient, responsible and disciplined are to be made to be so. What characterizes these strong people? If we look at political fields ranging from labour market and social policy to competition and innovation, pensions and financialization measures, one thing stands out, and this is the political wish to use policy as a tool with which to mould individuals into inherently future-oriented beings capable of creating their own fate. Good citizens are active, responsible, entrepreneurial and risk-taking, inherently capable of taking the future in their own hands (Andersson, 2010; Clarke, 2005). Futurity – to do with risk, anticipation, managing potential outcome and future change in people and markets – has emerged as a fundamental aspect of governmentality (Finlayson, 2003, 2009; Watson, 2009). New Labour embodied this futurity more than any other political movement, being constantly geared towards the management of the people's potential and towards the governing of aspirations and hopes of people (Sennett, 2006). Equality of opportunity, as the hallmark of contemporary political ideology, represents exactly this relocation of political content to the future – opportunity denoting constantly new future possibilities. Is this progressive? Well, it seems nice to believe that people can always do better, that they can be pushed to become the best that they have it in themselves to be. But there is also a tremendous paternalism in this, an authoritarianism that says, 'I know what future is best for you and what you are destined to become', an inherently utilitarian approach to people as *becomings* of future use.

Breaking out of the opportunity society

For a long time, the debate was that social democracy had to reclaim notions of freedom and opportunity, take them from the right and make them part of its own vision of politics. It did so by arguing that individual freedom had to be connected to the social good of the community as a whole. This argument was rapidly no longer about freedom but more about social control and social paternalism. It accepted essentially neoliberal notions that opportunity was somehow out there, magically spewed up by an ever more dynamic economy. This vision of the opportunity society is today next to useless. If there is no opportunity available, no automatic ladders of advancement and merit, no way out of the traps of contemporary capitalism, then notions of self-reliance, responsibility and opportunity become the elements of a politics of humiliation. A core aim of a new social democratic politics is to break out of such politics of humiliation and to see people not as manageable and exploitable entities, but as *persons* – persons gifted with the capacity of solidaristic action and with the capacity of political action; in other words, as competent citizens. What this leads to is nothing less than a revived notion of democracy, as something in which being strong, productive or efficient is not the first criterion of belonging, but in which everyone has the right to a future and the right to a stake in what that future should be.

Enough has been said about the depth of social democracy's crisis and about the problems emanating from the last decades' reformatting of social democratic policy. The time has come to try to think, again – but differently – about the social democratic project, about the kind of things that it wants to do, the vision of the world that it projects and the legacies it wants to bestow. I think that today this calls for a radical break with the last decades of social democratic politics and for a kind of going back to the roots – one that is, however, not nostalgic but utopian. This means looking back at what social democracy once developed as answers to fundamental dilemmas of capitalism, to do with the wholeness and fulfilment of people in a different and better future. For this reason I want to discuss, in this chapter, the particular links between social democracy, democracy and future.

The need for a new future

In Cormac McCarthy's book *The Road*, the world has come to an end, fires have devastated the face of the earth and human beings have no other food source than their own offspring. Against roaming cannibals and road bandits, a man defends his son, the possible saviour of humanity. To defend him, others must be killed, and to let him eat, others must be stopped from stealing the rare tin cans and fruit jars that remain from a lost era of opulence. The boy is a metaphor for humanity, lost as it is on a highway, in a burnt landscape where at times one must climb over ranges of incinerated cars. Where does it lead, this road? It hopelessly winds its way through the continent, to the shore of a dead ocean (McCarthy, 2010).

The Road may be, for climate change, what Rachel Carson's book *Silent Spring* was for the environmental movement. The importance of *Silent Spring* was that it led to action at the individual, national and global level. Action was not flawless, or perhaps not even particularly adept at saving the environment, but arguably progress was made. There is a limit, where insights into the devastating effects of our actions on the world around us stops being mobilizing and inductive to action, and starts being crippling instead. The return of dystopian thinking is one of the more worrying signs of the times. Indeed, how can we think the good society when the future of the world is looking so dark? The future is in a squeeze, a squeeze that can be efficiently illustrated by two clearly discernible global trends: the decreasing availability of fertile soil, due to climate change; and the need to reduce carbon emissions, due to the same process of climate change – partly at least by reducing the productivity of the remaining agrarian production. In a world with less food stuff and less land to grow it on, who is going to live and who is going to die? And, in a world dominated by rampant financial capitalism, how do we stop the speculative movements of financial capital from ravaging our very basic resources of water and calories, resources that financial capital has already clearly targeted as the source of the next derivative revolution? In a coming time of disaster, how do we defend democracy and democratic values from temptations to do with everything from enlightened Green dictatorship to utopias of pure white nations of Smallville? Arguably, not since the collective panic around the threat of nuclear war in the 1950s and 1960s has Western civilization been so much in the grips of fear about the future.

Future fear is not an irrational panic. It is, on the contrary, a socially rational kind of survival instinct, which extends into the imagined lives of one's children, and maybe even of their future ones. While our capabilities for rational planning may have a shorter scope, love can travel far into distant time. Future fear is also a well-founded feeling. There were good reasons in the 1960s to believe in the imminence of nuclear war, as there are good reasons in the present to believe that this world will be a very different place 20 or 30 years from now. But future fear is political dangerous, socially explosive and devastating on individual lives and on society as a whole, as is testified by the rise of xenophobia and hatred of Others in Europe in the aftermath of the financial crisis, by the steady advance of the extreme right and by the mobilization of robbed populations in Greece, Ireland or the UK. Future fear can lead to mobilization, but it also risks becoming the very opposite of enlightened action. The task of democratic politics in the present is this: to channel future fear into enlightened action.

This is not a question of inventing a new future narrative, a story with which to convince disenchanted electorates, or a brand name for a new politics. It is a question of building a new world – a laborious and difficult task, which must begin with theory and reasoning, with genuine social analysis and ideological debate. It begins, I propose, with understanding the future itself, as a problem that merits our attention. I propose that adequately analysing and responding to problems of future squeeze and future fear is the key to social democratic renewal and to a forceful argument about social democracy's role in today's and tomorrow's world. In order to gain a future, social democracy needs to think the future. Let's start, therefore, with the future, and with what the future requires from politics.

The future as a democratic problem

The future is not an easy thing to grapple with, because of its cognitive distance. Neither politics nor the social sciences are particularly well equipped to deal with it. Arguably the future is a social construction, meaning something created by social actors, including political ones; but it can also manifest itself in tangible ways and as such also become, in a sense, an actor (Latour, 2005). Climate change is an example of this: curves of rising temperatures or the eradication of arable soil tell us something about a material presence that is in the process of acquiring physical existence and that performs a form of action that is certainly the effect of all our actions, yet is almost immovable by our negotiations and interpretations. We cannot deny its objective existence, yet it is what we make it.

It might be proposed, more specifically, that the future is a particular democratic realm, or, if we like, a test for democracy. As pointed out by sophisticated observers such as the French historian and philosopher Pierre Rosanvallon, the future is the blind spot of democracy because it has no stakeholders and few defenders (Rosanvallon, 2008). Future generations have no vote bearing on the actions of the present. Yet the future is all our commons (Ostrom, 1990). The British sociologist Barbara Adam points to the discrepancy between individual people's ability to deal with the futures, for instance through the everyday actions implicit in caring for and raising their children, and the inability of capitalist societies to take a similar responsibility for the *timeprint*, the fact that all our actions have long-term consequences and will affect generations and stakeholders not yet living (Adam, 2005). This is a democratic paradox in contemporary societies, a source, as Adam writes, of disembeddedness and disconnection, and maybe also of a kind of collective sorrow. It is not, as Anthony Giddens has recently claimed, a new paradox of advanced modernity, but on the contrary one that has been debated as least since the late 1960s (Club of Rome, 1972; Giddens, 2009). Now it needs to be solved urgently, as is testified by the magnificent challenges of the financial crisis and of climate change – both of which are crises of futures.

To the future crises of financial capitalism and climate change we can add a third one, which is the crisis of people, not as derivatives of future growth or human capital (Andersson, 2010), but as holders of future aspirations. Can we uphold democracy and legitimate social structures if we deny young people a future, if politics convey a sense of exasperation and non-belonging? The tuition fees are, from this perspective, an assault on the young generation, but this is only one aspect of a world that seems to get tighter and more difficult for one to 'realize oneself' in. The revolutions in the Arab world, driven forward by a generation of young without hope of creating a space for themselves in societies plagued by unemployment and terror, are a reaction against such future loss. Democracies are upheld by a sense of future orientation, which in the past was often translated as an idea of progress; and this 'progress' meant 'more for everyone'. In the Western world today, this very idea of progress as a material process is part of our crisis. And so we need to find another concept of the future, one that breaks with the growth fetish (Hamilton, 2007), which has served as social glue for so long – one that replaces materialism and productivism with other values (FitzPatrick, 2004). Such a concept of the future cannot be realized by a story or a brand, but by a future to be built through inclusive politics, through transformations of democratic and economic structures, and by giving people a stake (Hutton, 1997). Otherwise, is my conjecture, social democracy will become more and more obsolete, while we witness the rise of a nostalgic, protectionist and increasingly dangerous neofascism in Europe.

Good futures

A lot of ink was spent, in the 1990s, on filling in the 'social' of social democracy, thereby breaking with historical associations to social*ism* as an economic and political doctrine. We are a social movement, we do not believe in -isms and ideologies, but we are concerned with making the world a little better, a little more social – or so it went. The trouble is that 'social' took the overhand over 'democracy' and led to the development of social policies that were certainly social, but also illiberal (King, 1999) and lacking in democratic content in their often explicit disdain of the principles of citizenship. The politics of aspiration – that is, the legitimate attempt to fill social citizenship with questions of mobility and self-reliance – became stuck in social control and economism. The debate over the democratic nature of politics fell away as something that might, with luck, follow from people getting richer, consuming more, feeling happier. This does not seem to have been the case. On the contrary, disenchantment and apathy can be seen as the very result of such politics (Hay, 2007).

Utopia is a difficult term. It was rejected, after 1989, as a blue print, as a mechanistic vision of the endpoints of social development and as guilty of having led to the totalitarian doctrines of Nazism and Stalinism (see for instance Mulgan, 1994). But utopia is essential to collective action and, it could be proposed, utopia has a central democratic function, which is that of giving us a reason to coexist and a sense of place in time. In the words of the communitarian philosopher Charles Taylor (2004), utopia is what places us in time and space, a standard to live by. Taylor's conception can be compared to how the Swedish socialist intellectual Ernst Wigforss once viewed the principle of equality as a provisory utopia, one that might never be fully realized, but without which we would be lost (for Ernst Wigforss, see Tilton, 1990).

Visions of the future are as many in society as we people are, but collective action requires some process capable of bringing that multitude of futures together into a common, not necessarily consensual, vision of what we believe to be universal, moral and ethical. In specific domains, actors often have radically different and conflictual visions of the future. Urban sociologists have shown, for instance, that New Labour's utopian dream of harmonious local communities is falsified when contrasted with local social reality, where in fact urban development remains full of conflicts over local futures, often driven by the material interests of outsourced urban management (Imrie and Raco, 2003). In the domain of natural resources, conflicts over land use or over key collective assets such as forests display a multitude of different visions, ranging from exploitation to conservation (Beland Lindahl, 2008). These are examples of controversy over the future. At the level of global climate politics, the magnitude of such future controversy and the difficulty in solving it is obvious. Democratic politics needs to handle these controversies over our common future in ways that are, precisely, democratic. It is in this sense of 'democratic' that we need to consider the difference between common futures and futures as consensus-based. In my view, common futures must take into account conflicts of interest, concerns with public and private and so on, and they must not attempt to ignore such clashes between visions of social development (see Mouffe, 2005). This is the reason why the emphasis on consensus in key debates such as the one on climate change is, while understandable, also problematic and plays right into the hands of climate deniers – as is testified in the UK by the Climate Gate scandal and in France by the storm around the Academy member Claude Allegre. However, in the process of rethinking how we can create democratic futures, we must realize that there are limits: some decisions are not ours to take. In other words, considering the *timeprint* as the sum of the future effects of our actions, many of which we will not live to see or feel, requires a weighing together of interests and visions where some things are protected as part of a future commons. From within the context of political theory, we might see it as a variation on Rousseau's famous statement that the principle of liberty requires the rejection of the right to sell oneself as a slave. We do not have the right to sell fundamental dimensions of future generations' freedom either – be they forests, clean air, fertile land or fundamental social infrastructure such as libraries or universities. Democracy requires the protection of key interests.

If we follow this line of thought, we arrive at a definition of *good* that has been nearly obsolete in political language in the last decades: it has to do with public goods, essential for freedom, and with the principles of citizenship not only at the national level but at the global level too (Petrella, 1996). In other words, there is a moral and ethical imperative not to sell out the forests that produce the oxygen and the living environment for future generations, or to let atolls in the Pacific sink. Such an argument can only be made at the level of ideology, ethics and interests – creating the basis for a discussion on how we might develop, in the global community, the institutions and policy instruments. It must include new forms of participation (some interesting work appears to be done in UK, with participatory processes around carbon budgets), which might provide a foundation for a new reformism.

It is impossible to do this without taking into account the moral, ethical, and even existential dimension of the future. In other words, it can only be done at the level of a democratic debate about the good society, leading to the formulation of a utopian goal to do with the content of what this social vision means, as well as with the process through which it may be realized. This is not utopia as a blueprint or mould for social development and individual behaviour, but as the democratic process of weighing future visions and future interest together, in a vision of a world in which the great number of people can live and be *whole*, as Raymond Williams once argued (Williams, 1983 (1958)). It is quite possible that we cannot be whole without a vision of our future. Research on communities struck by war, exile or economic depravation show that their loss is translated as a loss of future, after which lives become lived and felt as fragmented and fractured. Everyone needs a future, and many individual futures are only possible with some recourse to collective action. Collective action needs utopia as an ethical dimension a sense of what is right. It also needs a practical through which we can make what is right realizable. Within its framework, dissent and conflict must be possible, but politics must assume the interest of the long term. With such a meaning, utopia is a living principle of radical politics, never fix or frozen, but standing in a kind of ongoing dialogue with the future.

The above discussed necessitates the development of a new set of political institutions, of which some elements already exist. We have institutes for studies of the future and for long-term planning, for instance the one in Stockholm, which, under the aegis of Alva Myrdal and Olof Palme in the 1970s, developed a highly original form of weighing social science research and public participation as a process of democratically 'choosing futures' (Andersson, 2006). In Finland, since 1989, a standing futures committee is in charge of evaluating the futures of government policy, and all governments must present to it the future impact of their policies. In the Netherlands, the Scientific Council for Government (WRR) is charged with independent advice and strategic priorities for policy issues and has managed to keep such an independent and future critical position since the early 1970s despite the changing political climates. Let's contrast these examples with a British one – the Strategy Unit, which was politicized under Blair and charged with 'blue skies thinking', not with a concern with the future as such. At the global level blue sky thinking is much more difficult, and maybe it is time to revive historic utopian ideas of world government (ideas that engaged for instance several British Labour Party members of parliament), or the federalism of the early peace movement. It seems clear that the haggling over standards and emission rights in the global climate arena is more prone to protecting various national interests than the future of the world, but this may of course change. I want to move on, however, to a final point with direct implications for social democratic ideology and identity: namely what I call the value theory, which is not an allusion to Marx' theory of surplus value but might rather be translated as the need to make a moral and ethical argument about the limits of capitalism and about the importance of alternative values to the economic.

Social democracy's value theory

Social democracy is a movement that has, throughout history, been tempted by managerialism and technocracy; but it is also defined by its utopian stance and by the debate on the hierarchy of economic, social and cultural values. As the American political scientist Sheri Berman (2006) writes, the historical importance of social democracy was that it won the argument about the primacy of politics – the argument that principles of equality and democracy were more important than principles of accumulation and market efficiency. This is already a highly positive reading in Berman's version, but alas, this is where social democracy has most significantly gone lost. Social Democratic Parties – in Sweden, Britain, Germany – have become completely absorbed, in recent decades, in the ever-growing belief in the possibility of economic growth and market mechanisms to solve all other problems. Ethical arguments about the devastating effects of capitalism on social community, the role of the principle of equality as the guiding star of social development, the role of social citizenship and collective goods for democracy, were lost, or turned on their heads in favour of ideas about efficient market structures and individual competition. It is impossible to think the good future without thinking in terms of the values that should govern this future. Today both the principle of equality and that of democracy are in crisis – the first, a shunned term, and the second, presumed to be in good shape while the evidence to the contrary is growing around us.

As growth falters as an overriding value of social activities, we must ask the question of what could possibly take its place as the legitimizing principle of social organization. I would suggest that part of the crisis of social democracy is its massive constituency crisis, by which I mean not so much the fact that people are no longer voting for labour parties, or that membership is declining – which are significant problems in their own right – but rather the more abstract problem that social democracy seems not to believe in the good of people any more. In a time dominated by financial and climate crisis, our hope must be that not only politics, but citizens too will, first of all, rise to the occasion and believe in the possibility of a better future, and, secondly, be prepared to act for it. But there are many obstacles in the present towards such people, enlightened and competent about the future. Part of the problem is that politics has shunned the rights-side of social citizenship, and so it has left us with a notion of citizenship that is narrow and limited to a core obligation towards the 'good' of society. What about the right, for instance, to be regarded as a competent citizen, able to say something about societal decisions, or the right to an education not geared towards the creation of future human capital, but towards future competent citizens?

In the 1950s and 1960s there were big debates in Western societies about the dangers of specialization and expert rule. Indeed it was in this context that Aldous Huxley wrote his *Brave New World* (2003) and Michael Young his satire on the dangers of meritocracy, *The Rise of the Meritocracy* (1958). In the present, many things in society that have a long-time print – take financial derivates as an example – are almost impossible for anyone but a small clique of enlightened experts to understand. The fame of self-appointed experts such as Nouriel Robini, the economics professor who foresaw the financial crisis and is currently rated one of the most influential global experts on policy matters, is exactly that they claim to know the impact on our future of the things that we don't understand. The gap between the abstract, and thus somehow depoliticized, nature of financial derivatives and the absolutely devastating effect that these things may have on our lives is enormous. Such a gap, between the things I know and what might destroy me, is conducive to future fear. It strips masses of people of their competence about the future and of their feeling of having a legitimate stake in the future. The population of Iceland went overnight from the certainty of living in one of the best societies of the world to poverty and depression. It is a good thing for Iceland that the Icelanders have managed to turn grief into large-scale public debates, outdoors theatre and public hearings. In Greece, the situation appears to be taking a different route.

For all the reasons here outlined, the future is an urgent issue, which needs to be dealt with, but not in terms of finding the plot or creating the future vision or narrative, the big story that will sell social democracy to disenchanted voters. My suggestion is that we need to think about the future itself, as a political problem in its own right, and also as a fundamental challenge to reformist policies – a challenge in which, in fact, possibly the keys to the good society lie.

12
The National in the Network Society: UK Uncut, the English Defence League and the Challenge for Social Democracy

Ben Little and Deborah Grayson

Introduction

Social democracy, as embodied in the institutions created in the post-war settlement, is on the brink of collapse. As Social Democratic Parties struggle to re-imagine themselves after a string of electoral defeats across Europe, unrestrained neoliberalism is consolidating its hold on power. This moment of political vacuum on the left is leaving Europe-wide austerity measures almost unopposed by the political mainstream. But it is also taking place at a time when the power of new technologies to facilitate dissent and make demands for democratic representation can no longer be dismissed as faddish. From Barack Obama's unlikely presidential nomination to the recent revolutionary waves in the Middle East, new social networking tools are having palpable effects within the formal political sphere. And new forms of popular movements, which we term 'identity networks' – like the Tea Party in the USA and the student opposition to fee rises in the UK – are wielding power in ways to which formal political structures are struggling to respond. This chapter seeks to describe these shifts in the possibilities of collective action and to propose the beginnings of a new relationship between Social Democratic Parties and the emerging 'identity networks' of the left, through a reclamation of the discourse of the nation.

Although the nation and the network have had very different intellectual lives and are often described as oppositional – the stronger the sense of network, the weaker the attachment to the nation – it is our contention that the current crisis of social democracy in Europe can only be overcome through an appreciation of the way these concepts are starting to connect. This is not techno-fetishism: the technology does not determine the outcome, but it does transform the realm of what is possible. Across Europe, the far-right seem to be far more comfortable in this emerging ideological space; and, as neo-fascist electoral success spreads even as far as such bastions of tolerance as Sweden and Norway, it becomes ever more urgent for the left to start engaging with this organizational and intellectual conjunction. A pan-European perspective is important, and we have much to learn from the patterning of events across the continent, although without losing sight of the complexity of the particular within specific localities. We hope that this chapter will remain of interest to a wider European readership, despite our primary focus on the implications of recent developments within the United Kingdom.

In this chapter we argue that there are emerging popular movements on both left and right, which are savvy to the transformations underway: they are opposing forces on the front line of new political configurations, made possible by the increasing accessibility of sophisticated and scalable tools of digital communication. Yet the battle lines go beyond the politics of the street and deep into the foundations of our established ideologies. To confront how the politics of the left must adapt its thinking to this new era, a new political configuration will need to re-articulate the relationship between the local, the national and the global through the lens of the material connections between people and things that social network technologies make apparent[1].

Our politics must reshape itself in an era when social networks become the key locus of struggle, not just for the spirit of the nation, but also for policy making, service delivery and the market. Moreover, social democracy can and should adapt to this new terrain for its own sake, because the cultural shifts happening around digital network technologies could potentially be the heralds of a new order, which is both *more* social and *more* democratic. The concomitant risk is that, if we do not, networks will come to be dominated by corporate interests and the far-right, which seek to use them for anti-social and undemocratic ends.

For social democracy, the techno-cultural shift brought about by the democratization of digital network technologies means there is a need to reconcile two challenges that are currently understood as separate, even oppositional. The first is to show how social democracy might reincorporate the national into the politics of a re-imagined state in order to build consent for a programme of equality; the second is to rectify the inadequacy of centralized state control in the network society.

To explain the connection between these two tasks, the term 'network society' needs some breaking down. The 'networks' referred to are multiple. Coined by Manuel Castells in the mid-1990s, the term initially referred to the networks of *global capital flows*. Over time, with the mass take-up of mobile phones and the emergence of blogging and other social media, the concept has had to be expanded to include cultural and social life. In this way, the possibilities of 'mass self-communication' (2009, 65–72) facilitated by *digital* networks have started to make explicit the *material* networks of peoples' lived experience. We must now understand the 'network society' as a way of describing the state of modern capitalism, the relationship between technologies of personal communication and culture, and the way in which we form and maintain relationships, both individually and collectively. All three of these phenomena, separately and in conjunction, are radically changing our relationships to the 'imagined communities' of place, ethnicity and nation (Castells, 2009; Anderson, 1991). Within this new conceptual space, politics is changing fast; coalitions of interest are shifting rapidly; novel ideologies are being formed and old ones are being revived.

The network, the state and the crisis of the nation

To many, it will be seem something of an overstatement that websites and Internet services such as Facebook and Twitter should cause a crisis for social democracy. Yet in 2006 Yochai Benkler was already defending such a position from accusations that it was dated:

> It seems passé today to speak of 'the Internet revolution.' In some academic circles, it is positively naïve. But it should not be. The change brought about by the networked information environment is deep. It is structural. It goes to the very foundations of how liberal markets and liberal democracies have co-evolved for almost two centuries. (Benkler, 2006, 1)

This is a crisis point for modern politics, as, since the French Revolution and the *Declaration of the Rights of Man*, 'nationalism and democracy [have been fused] in an apparently irresistible combination' (Gamble, 1981, 133), and the modern state emerged from this marriage between territory and political representation. The European left has become afraid of using the nation to build its politics, believing instead that the idea of the state stands on its own terms. Yet, without an alternative frame for articulating the relationship between place and power, the result has been the alienation of core working class votes, decreasing voter turnout and the narrowing of social democracy to the politics of urban liberal elites. Without a narrative of the national, identities become increasingly constructed around leisure interests or the consumption of global brands, further weakening the relationship between citizen and state. In the 'network society', where national borders are permeable to capital, commodity and communication flows, the credibility of the nationally bound democracy comes under threat.

Why does the nation still matter? Because we have an austerity package to resist and the prospect of another global recession, not to mention the need to decarbonize rapidly; because the solutions to these problems require a renewed sense of a relationship between current generations and those to come; and because we desperately need a form of governance that has the consent and involvement of the majority in order to implement a programme that fulfils these aims. It is possible that the future holds something very different – some as yet unimagined form of networked syndicalism, or a post-statist model of social welfare. For now, we need to use what we have to hand: the emotive power of the nation as an idea that creates a relationship between the present and the future through the idiom of shared space, and the force of the state as the only power that can stand up to unbridled capitalism.

The fears of revisiting nationalism, which date to the 1930s and 1940s, forget that it was initially *the* radical enlightenment movement in Europe and an assertion of the fundamental rights of the people against the arbitrary powers of church, monarch and aristocracy. 'What is a nation?' asked Abbe Sieyes in his inflammatory 1789 pamphlet. 'A body of people who join together to live under common laws and be represented by the same legislative assembly.' If the nobility and the church insisted on living under different laws, then they should be excluded from the nation; the third estate, those living under common law, was 'everything' (Sieyes, 1789). While this is not, of course, advocating a modern-day Terror, it recognizes the French Revolution as foundational to the development of liberal democracy across the world. A return to Sieyes' civic understanding of the nation means that it should not only be possible, but desirable, for the idea to be reclaimed as a space for solidarity, fundamental rights and equality, in opposition to that of multi-national corporations, international celebrity culture and the 'weightless millionaires', who seem to exist beyond the realm of the nations that the rest of us inhabit, and who refuse to be subject to their laws.

British social democracy has presented itself as powerless against these power-brokers of globalization, as it is bound to the state and its borders. Yet there was a paradox implicit in the defunct 'Third Way' politics of New Labour's view of globalization and of the knowledge economy: on the one hand, these ideas claim that capital is no longer subject to states but is free to roam where it pleases, while on the other hand capital *requires* nations to compete with one another to function. As Paul Hirst pointed out in 1999, 'if world free markets really prevailed and were ungovernable then national public policy would be irrelevant, and the voices that demand adaptation to global competitive pressures would be silent' (Hirst, 1999, 12). Social democracy, unlike neoliberalism, is bound to the idea of the nation: states remain nation-states and their power can be reasserted in those terms. The concept of the nation can be the locus of struggle against capitalist excess.[2]

We need to embrace a new vision of nationalism, 'a civic identity which exists alongside other identities' (Johnson, 2010, 80), in which the nation is not an ethnically determined relationship with a territory, but the conceptual space of a social contract that binds people, collective life and the processes of governance together against the atomizing forces of capital. The discovery of a progressive civic nationalism may not be the desired direction for many on the left, but it is an important strategic move that may well be transcended in the future, once the immediate challenges have been faced.

The risk of digital networks facilitating the politics of the right is more real and more frightening than a left engagement with nation. Networked right-activism has powerfully manifested itself in the Tea Party movement in the USA and in the English Defence League in the UK. Like previous far-right movements, these virulent mobilizations of prejudice and reaction are dominating the discourse of the nation and shaping its politics. The difference is that now they are aligned, not just to the inequalities of racial exclusion, but also to an ideal of the stateless nation and to the retrenchment of the redistributive mechanisms of modern governance. These movements on the right have spread rapidly through digital networks, and opposition to them has been slow. This is partly because, after the successful use of such technologies in Barack Obama's election campaign, the left smugly thought that the terrain of the digital network was theirs, even as Blue State Digital (the organization behind the democratic electoral machine) has sold itself to a global advertising giant. But the success of these divisive movements is also partly due to the fact that the new right is occupying a real gap in the political imagination – and their grievances are material, even if their targets are born of hatred, misinformation and fear.

We believe that a countervailing left politics is already being built in the new green movement and in the pro-tax/anti-cuts protests. While these movements are not intrinsically social democratic, alliances can and should be made with them in the face of seemingly intractable problems across the spectrum of left concerns. Realistically, social democracy, if it reinvents itself and its relation to place, the nation and the network, is perhaps the only political model that can win consent for the necessary transformations for a greener and fairer economy while maintaining a commitment to fundamental rights. In short, we need a politics that is prepared to embrace and use state power, albeit in a less centralized and technocratic way than it has to date. We need a confident state that stands up to the anti-government discourse of the right and keeps spending; but we also need a state that trusts its people enough to relinquish control and allow the creativity, energy and power of those pursuing social democratic ends outside formal political processes to re-imagine our nation.

Transformations of the 'network society'

To realize the potential power of these social changes, we must try to understand better how the techno-cultural shifts in the move towards a horizontal network society challenge political centralism and reorganize our economic lives. While embedded in history, the forms of social relating we wish to examine are necessarily novel; the speed of technological change, the rapidity of its spread across the globe and the sheer number of people making connections with one another across space have created challenges and possibilities unimaginable just two decades ago. To chart this transformation, we will remain within the frame of the sociologist Manuel Castells and of his work over the last 15 years, borrowing some of his terminology and developing it, to describe briefly what we see as the emerging political struggles of contemporary Britain.

The Information Age, Castells' weighty trilogy produced in the second half of the 1990s, begins with the *Rise of the Network Society* (1996), in which networks are seen primarily as those of financial capital, which operate in opposition to human values and needs:

> People increasingly organise their meaning not around what they do but on the basis of what they are, or believe they are. Meanwhile, on the other hand, global networks of instrumental exchanges

selectively switch on and off individuals, groups, regions, and even countries, according to their relevance in fulfilling the goals processed in the network, in a relentless flow of strategic decisions. It follows a fundamental split between abstract, universal instrumentalism, and historically rooted, particularistic identities. Our societies are increasingly structured around a bipolar opposition between the Net and the Self. (Castells, 1996, 3)

This new order provides opportunities for those who are seen to be of value to the network (highly educated, flexible, 'self-programmable'), who gain value from each connection; but it also excludes those seen to be valueless, making it harder for them to accrue value. In response to this growing inequality, those excluded ('the computer illiterate [...] consumptionless groups, and [...] under-communicated territories', p. 25) begin to form 'resistance identities' around this disconnection, a process that leads to the growing importance of local, ethnic or religious identities. They use idioms of territory, which may still coincide with the state; but states have 'lost much of [their] sovereignty' (Castells, 1997, 419), and, besides, the state is generally rightly understood as colluding with the oppressive forces of capital.

Separated by space, this global proletariat of 'generic labour' finds collective action on the basis of class to be less and less possible (p. 476). Its members have common grievances, but are inherently isolated: 'However these identities resist, they barely communicate [...] with each other because they are built around sharply distinct principles, defining an "in" and "out"' (p. 421). In contrast to resistance identities, 'project identities', built around issues such as feminism and environmentalism, aim to transform society as a whole, asserting a species-wide commonality of experience. But, without the mechanism of the interactive digital network, Castells cannot conceive of how these 'networks of social change' (p. 428) will be able to mobilize the power of local identity to global ends.

His perspective has changed somewhat five years later, in *The Information Society and the Welfare State* (2002), which looks at information and communication technology (ICT) development in Finland while contrasting it to the situation in Silicon Valley and Singapore. The combination of rapid dissemination of ICT equipment and skills has led, by this point, to Finland being one of the world leaders in the telecoms industry; but it has achieved this in conjunction with generous welfare provision, creating a 'socially sustainable network society' (2002, 14) rather than one in which capital networks are at odds with human selves. By creating an 'informational welfare state' to deliver services, by supporting the development of 'social hackerism' – the beginnings of the 'generative framework' of Zitrain (2008), where resources and space are given by the state for actions external to the state – and by understanding these things as *part* of a strong Finnish national identity rather than as opposed to it, Finland has avoided many of the oppositions Castells warned of in *The Rise of the Network Society*.

His excitement at the power of digital tools to create meaningful alternatives to the logic of capital flows becomes even more palpable in his most recent book, *Communication Power* (2009). By now Web 2.0 has emerged, occupying a central part in the lives of most of the world's rich and of ever-growing numbers of the world's poor. 'We do not watch internet, as we watch TV. In practice, Internet users [...] *live* with the Internet' (Castells, 2009, 64). This opens up new political possibilities, because of the 'potential synergy between the rise of mass self communication and the autonomous capacity of civil societies around the world to shape the process of social change' (p. 303).

Leading on from his construction of 'project identities', Castells notes that 'the Internet has played an increasingly important role in the global movement to prevent global warming' (p. 325). However, by focusing on the various online tools used by Friends of the Earth or by the Stop Climate Change Coalition to raise their profile or to mobilize action on or offline (pp. 323–325), Castells misses what is truly novel about the new green movement that has emerged in the last ten years: its growing plurality and diversity, the alliances being formed between previously disconnected issues (for example, links with trade unions) and its ability to link up 'resistance identities' embedded in localities. These linkages are what we term 'identity networks'. They create political impact through mass horizontal action, 'local at all points', like Latour's railroad train, even if 'it takes you from Brest to Vladivostock' (Latour, 1993, 117). Rather than Al Gore as the celebrity spokesman for the environmental project identity – a 'weightless millionaire' if ever there was one – there are emerging figureheads in the battle against climate change, and they are very different.

Identity networks

It is our contention that the new green movement has developed, in the last ten years, from being polarized between the 'resistance identities' of individual battles over specific locations and the 'project identities' concerned with global emissions, to a more subtle and nuanced 'identity network'. Friends of the Earth and Stop Climate Chaos were pivotal in passing the Climate Change Bill in 2008, which made the UK the first country to commit legally to an 80 per cent cut in carbon emissions by 2050, but this was essentially an old-school lobbying job, operating through fairly traditional channels, with some cosmetic online tinkering.

An example of where the 'identity network' can be seen at work is in the loose coalition formed to stop the building of a third runway at Heathrow, mapped by John Stewart in *Victory Against All Odds: How the Heathrow Campaign Was Won* (2010). The campaign drew together a potent combination of groups, organizations and individuals – the West Londoners connected through the noise pollution of the planes over their heads Heathrow Association for the Control of Aircraft Noise (HACAN), the villagers of Sipson, Harlington and Harmondsworth fighting the destruction of their homes No Third Runway Action Group (NoTRAG), the celebrities who bought and publicized the Greenpeace 'Airplot' (Emma Thompson, Zac Goldsmith, Alistair McGowan), the politicians from all parties who kept the issue alive in Parliament (John McDonnell, John Gummer) and the activists in Climate Camp and Plane Stupid, who linked the debate to the global fight against climate change. While remaining separate, tactics and resources were shared, personal connections were formed, and the actants involved were transformed.

Climate Camp made itself 'local' for a week by holding the 2007 camp in a field next to the airport; celebrities made themselves neighbours by buying the Airplot; John McDonnell took direct action, picking up the mace in the House of Commons; HACAN held 40 public meetings attended by 20,000 during the official consultation period, the end of which was publicized by Plane Stupid's headline grabbing banner which was dropped off the Houses of Parliament. Throughout the campaign, global and local, online and offline, 'project identities' and 'resistance identities' were blended to make a compelling case that this was an authentic expression of 'the people' against a corporate giant and a remote and unrepresentative state. It was understood *simultaneously as* an issue affecting the villagers of Sipson, the residents of West London, the millions of other locals affected by airport expansion (connected through the AirportWatch network) and the billions around the world who will suffer from climate change in their own localities. Thousands signed up online to become 'beneficial owners' of the Greenpeace Airplot, a piece of land in the proposed path of the new runway, which was chalked in giant letters, so as to be visible from the planes above it, with the emotive phrase: 'Our Climate, Our Land' (Greenpeace, 2009). And these transformations have had effects beyond the immediate aims of the campaign. Activists who 'adopted' residents have remained friends with them. John McDonnell has become a frequent spokesperson on climate change in Parliament. The Airplot has become a community garden. Members of Plane Stupid bought a house next to the airport and have now set up Transition Town Sipson.

Identity networks can mobilize on a substantial scale and have real political effects, creating solidarity across space while maintaining the complexity of the particular. But the network that formed to stop the third runway emerged in a vacuum of the nation as a sphere of political action. It constructed a narrative that tied the disparate project and resistance identities together in a way that not only asserted the interest of the various participants of the campaign on global and local scales against the intermediary of the national; it was also a campaign that was intrinsically anti-statal, peaking with the banner drop declaring the Palace of Westminster to be the headquarters of BAA Ltd.

This is not a criticism of the campaign. What emerged was a semi-organic strategy to combat an abuse of state power that put local and global concerns at odds with a limited vision of the national interest. This limited vision is one in which politicians see the state as a weak force against the tides of globalization and the fluidity of capital. Its role becomes nothing more than to ensure that the nation is not 'switched off' in the logic of Castells' network society – indeed, it could be argued that the entire Third Way policy framework championed by the former New Labour government was predicated on the idea that politicians were powerless to do anything except mitigate the worst excess of global capital through modest redistribution. The Heathrow campaign refused to accept that notion and won. They won partly because they were dogged, determined and right, but they also won because, while New Labour was operating under the logics of the network society of the 1990s, where global capital was king, the campaign was at the vanguard of the new, democratized social network society, in which capital is just one way of forming links between people and groups. Contrary to the arguments of BAA, the victory of the Heathrow campaign did not mean some sudden loss of British competitiveness in the global economy. Instead it provided a model for other protest groups across Europe (and indeed across the world) to follow. For the 'weightless millionaires' of network capitalism, this is a wakeup call. Capital may be highly fluid and mobile, but it multiplies in places that are very much physical and real. It needs access to markets and infrastructure – things that are provided by nation-states. There is a political strength in this realization that state and nation have the power to control who, how and why the interaction between people and capital occurs.

Thus we are at a moment for social democracy to reassert itself alongside the state, re-imagined as inextricably linked to the idea of a nation of people under common law and with common values. The battle against library closures in the UK (part of the conservative/liberal democrat government's austerity drive) is adopting the sort of identity network model to embrace it as we write: while each fight is against an individual council, they are connected through online tools like falseeconomy.org.uk and sharing messages and tactics – such as 'mass borrowing' all the books in the library in protest (BBC, 2011a, 2011b). The geographical attachment to the particular becomes simultaneously a national attachment to the idea of literacy, education and learning as a public good. These sorts of campaigns enable the democratic left to build a consensus around core values: the local group ties to a national message that asserts a universal right. Literacy is a common good, which we do not compete over; its benefit grows for all as more of us become literate.

This linking of the local to the national is even more palpable in the actions of UK Uncut, a non-hierarchical anti-tax avoidance protest movement that scaled up from a one-off event to dozens of regular protests across the country in a matter of weeks. By creating a loose network with an open 'wiki-style' collaborative website at its heart (ukuncut.org.uk), it has succeeded in orchestrating action in a national frame while maintaining local autonomy: marrying social democratic principles with a participatory, informal organizational structure that is functionally leaderless. More significantly, its traditional left-wing calls for a fair tax-and-spend system, alongside an assault on wealthy tax dodgers and multi-national corporations, has won approval from such bastions of tradition as the *Daily Mail* in its appeal to a 'fair play' model of Britishness (*Daily Mail*, 2010).

This recourse to national identity refocuses attention on the real villains of the 'network society' by targeting the double standards previously assumed to be the right of the mobile elite in a global capitalist society. It is the call of Sieyes revisited, the assertion of the rights of the Third Estate against those who consider themselves beyond the common law of the nation. Through the vistas of the network society, asking people to pay their taxes locally is a revolutionary call, and it may well spread. As we write, US and Canadian 'Uncuts' have been launched, and the organization is starting to build European connections and to expand its targets to include the tax havens that make such a system possible. Defending the nation in this manner becomes a global good that values the equally strong assertions of fellow nations. This could be the spirit of a new nationalism, powered by a social democratic identity network that builds its ideology upon fair taxation, cross-cultural solidarity and the rights and privileges of an open and interactive model of empowered citizenship.

The 'wrong sort' of identity network

While anti-cuts campaigners are rediscovering the link between national values and state provision, the rise of the English Defense League (EDL) is a consequence of the disconnection between statist governance and the discourse of nationhood. Its members play on the localism agenda, telling those left behind by globalization that their geographical ties make them important and deserving of privilege. As a global phenomenon, the resistance identities that drive this new localist fascism are increasingly finding common ground with similar movements in other countries, despite their different nationalisms; 'identity networks' are not just the property of the left, the greens, the privileged or those we would naturally think of as 'international'. The British far-right now participates in online and off-line networks across Europe and the Atlantic, made up of like-minded people who share their concerns, fears and prejudices. Participation in far-right networks can transform their understanding of their own disadvantage and engender a vital sense of agency in the world in which they are powerless. Rather than being a relic of an old East End of London or of the post-industrial northern England, the EDL is made up of active participants in twenty-first century global neo-fascism, a movement reported by the media and influencing governments across Europe and North America.

How can the left respond to this threat? Certainly not merely through the mechanisms of increased central control. Fighting the EDL on the streets, locking up its members or banning them for inciting racial hatred plays into the narrative of victimization that attracted groups of alienated young men in the first place. Just as the increased surveillance and the infringement of civil liberties following September 11 have further distanced young British Muslims from the state – indeed, have transformed their sense of identity so that, for many, religion has become its most central aspect (Saeed, 2008) – trying to stamp out the EDL by force fundamentally misunderstands it aims. Unlike the National Front in the 1970s, which sought to demonstrate power through overt clashes with anti-fascists and police, the EDL is not attempting to take on the state on its own terms (Burghart and Zeskind, 2010). It exercises a different sort of power, stoking up existing tensions within limited geographical areas and giving its actions collective force by sharing information, strategies, resources and press contacts through horizontal, digitally mediated networks. The EDL pose a new sort of threat and will require new sorts of solutions, which it would be foolish to pretend we have already worked out; but building links between isolated 'locals' along the lines of Hope Not Hate's successful campaigns against the British National Party, combined with the left re-articulating the space of the national, might offer a way forward.

As new digital technologies become more widely available, they offer both sides of the political divide the opportunity to build or maintain identity networks, either with similarly alienated groups, those in solidarity with common political projects, or with people experiencing comparable forms of oppression around the world. When linked to fundamental principles of equality and respect or to the environment, these identity networks can be transformative and emancipatory, but there is also the possibility of reactionary localisms and fragmentary cultural fundamentalisms. The processes and technologies that have created the alterglobalization and new green movements, linked up the EDL with the Tea Party and fuelled Islamic fundamentalism have similar roots – but can result in very different political outcomes.

Conclusion

Political power is increasingly being wielded by those who embrace the network logic. Movements are getting organized and acting without the formalized structures expected by political parties, and yet they are shaping the trajectory of politics and forcing policy makers to meet them and their agendas. From the Tea Party in the USA to the student occupations of 2010 in the UK, these movements are remoulding the political space in which decisions are made. They are intrinsically opposite to elite structures and resilient enough not to be easily suppressed, operating to a 'starfish' model that cannot be decapitated (Brafman and Beckstrom, 2006).

There has been a tendency to techno-fetishism that sees digital media as inherently emancipatory, and the chief threats to their ability to deliver equality as coming from the state and the corporations that dominate the internet (Hands, 2011). This argument fails to see that a politics based around networks could be profoundly different, depending upon its ideological frame. Networks are ambivalent to the priorities of previous political constructions: they can deliver the equality project of the left or the hatred and bigotry of the far-right. There are many reasons to be hopeful, and there is a wealth of ideas emerging around collaborative consumption (Botsman and Rogers, 2010), co-production (NEF, 2008), corporate cooperativism (Grant, 2010), Transition Towns (Hopkins, 2006), wikigovernment (Novack, 2009) and so on. Any number of progressive political programmes could emerge out of the current moment – from an internationalist networked syndicalism that flourishes in the spaces that capitalism leaves behind to a digital corporate welfarism emerging out of the Finnish experience recounted by Castells.

Historically, we have understood territorial identities as inherently oppositional, or in competition with one another. In reaction to this, the trend on the left has been to adopt a global outlook, where people that are attached to territories are seen as either backward or fascists. While the desire to transcend parochialism has been well intentioned, the result has been left-wing parties ceasing to be able to speak to people who feel that their relationship to place is important. This is the crisis of social democracy: that the left has nothing to say to the white European working class. We need to find a way to conceive of territorial identities that doesn't pit them against other territorial identities in a kind of zero-sum competition or, worse, stoke up conflicts between 'locals' and immigrants.

The best sorts of identity networks are beginning to show us the way to a new cooperative politics of interdependent territorialities. While we are working out what it is that comes next – and there are really good signs, and lots of ideas, but they aren't there yet – we need to hold onto the nation and the state in order to create the space for the next thing to flourish. The state has been the best mechanism for delivering equality to date, and the nation still commands an emotive connection to past and future that will be essential for building consent for a politics not solely based on the concerns of the present. The marriage of those two things remains powerful. The leftist identity network, whether green or anti-tax avoidance, demonstrates how we can create a positive-sum set of attachments through territorial identity that work together for the benefit of everyone, and can connect the twentieth-century project identities with a revitalized social democracy for the twenty-first century. The way in which Social Democratic Parties recognize this challenge will determine whether they remain a viable political force.

Notes

1. At its most basic level this 'making apparent' consists of simple lists of connections – to people, institutions, events and products – that sites like Facebook or Twitter make public to differing degrees. At a deeper level, these technologies have the potential to transform our social relations in a profound way. What they offer is a social efficiency mechanism in the same way that previous ICT developments offered economic efficiencies. The impact this will have on relationships, markets and politics is yet to be seen.
2. That the weak nation plays into the hands of large corporations is currently bring illustrated in the depiction of the UK as 'Broken Britain', forced to privatise public services because of 'the markets', slash spending for fear of a neo-liberal academic deciding we should lose our triple A credit rating, and unable to collect corporate tax even when deemed entitled to by the European court! (Hawkes, 2011).

Part VI
Conclusion

The Way Ahead

Henning Meyer and Jonathan Rutherford

The immediate political future will be dominated by the economy and the pace of recovery of our national economies. Social democratic policies around the deficit and around future growth are crucial, but alone they will not achieve electoral success. The issue of the economy is hegemonic, and not solely about management and technical competence. Social democracy needs a much broader political approach, which should encompass culture, society and nation. There is an urgent need to begin replenishing its intellectual life. We have to find sources of political, cultural and philosophical vitality and new ways of thinking and organizing. Social democratic parties need to make the transition from government mode to leadership of a movement, and then find ways of sustaining the movement back to government.

Social democracy is not facing a powerful hegemony, as it did in the 1990s. The financial crash has broken the neo-liberal economic order and exposed its dysfunctional nature. But neo-liberalism has not been politically defeated. There is currently no viable alternative political economy on offer. The task is to create one. The stakes are much higher than in the early nineties, during the formation of Third Way politics. Today the political terrain is fractured and open to realignment. There is a growing xenophobic right, which, together with left and green parties, has taken votes away from social democratic parties. In the wake of the 2008 financial crash, there is a significant manoeuvring in a 'war of position' of shifting social forces.

In the post-crash era we need to engage with the new conditions, rebuild political movements and national coalitions and transform our cultures and societies around social and democratic values and priorities. This involves not simply 'listening to people' but creating national political leaderships that involve dialogue as the basis for building relationships and trust. People want to know what social democrats believe in, then they want to know what we are going to do, and then they'll decide whether or not to vote for us. Navigating the transition from Third Way politics to a new revisionism will be politically difficult in the face of a right-wing media, hostile financial markets and a significant amount of public scepticism. It will require foundational thinking rather than simply a new set of policies.

What is social democracy, and what is it for? What kind of society does it seek to create? What is its political economy? What is its ethics and what does it think about the meaning of life? What is its understanding of our different cultures and societies, and who we are as individuals? Does it practice what it preaches? Whatever the answers are to these questions – and we have attempted to address them in this book – they are not what they would have been 20, or even 10 years ago.

Rethinking European social democracy needs to be orchestrated around these kinds of foundational questions, so that it may add up to something more than the sum of its different national parties. Each one needs to contribute to, and be part of, a larger story about its meaning and historical purpose in Europe. Without authentic and durable conviction expressed in our values and aims, European social democracy will end up with a superficial politics of tactics and positioning that plaster over its failures and ailing political philosophy. It will be fragmented by national differences, buckle at the first confrontation with its enemies and be unable to weather setbacks and 'events'.

In the years ahead, European social democracy will need to establish a strategic, purposeful politics that has enduring, authentic conviction. This will provide the lodestone for addressing the tactical questions of how to build popular support and win elections. A strong, coherent story will enable it to move forward step by step towards the kind of social Europe we want to live in.

This kind of deeper and longer term work will shape the future of Europe for generations. It will mark it out as a new revisionism that will take place at a national and European level, and both within and outside our national political parties. It will be integrated into policy formation and party reform, and it will have a synergy with the development of local community organizing. It will embed itself in the local and from there build upwards, to a pan-European network of parties, alliances, social movements and labour organizations. It will be the most significant systemic change to social democratic parties across Europe since their formation.

By orchestrating think tanks, policy formation, deliberative fora with party members and the public, and community organizing, and by mobilizing academics and civil society organizations, social democratic parties can do what the New Right in the UK did so brilliantly in the 1970s and 1980s and facilitate the groundwork for a new, decades-long hegemony of the centre-left. The historical conditions exist for this hegemony; what it needs is the political leadership and determination to see it through.

Our original intention when we first met in Berlin in 2008 was to begin this process and build a new axis around the SPD and Labour, which will provide a philosophical and political frame for a revived European social democracy. The declaration Building a Good Society outlined the intention. This book is a first attempt to begin adding substance to the frame. In the years ahead we need to give this emerging politics intellectual coherence, moral purpose and political direction. We will need to dig deep, philosophically and historically, in order to create the foundations on which to build a demotic language that resonates with people's life experiences and hopes. We will need to link our theoretical work to the practical business of community organizing and develop good dialogue with organizations and movements across the civil society. And we will need to share our experiences and knowledge across nations.

In the wake of the Third Way, what will come next? We must persist in working our way towards an answer. There is a risk that we will not. The force of inertia within our own parties, combined with the latter's political weakness, could cause their leaderships to falter. Political timidity will turn us away from taking necessary risks. We could do worse than develop a dialogue together that gives us courage and strength, and out of which we can create a social democracy for these difficult times. Let's begin.

Appendix

Building the Good Society – The Project of the Democratic Left
Jon Cruddas and Andrea Nahles

Europe at a turning point

Europe is at a turning point. Our banks are not working, businesses are collapsing and unemployment is increasing. The economic wreckage of market failure is spreading across the continent.

But this is not just a crisis of capitalism. It is also a failure of democracy and society to regulate and manage the power of the market. At this moment of crisis we reject the attempt to turn back to the 'business as usual' of unsustainable growth, inequality and anxiety economics. But we recognize too that there is no golden age of social democracy to go back to either.

The future is uncertain and full of threats; before us lie the dangers of climate change, the end of oil and growing social dislocation. But it is also a moment full of opportunities and promise: to revitalize our common purpose and fulfil the European dream of freedom and equality for all. To face these threats and realize this promise demands a new political approach.

On the tenth anniversary of the Blair–Schroeder declaration of a European Third Way, the democratic left offers an alternative project: the good society.

This politics of the good society is about democracy, community and pluralism. It is democratic because only the free participation of each individual can guarantee true freedom and progress. It is collective because it is grounded in the recognition of our interdependency and common interest. And it is pluralist because it knows that, from a diversity of political institutions, forms of economic activity and individual cultural identities, society can derive the energy and inventiveness to create a better world. To achieve a good society based on these values we are committed to:

- restoring the primacy of politics and rejecting the subordination of political to economic interests;
- remaking the relationship between the individual and the state in a democratic partnership;
- creating a democratic state that is accountable and more transparent, strengthening our institutions of democracy at all levels, including the economy;
- enlarging and defending individual civil liberties;
- reasserting the interests of the common good, such as education, health and welfare, over the market;
- redistributing the risk, wealth and power associated with class, race and gender to create a more egalitarian society;

- recognizing and respecting differences of race, religion and culture;
- putting the needs of people and of the planet before profit.

The foundation of the good society is an ecologically sustainable and equitable economic development for the good of all. There are no short-cuts or ready-made blueprints. Instead, on the basis of these values and aspirations, we will take each step together, and in this way we will make our world a better place to live in. As Willy Brandt said: 'What we need is the synthesis of practical thinking and idealistic striving.'

Working in our own national arenas we can achieve a great deal, but we need to recognize that capital has gone global while democracy has remained largely stuck at nation state level. This statement brings together social democrats from Germany and Britain, and in doing so makes each stronger. The next stage is to use this exploratory text to build a pan-European network of social democrats who, like us, don't want to turn back to the past but are looking ahead to build the good society.

Learning from experience

In June 1999, Tony Blair and Gerhard Schroeder, the prime minister of Britain and the chancellor of Germany, published a joint declaration of European social democracy. Their statement brought together the ideas of the British Third Way and of the German Neue Mitte. They claimed that this new model of social democracy had found widespread acceptance: 'Social democrats are in government in almost all the countries of the union.' Today the reverse is true. Social democrats are out of government in almost all the countries of the union.

The historic stage of social democracy associated with the Third Way and the Neue Mitte was a response to the long period of right-wing dominance that had taken hold following the economic crisis of the 1970s. A new historic stage of capitalism had emerged, destroying the post-war welfare consensus and establishing a new consensus, around neo-liberal values and a free market economy.

The electoral successes of the Third Way and Neue Mitte were tempered by compromises and limitations. Neither New Labour nor the Social Democratic Party (SPD) were able to build lasting coalitions for transformational change. In the 2005 election both parties had millions fewer votes than in 1997 and 1998, and both have lost out in local and regional elections. Substantial numbers of traditional working-class supporters have lost faith in New Labour and in the SPD as the historical advocates of their interests. Many abstain from voting, while an increasing minority identify with other parties, which would claim to represent their interests, such as the leftist 'Die Linke' in Germany, and – of greater concern – the fascist British National Party (BNP) in Britain. The institutions and cultures of the working class that sustained Labour and the SPD through the twentieth century have either disappeared or lost their social vitality.

The Third Way and the Neue Mitte models of social democracy uncritically embraced the new globalized capitalism. In doing so, they underestimated the destructive potential of under-regulated markets. They misunderstood the structural changes taking place in European societies. They believed that a class-based society had given way to a more individualized, meritocratic culture. But the new capitalism has not created a classless society. Under market-led globalization the economic boom created unprecedented levels of affluence, but Third Way politics was not able to prevent this affluence from dividing societies. After a decade of social democratic government, class inequality remains the defining structure of society. Success in education and life chances in general continue to depend on family background.

The era of neo-liberalism was always going to end in self-destruction. Now the economic crash has created a turning point. We have a choice: we can go back to how things were before – the unsustainable growth, the individualized and consumerized world of free markets, high levels of inequality and anxiety, and the failure to confront the danger of climate change. Or we can define a new vision of progress, one based on justice, sustainability and security, in which there is a balance in our lives between producing and consuming and a balance between work and our lives as individuals and members of society. There is an alternative, and it must be constructed at a European level.

The good society

Our values of freedom, equality, solidarity and sustainability promise a better world, free of poverty, exploitation and fear. We have a vision of the good society and a more egalitarian economy, which will create a secure, green and fair future. But to achieve it capitalism must now become accountable to democracy; and democracy will need to be renewed and deepened so that it is fit for the task. A good society cannot be built from the top down, but can only come from a movement made by and for the people. Creating the good society will be the greatest challenge of our time and it will shape the lives of generations to come.

Our values

A new model of social democracy begins with our values. On these we can build the good society.

In this new global age we must live together as free and equal individuals in multicultural societies, and as citizens of Europe. We must build political institutions that create a sense of belonging in a just society, and we must reach out to the rest of humanity by creating democratic forms of global governance.

The ideal of a better, fairer and more open world resonates among millions of people who are searching for new ways to live together. It is a hope expressed in global and local social movements, countless single-issue campaigns, community actions, pressure groups and a multitude of informal individual engagements with political, charitable and social issues. The task of the democratic left is to develop the idea of a shared common good through argument, collective political action and campaigning among the people.

The good society is about solidarity and social justice. Solidarity creates trust, which in turn provides the foundation for individual freedom. Freedom grows out of feelings of safety, a sense of belonging and the experience of esteem and respect. These are the fundamental preconditions for the good society. We seek a life of self-invention and self-fulfilment. This desire for self-fulfilment involves the right of everyone to achieve his and her own unique way of being human.

But this is not the selfishness of market capitalism, because to dispute this right in others is to fail to live on its own terms. Solidarity expresses our interdependency. In a globalized world solidarity has no boundaries.

The notion of autonomy is central to a future in which people have the greatest possible control over their lives. Autonomy is not licence; it carries with it the obligations and constraints of living with others. It requires that each citizen has the resources – money, time, relationships and political recognition – to make a good life for him- or herself. This means the right to decent work, education and social security. The market cannot distribute freedom fairly, and so a wider political community must be created in order to decide the just distribution of resources. Individual autonomy is the product of a political community. Democracy and its renewal are central to the politics of the good society.

The guiding principle of the good society is justice, the ethical core of which is equality. Each individual is irreplaceable and of equal worth. In the good society each is afforded equal respect, security and chances in life, regardless of background. Discrimination based on class, racism, homophobia and prejudice against women is outlawed and rigorously contested in culture, education and the workplace.

Framing all these values is ecological sustainability. The good society is part of the planet and attuned to its ecology. It develops ways of flourishing within the constraints imposed on it.

A fair and sustainable economy

At the centre of the good society is the individual as productive agent. Only by reorganizing the system of production can we create a society of freedom and equality. The neo-liberal consensus did not deliver the individual freedom it promised. It created a 'winner takes all' culture of capitalism, which has damaged society and hence also the individual. It failed to create free, self-regulating markets.

We need to develop a new kind of economy, rooted in the values and institutions of the good society. It will be one characterized by a variety of different economic structures and forms of ownership. It will make sure that workers co-determine economic decisions in their companies. From this economic pluralism we can ensure there is no going back to the globally unbalanced economic growth that led to the crisis.

We need an ecologically sustainable development that meets human needs equitably and improves the quality of life of all. Climate change, peak oil and the need for energy and food security demand large-scale economic transformations. The time has come to start to discuss and then implement a new model of prosperity, which can be globalized but without leading to ecological disaster. Quality growth, meaningful work and technological progress can lead to more wealth and a better quality of life, but markets alone cannot achieve these goals. The future will demand a more active state, engaging with long-term economic planning and development to build a sustainable economy.

The reform of the economy can begin with the government taking services of general interest – utilities, transport, post, banks and public services – back into public ownership or placing them under public control, where this is the most accountable, equitable and economically sustainable way of guaranteeing these services. New rules for markets have to be established and stronger incentives fashioned for a more sustainable economy.

The market state and its agencies need to be transformed into a civic state that is democratized and made more responsive to individual citizens and small businesses. We need to balance a strong centre with effective power at local level for economic and social development. The advocacy roles of civil society organizations and of trade unions need to be strengthened.

The primacy of politics over the financial markets has to be restored. In the banking sector a plurality of customer-focused business models must be established, so as to include commercial banks, mutuals, regional and community banks and credit societies, all operating on a variety of scales. We have to make sure that the banking sector is restructured and that it develops transparent and accountable forms of corporate governance. A new regulatory and supervisory framework will define the role and practice of banking and the system of executive remuneration. Only the government, with its democratic authority, global alliances and tax revenues, can achieve the necessary level of reconstruction.

The economic crisis requires new global alliances; countries must start working together rather than continuing the race to the bottom. We need international and European regulation of financial markets. Transnational corporations must be made subject to democratic oversight through the introduction of a global economic democracy with defined rights of information, consultation and co-determination of workers' representatives. Private ratings agencies, which have a huge influence on economic performance, need reform and supervision by public authority. The liberalization and globalization of capital has redistributed wealth from poor economies to the rich and increased the systemic risk of worldwide economic collapse. Capital controls, the closing down of tax havens and the taxation of global financial transactions are needed to aid economic development and to protect vulnerable economies.

A new industrial policy should map out the future priorities and needs of Europe and of its national economies. Manufacturing is in decline as a share of gross domestic product (GDP). Industrial employment is falling and wages have been stagnating. Domestic demand has been falling too, and in some countries the gap was filled by cheap mortgage-backed credit. That short-cut option to economic growth is now closed. Core structures of industry have to be maintained and modernized, because they secure employment and provide a basis for the services sector.

We have depended on the global economic imbalance between the huge trade surpluses of some economies and the deficits of others. This is unsustainable and we have to rethink how, regionally in Europe and globally, we can have more balanced trade relationships.

Economic policy must ensure a diversity of business models and forms of economic ownership. We do not want to substitute monopoly capitalism for state monopoly. But we want markets to be regulated for the common good and for the greatest possible degree of economic pluralism. Government at different levels, including local states, should be encouraged to raise funds on the capital markets, issue mortgages and raise funding from bonds for their own infrastructure projects.

New green markets and a renewable technologies industry need developing, both for a carbon neutral economy and for energy security. In the short to medium term, the most effective solution to fight climate change is to establish a global carbon market based on a cap-and-trade system. In the meantime, energy efficiency should be at the heart of the response to the economic crisis, as this is the fastest route to take for both job creation and emissions control. A Green Strategy needs to be developed and coordinated by governments across Europe. Advances and price reductions in large-scale renewable technologies have the potential to replace carbon-intensive power-plants and nuclear energy. To ensure affordable warmth, the energy markets and prices must be regulated and the energy companies brought to account.

The knowledge economy matters, and we must focus on investment in innovation and on the generation of high value added products. But economic activity related to knowledge and culture must be extended beyond the limits of its current privileged zones, and its demands should not be prioritized over the rest of the economy.

The market is failing to deliver high quality research and development. Organization and product transforming and enhancing innovation require substantial initial government funding and a strong venture capital market aligned to it. Success needs buoyant, assertive and confident institutional cultures of risk-taking. Such conditions do not currently exist in higher education. Instead, universities driven by commercial imperatives and performance indicators are neglecting the convivial cultures in which innovation happens and ideas and communication flow. The higher education system must be decoupled from the market and from commercial imperatives and treated as a public good.

The full potential of the services sector has to be developed, especially in the fields of education and training, and in health, care and social services.

We need a new system of agriculture, both local and global. Investment should be made in a sustainable organic food system, where food is produced, prepared and consumed locally and where wealth created remains within local communities.

Good work and social security

We must work for a social Europe in which people come before profits and where society asserts its interests over those of the market. This means economies that prioritize full employment, fair levels of pay, and labour market rights that guarantee good conditions and protect workers against discrimination and exploitation. A social Europe stands for social insurance against sickness, unemployment, poverty and disability, and for good value pensions in old age. Economic democracy is a central issue. A social Europe must extend beyond work, to decent housing, high quality energy and transportation networks, good quality health care services, egalitarian education systems and skills training that prepares individuals for a good life as well as for good work. This agenda is a competitive asset in a globalized economy, not an obstacle to economic success.

We need a mix of cash benefits and social infrastructure to lift people out of poverty and to help stimulate demand. The tax system must contribute to a more equitable distribution of income and wealth. Low wage earners should not pay taxes. Those at the top must start paying their fair share, and legislation must tighten tax loopholes and tax avoidance schemes.

Welfare policies that provide preventive approaches are important and should be strengthened, but they must not be used to disguise cuts in benefits. Fixation on personal responsibility can create anxiety and social insecurity among the most vulnerable people in society, especially in a recession. People need help in order to lead dignified lives, free from poverty and social exclusion. Social benefits are a right of citizenship and should help people manage changes and vulnerable situations over the whole life course.

Pensions are about the total economic system, and they will play a key role in social investment strategies and wealth redistribution. The longevity revolution and the failure of financial markets to guarantee decent returns on personal pension plans make social insurance an economic priority. In the last decade, the replacement of defined benefit schemes with defined contribution schemes has created a fundamental shift of wealth in favour of the rich. They have transferred risk from the state and business onto the individual. This trend must be reversed in favour of public pay-as-you-go systems for both the private and the public sectors.

Labour market policies face the challenge of flexibility. The growth in short-term contracts, agency work, sub-contracting and use of the 'self-employed' has often left workers with fewer rights. Growth in employment has been both in low skill/low wage jobs in poor conditions and in high skill/high wage jobs, but sometimes also in difficult contractual and working conditions. The growing use of temporary and agency workers is spreading these conditions to other parts of the economy. Regulation can end low pay, low skill and casualized labour. Strong trade unions are the best defence against exploitation. Work and quality of life can be improved by introducing a living wage. But we must ensure that conditions of employment *are* compatible with caring responsibilities. The skills agenda should be extended, but also democratized and radicalized, so that it can provide the means not only to 'good work' but also to a good life.

A new politics of democracy

The institutions that have, in the past, given people access to political ideas and activity, such as trade unions, churches and political parties, face the challenge of a steep decline in membership. Many people are disaffected with representative democracy. They have lost confidence in politicians and political parties. We live in societies where large numbers are pessimistic about our future. This is because, for 30 years, our democracies have offered only one vision of society: that governed by markets and profit. The economic crisis is a crisis of democracy, but it also provides the opportunity to revitalize politics.

Despite the disillusionment with political parties, there are extraordinary levels of political, cultural and community activism in our societies. Politics has become more individualized and ethical, and it is rooted in a diversity of beliefs and lifestyles. The old collective styles and political monocultures are being rejected by some. These developments are stimulating a search for new kinds of democratic political structures and cultures, which reconnect institutions of political power with social movements and political constituencies. Community empowerment and campaigns around social justice and sustainability are becoming more vigorous.

Power must begin at the bottom and be delegated upward. We cannot create the collective agents of social change; people can only empower themselves. But we can strengthen democracy and thus create the conditions for the emergence of these agents and our capacity to build alliances with them. With real power and policy-making influence, they can develop the ethos of democracy.

We need a new culture of freedom of information and more open access to the media. Networks and databases facilitated by the web are of growing importance in campaigning, bringing political power to account and mobilizing popular opinion. Political parties remain an essential part of our democracies. They provide institutional continuity, while networks are often transient. There is much to be gained by synergies between the two. For this to happen, parties will need to allow their own cultures and organizations to be opened up and democratized in the process.

We must, in the words of Willy Brandt, 'dare more democracy'. We need to strengthen our democratic cultures by introducing electoral reform where it is needed and by increasing the opportunities for active participation and deliberative decision-making processes also inside our parties. This is a precondition for strong Social Democratic and Labour Parties in Europe. The time of top-down communication is over. The same is true for technocratic governments, which tell people about necessities rather than persuade them through reasons. People do not believe in spin-doctors any more.

The main task in the years ahead will be to create and consolidate political trust in public life. Trust is the basis of all political and social action. It is best created by bringing people together to agree on common aims and decisions, not by excluding them. It is achieved by initiating and engaging in open debate, not by seeking to avoid it.

In the process of democratic renewal, nation states can and must do more, alone and together. But it is the political community of Europe that must be used if the economic crisis is to be a turning point for a new future and not a return to the failed politics of the past. The European ideal of a continent of secure citizens who all live as freely and fully as they can, in sustainable and just societies, is within our grasp. But it will take a leap of imagination and powerful ambition to make it happen.

A politics for a better Europe

A politics for a social Europe

Europe needs a 'post-Lisbon Strategy' that is based on the concept of 'social productivity'. Social productivity is about social growth: increasing the social value and quality of work, accounting for the environmental and social costs of markets and developing sustainable patterns of consumption. The well-being of citizens and the general quality of life must be improved beyond simple numerical and monetary values. Wealth needs to be redistributed in a more egalitarian manner. Effective regulatory standards need to be introduced to guarantee good, affordable and comprehensive public services, fair wages, good working conditions, free education for all and a human approach to immigration and global solidarity.

The financial economy

Our strategy for a social Europe must begin by tackling the economic crisis. By working together we will set the foundations for a Europe of greater cooperation, fairness and social justice. Member states are pursuing their own separate policies, often at the expense of their European Union (EU) partners. There is an urgent need for a coordinated Europe-wide fiscal stimulus. The multiplier on coordinated fiscal expansion is much greater than for any individual country. In a coordinated response, the trade-off between increased debt and effective stimulus is much better for the EU as a whole than it is for any one country.

We need to introduce European-wide reforms in financial and economic governance. The regulation of financial market actors in Europe is not sufficient. A European supervisory institution can enforce adequate capital requirements, increase transparency in financial market actors' investment behaviour and facilitate efficient information exchange between national supervisory authorities. European financial markets must become a source of stability and development in a production-orientated European economy. The emphasis on achieving shareholder value hinders capital investments in fixed assets, and thereby growth and employment.

To this end we need to reform the European Central Bank and the European Monetary Union. This will improve the prospects of Britain applying to join the Euro. The mandate for the European Central Bank needs to be broadened in the form of a law that the Council and Parliament can also amend. As well as price stability, the mandate should permit other social objectives where necessary. These objectives would include the prevention and reduction of unemployment, the stability of the financial system, support for other EU economic policies and monetary cooperation with outside powers.

The EU's central budget needs to be significantly increased, and it must be able to redistribute considerably more resources than at present. Alongside this reform, the Commission must have the right, when supported by Council and Parliament, to run deficits.

The Stability and Growth Pact should be replaced by an agreement on the coordination of member state budgetary policies. Coordination and centralization are to some extent alternatives here; the greater and more reliable the coordination, the smaller the central budget could be – but between them the two measures must make possible some control over aggregate tax and spending policies in the EU.

Employment and social security

Different national paths constitute a source of strength in the EU. To achieve a social Europe does not mean enforcing a single system on all nations, but agreeing on a set of welfare outcomes. A European minimum wage, corresponding to the national average income, would help to limit the increasing wage differentials in Europe and to prevent 'social dumping'. To push forward its implementation will require an organization similar to Britain's Low Pay Commission, with a remit for campaigning and working closely with the trade unions.

The series of European Court rulings – the Laval, Viking and Rueffert cases – have deregulated labour markets by changing the terms of the 1996 Posting of Workers Directive. This now needs reform to restore collective bargaining and workers' rights to strike, and to establish equality for posted and migrant workers across Europe.

Europe needs fair policies on taxation. Current tax competition in Europe is leading to a shifting of the tax burden from companies to individual income and consumption. This is regressive and unjust, and there needs to be a harmonization of corporate tax policy to safeguard the financial basis of national social security systems. In the medium term the European Union should have its own financial resources, based on a European corporate tax and a European financial transactions tax. Offshore tax havens should be outlawed, and corporate profits should be taxed in the countries where they are earned.

Energy security and sustainability

Europe must become the most ecologically sustainable economy in the world. If the US is starting a competition to become the 'greenest economy in the world', Europe must take part in this race because all humankind will win. We need Europe-wide green standards for power stations that adopt a series of successively tougher targets for emissions standards, which will drive the introduction of carbon capture and storage. An efficiency target for electricity generation, which is similar to that proposed for cars in the EU, would make it difficult for a government to allow the construction of new coal-fired power stations without some form of carbon capture technology attached.

Balancing the grid at an EU-wide level will reduce the need for coal and will improve energy security by reducing reliance on foreign oil and gas. It will make significant cuts in carbon emissions and in the long run bring down fuel bills too. The current bilateral schemes that are being negotiated need to be extended across Europe.

Global social justice

A social Europe must work for global trade justice. The EU is still pursuing an aggressive free trade agenda. It is currently negotiating Economic Partnership Agreements with African, Caribbean and Pacific countries that pose a serious risk to the development of the countries involved. The EU's latest 'Global Europe' trade strategy is trying to force dozens more countries into even more extreme free trade agreements for the benefit of big business. We need a full-scale review of EU trade policy and a new strategy that puts the rights of poor and marginalized people at its centre. Trade policy needs to be made more democratic and accountable, and it must include much greater sharing of information and real participation from the civil society.

European democracy

To strengthen European democracy in the economy, we should use the potential of introducing supervisory boards through European Public Companies (SEs) for stakeholders in order to co-determine control over the management board.

The EU needs to build a European-wide civic culture, which will engage in voting, sustain its democratic institutions and subject them to scrutiny. The EU needs to trigger public debate before taking its major decisions. To respond to popular opinion, the European Parliament, which is directly elected by the people, needs to get the right to initiate legislation and to elect the Commission's president.

Invitation to debate

This appendix lays out the principles of the good society. But the project of the good society has to be developed by society itself, through debate and action. We therefore invite civil society, social movements, trade unions and members of our parties and of those in all other European nations to discuss and further develop the ideas set out in this proposal. Our invitation to debate extends to everyone who wants a more socially just, sustainable and democratic Europe.

This is just the beginning.

About the authors

Jon Cruddas is MP for Dagenham

Andrea Nahles is Vice-President of the Social Democratic Party of Germany (SPD), a member of Bundestag and spokesperson for labour and social affairs of the SPD group in the Bundestag.

8 April 2009

Bibliography

Adam, B. (2005), *Future Matters* (Amsterdam: Brill).
Ainley, P. and M. Allen (2010), *Lost Generation* (London: Continuum).
Akerlof, G. A. and R. J. Shiller (2010), *Animal Spirits* (Princeton, NJ: Princeton University Press).
Alesina, A., R. Di Tella and R. Maculloch (2004), 'Inequality and Happiness: Are Europeans and Americans Different?', *Journal of Public Economics* 88, pp. 2009–2042.
Amato, G. (1997), *Antitrust and the Bounds of Power* (Oxford: Hart).
Anderson, B. (1991), *Imagined Communities* (London: Verso).
Andersson, J. (2006), 'Choosing Futures: The Construction of Swedish Futures Studies 1967–1972', *International Review of Social History* 51, pp. 277–295.
Andersson, J. (2010), *The Library and the Workshop. Social Democracy and Capitalism in an Age of Knowledge* (Palo Alto: Stanford University Press).
Andrews, F. M. and S. B. Withey (1976), *Social Indicators of Well-Being: Americans' Perceptions of Life Quality* (New York: Plenum Press).
Arendt, H. (1998), *The Human Condition* (Chicago: Chicago University Press).
Baldwin, P. (1990), *The Politics of Social Solidarity: Class Bases of the European Welfare State 1875–1975* (Cambridge: Cambridge University Press).
Bălțătescu, S. (2007), 'Banii n-aduc fericirea? Influența venitului asupra bunăstării subiective în România postdecembristă'. [English: Money doesn't buy happiness? The influence of income on subjective well-being in post-communist Romania], in F. Chipea, I. Cioară, A. Hatos, M. Marian and C. Sas (eds) *Cultură, dezvoltare, identitate. Perspective actuale* (București: Editura Expert), pp. 295–306.
Barnett, A. (2010), 'Forces Stacked against Modern Liberty', in R. Bechler (ed.) (2009) *The Convention on Modern Liberty: The British Debate on Fundamental Rights and Freedoms* (Exeter: Imprint http://www.opendemocracy.net/ourkingdom/anthony-barnett/forces-stacked-against-modern-liberty, accessed 13 February 2011).
Bartolini, S. (2007), *The Political Mobilisation of the European Left 1860–1960: The Class Cleavage* (Cambridge: Cambridge University Press).
Bavelas, J. B., N. Chovil, D. A. Lavrie and A. Wade (1992), 'Interactive Gestures', *Discourse Processes* 15(4), pp. 469–489.
BBC (2011a), *Buckinghamshire Library Emptied in Cuts Protest*, 17 January (http://www.bbc.co.uk/news/uk-england-beds-bucks-herts-12204369, accessed 13 February 2011).
BBC (2011b), 'Isle of Wight Library Protestors Plan "mass borrow"', 21 January (http://www.bbc.co.uk/news/uk-england-hampshire-12248991, accessed 13 February 2011).
Beck, U. (1992), *Risk Society: Towards a New Modernity: Theory Culture and Society* (London: Sage).
Behland Lindhal, K. (2008), Frame Analysis, place perceptions and the politics of natural resource management, PhD (Uppsala: Swedish University of Agriculture).

Benedict, R. (1968), *Patterns of Culture* (London: Routledge and Kegan Paul).
Benkler, Y. (2006), *The Wealth of Networks: How Social Production Transforms Markets and Freedom* (New Haven, London: Yale University Press).
Berger, S. (1994), *The British Labour Party and the German Social Democrats, 1900–1931. A Comparative Study* (Oxford: Clarendon).
Berger, S. (2006), 'Internationalismus als Lippenbekenntnis? Die transnationale Kooperation sozialdemokratischer Parteien in der Zwischenkriegszeit', in J. Mittag (ed.) *Politische Parteien und europäische Integration: Entwicklung und Perspektiven transnationaler Parteienkooperation in Europa* (Essen: Klartext) pp. 197–204.
Berger, S. and D. Broughton (eds) (1995), *The Force of Labour. The Western European Labour Movement and the Working Class in the Twentieth Century* (Oxford: Berg).
Berman, S. (1998), *The Social Democratic Moment. Ideas and Politics in the Making of Interwar Europe* (Cambridge, MA: Harvard University Press).
Berman, S. (2006), *The Primacy of Politics. Social Democracy and the Making of Europe's 20th Century* (New York: Cambridge University Press).
Bernanke, B. (2010), *Speech on The Economics of Happiness, University of South Carolina Commencement Ceremony, Columbia*, South Carolina, 8 May 2010.
Bernstein, E. (1993), *The Preconditions of Socialism and the Tasks of Social Democracy*, in H. Tudor (ed.) *The Preconditions of Socialism* (Cambridge: Cambridge University Press).
Blair, T. (1998), *The Third Way* (London: Fabian Society).
Blair, T. (2001), Speech to Labour Party Conference, (http://www.guardian.co.uk/politics/2001/oct/02/labourconference.labour6, accessed 13 February 2011).
Blair,T. (2004), 'Swinging Sixties Speech' Somerstown, London, 19 July.
Blair, T. Labour Party Conference Speech (2005) (http://www.guardian.co.uk/uk/2005/sep/27/labourconference.speeches), 13 February 2011.
Blond, P. (2009), 'The Necessity of Virtue', The Tablet, 23 May.
BNP (2005), *The Peak Oil Report* (online: no longer available).
Bok, D. (2010), *The Politics of Happiness: What Government Can Learn from the New Research on Well-Being* (Princeton: Princeton University Press).
Botsman, R. and R. Rogers (2010), *What's Mine Is Yours: How Collaborative Consumption Is Changing the Way We Live* (London: Harper Collins).
Brafman, O. and R. A. Beckstrom (2006), *The Starfish and the Spider: The Unstoppable Power of Leaderless Organizations* (New York: Portfolio).
Braunthal, J. (1966 – 1980), *History of the International*, 3 vols (London: Gollancz).
Breuilly, J. (1992), *Labour and Liberalism in Nineteenth-Century Europe: Essays in Comparative History* (Manchester: Manchester University Press).
Breuilly, J. (1994), *Labour and Liberalism in Nineteenth-Century Europe: Essays in Comparative History* (Manchester: Manchester University Press).
Bull, M. J. and P. Heywood (1994), *West European Communist Parties after the Revolutions of 1989* (Basingstoke: Palgrave Macmillan).
Burghart, D. and L. Zeskind (2010), 'Tea Party Nationalism: A Special Investigation', *Searchlight Magazine* 424, October 2010.
Cacioppo, J. T. and W. Patrick (2008), *Loneliness, Human Nature and the Need for Social Connections* (New York: W.W. Norton & Company), p. 11.
Callaghan, J. (2006), 'Old Social Democracy, New Social Movements and Social Democratic Programmatic Renewal, 1968–2000', in J. Callaghan and I. Favretto

(eds) *Transitions in Social Democracy: Cultural and Ideological Problems of the Golden Age* (Manchester: Manchester University Press), pp. 177–193.

Campbell, A., P. E. Converse and W. L. Rodgers (1976), *The Quality of American Life: Perceptions, Evaluations, and Satisfactions* (New York: Russell Sage Foundation).

Carr, J. (1985), *Helmut Schmidt: Helmsman of Germany* (New York: St Martin's Press).

Castells, M. (1996), *The Rise of the Network Society* (Oxford: Blackwell).

Castells, M. (2009), *Communication Power* (Oxford: Oxford University Press).

Castells, M. (2010), *The Power of Identity*, 2nd edn (Oxford: Wiley-Blackwell).

Clark, A. and A. J. Oswald (1994), 'Unhappiness and Unemployment', *Economic Journal* 104, pp. 648–659.

Castles, F. G. (1976), *The Social Democratic Image of Society* (London and Boston, MA: Routledge & Kegan).

Clark, A., P. Frijters and M. A. Shields (2008), 'Relative Income, Happiness and Utility: An Explanation for the Easterlin Paradox and Other Puzzles', *Journal of Economic Literature* 46, pp. 95–144.

Clarke, J. (2005), 'New Labour's New Subjects', *Critical Social Policy* 25(4), pp. 425–463.

Meadows, D. H., D. L. Meadows, J. Randers and W. W. Behrens. (1972), *The Limits to Growth*, Club of Rome.

Collignon, S. (2003), *The European Republic. Reflections on the Political Economy of a Future Constitution* (London: The Federal Trust), www.stefancollignon.eu), accessed 15 January 2011.

Collignon, S. (2008), 'Why Europe Is Not Becoming the World's Most Competitive Economy. The Lisbon Strategy, Macroeconomic Stability and the Dilemma of Governance without Governments', *International Journal of Public Policy* 3(1/2).

Collignon, S. (2010), 'The Moral Economy of Money and the Future of European Capitalism', in L. S. Talani (ed.), *The Global Crash: Towards a New Financial Regulatory Regime?* (London: Palgrave Macmillan) (http://www.stefancollignon.de/PDF/Moraleconomyofmoneyandfuture_of_capitalism7.pdf.

Collignon, S. and D. Schwarzer (2003), *Private Sector Involvement in the Euro. The Power of Ideas* (London: Routledge).

Collins, H. (2001), 'Is There a Third Way in Labour Law?', in A. Giddens (ed.) *The Global Third Way Debate* (Cambridge: Polity Press), pp. 300–314.

Credit Action Debt Statistics, www.CreditAction.org.uk.

Cuperus, R. (2010), 'A Good Society Not Only for Academic Professionals!', *Social Europe Website* (http://www.social-europe.eu/2009/11/a-good-society-not-only-for-academic-professionals/?pfstyle=wp, accessed 2 December 2010).

Dahrendorf, R. (1990), *Reflections on the Revolutions in Europe* (London: Chatto and Windus).

Daily Mail (2010), 'Mayhem in Oxford St as Protesters Target Stores Including Topshop's Flagship Branch over Firms Avoiding Tax Bills', 5 December 2010 (http://www.dailymail.co.uk/news/article-1335632/Sir-Philip-Greens-flagship-Topshop-closes-protests-taxes-cause-mayhem.html, accessed 13 February 2011).

Day, S. (2005), 'Developing a Conceptual Understanding of Europe's Transnational Parties (With a Specific Focus on the Party of European Socialists)', *Journal of Contemporary European Studies* 12(1), pp. 59–77.

Day, S. and J. Shaw (2006), 'Transnational Political Parties', in R. Bellamy, D. Castiglione and J. Shaw (eds) *Making European Citizens* (London: Palgrave Macmillan), pp. 99–117.

Deaton, A. (2008), 'Income, Health and Well-Being around the World: Evidence from the Gallup World Poll', *Journal of Economic Perspectives* 22(2), pp. 53–72.

Devin, G. (1993), *L'Internationale socialiste: Histoire et sociologie du socialisme international (1945–1990)* (Paris: Presses de la Fondation des Sciences Politiques).

Diener, E. and E. M. Suh (1999), 'National Differences in Subjective Well-Being', in D. Kahnemann, E. Diener and N. Schwarz (eds) *Well-Being: The Foundations of Hedonic Psychology* (New York: Russell Sage Foundation), pp. 434–451.

Diener, E. and S. Oishi (2004), 'Are Scandinavians Happier than Asians? Issues in Comparing Nations on Subjective Well-Being', *Politics and Economics of Asia* 10(1), pp. 1–25.

Diener, E., E. M. Suh, R. E.Lucas and H. L.Smith (1999), 'Subjective Well-Being: Three Decades of Progress', *Psychological Bulletin* 125(2), pp. 276–302.

Diener, E., R. Lucas, U. Shimmack and J. F. Helliwell (2009), *Well-being for Public Policy* (Oxford: Oxford University Press).

Diener, E., R. A. Emmons, R. J. Larsen and S. Griffin (1985), 'The Satisfaction with Life Scale', *Journal of Personality Assessment* 49, pp. 71–75.

Dimitrakopolous, D. G. (2011), *Social Democracy and European Integration: The Politics of Preference Formation* (London: Routledge).

Dolan, P., T. Peasgood and M. White (2008), 'Do We Really Know What Makes Us Happy? A Review of the Economic Literature on the Factors Associated with Subjective Well-Being', *Journal of Economic Psychology* 29(1), pp. 94–122.

Dorey, P. (1995), *The Conservative Party and the Trade Unions* (London: Routledge).

Dullien, S. and H. Herr (2010), 'EU Financial Market Reform. International Policy Analysis 2010' (Friedrich Ebert Foundation, http://library.fes.de/pdf-files/id/ipa/07242.pdf, accessed 12 January 2011).

Dullien, S., H. Herr and C. Kellermann (2011), *Decent Capitalism. A Blueprint for Reforming Our Economies* (London: Pluto Publishers).

Edahiro J. (2010), 'Letter from Japan', *Resurgence Magazine*, 262, October 2010 (http://www.resurgence.org/magazine/article3174-letter-from-japan.html, accessed 13 February 2011).

Edinger, L. J. (1965), *Kurt Schumacher: A Study in Personality and Political Behaviour* (New York: Columbia University Press).

Eley, G. (2002), *Forging Democracy. The History of the Left in Europe, 1850–2000* (Oxford: Oxford University Press).

Engels, J. Niklas and G. Maaß (eds), *The View from Europe: Analyses of the Crisis of Social Democracy after the 2009 German Federal Elections*. (Friedrich Ebert Stiftung: http://library.fes.de/pdf-files/id/ipa/06941.pdf, accessed 15 January 2011).

European Commission (5 December 1993), *Growth, Competitiveness, and Employment: The Challenges and Ways Forward into the 21st Century*. White Paper /* COM/93/700FINAL */.

European Commission (November 2008), Demographic Challenges for European Regions, http://ec.europa.eu/regional_policy/sources/docoffic/working/regions 2020/pdf/regions2020_demographic.pdf.

European Commission (2010a), *http://ec.europa.eu/economy_finance/articles/eu_economic_situation/pdf/com2010_522en.pdf "\ o" Proposal for a Council Regulation*

Amending Regulation (EC) No 1467/97 on Speeding up and Clarifying the Implementation of the Excessive Deficit Procedure" Proposal for a Council Regulation Amending Regulation (EC) No 1467/97 on Speeding up and Clarifying the Implementation of the Excessive Deficit Procedure (http://ec.europa.eu/economy_finance/articles/ eu_economic_situation/pdf/r com2010_522en.pdf, accessed 5 December 2010).

European Commission (2010b), *Proposal for a Regulation amending Regulation (EC) No 1466/97 on the Strengthening of the Surveillance of Budgetary Positions and the Surveillance and Coordination of Economic Policies* (http://ec.europa.eu/ economy_finance/articles/eu_economic_situation/pdf/com2010_526en.pdf, accessed 6 December 2010).

Faux, J. (1999) 'Lost on the Third Way', *Dissent* 46(2), pp. 67–76.

Favretto, I. (2006), 'The Italian Left and the Affluent Society', in J. Callaghan and I. Favretto (eds) *Transitions in Social Democracy* (Manchester: Manchester University Press), pp. 163–176.

Felce, D. and J. Perry (1993), *Quality of Life: A Contribution to Its Definition and Measurement* (Bangor: University of Wales).

Finlayson, A. (2003), *Making Sense of New Labour* (London: Lawrence and Wishart).

Finlayson, A. (2009), 'Financialisation', *British Journal of Politics and International Relations* 11(3), pp. 422–437.

FitzPatrick, T. (2004), 'A Post-Productivist Future for Social Democracy?', *Social Policy and Society* 3(3), pp. 213–222.

Frey, B. S. (2008), *Happiness: A Revolution in Economics* (Cambridge, MA: MIT Press).

Fukuyama, F. (1992), *The End of History and the Last Man* (New York: Simon and Schuster).

Fukuyama, F. (1997), *The End of Order* (London: Social Market Foundation).

Fülberth, G. (2009), *'Doch wenn sich die Dinge ändern' – Die Linke* (Berlin: Papyrossa).

Gabriel, Sigmar (2010), 'So kommt die SPD wieder in die Mitte der Gesellschaft', *Berliner Republik* 1 (http://www.b-republik.de/aktuelle-ausgabe/so-kommt-die-spd-wieder-in-die-mitte-der-gesellschaft, accessed February 2010).

Galbraith, J. K. (1952), *American Capitalism: The Concept of Counter-Vailing Power* (Boston: Houghton-Mifflin).

Galbraith, J. K. (1959), *The Affluent Society* (London: Hamish Hamilton).

Gallese, V. (2003), 'The Roots of Empathy: The Shared Manifold Hypothesis and the Neural Basis of Intersubjectivity', *Psychopathology* 36, pp. 171–180.

Gallese, V., L. Fadiga, L. Fogassi and G. Rizzolatti (1996), 'Action Recognition in the Premotor Cortex', *Brain* 119, pp. 593–609.

Gallie, W. (1956), 'Essentially Contested Concepts', *Proceedings of the Aristotelian Society* 56, pp. 167–198.

Gamble, A. (1981), *An Introduction to Modern Social and Political Thought* (London: Palgrave Macmillan).

Garry, J., M. Marsh and R. Sinnott (2005), ' "Second-Order" versus "Issue-Voting" Effects in EU Referendums: Evidence from the Irish Nice Treaty Referendums', *European Union Politics* 6(2), pp. 201–221.

Gertner, J. (2010), 'The Rise and Fall of the G.D.P.', *New York Times*, MM60.

Giddens, A. (1991), *Modernity and Self Identity: Self and Society in the Late Modern Age* (Cambridge: Polity Press).
Giddens, A. (1994), *Beyond Left and Right: The Future of Radical Politics* (Cambridge: Polity Press).
Giddens, A. (1998), *The Third Way: The Renewal of Social Democracy* (Cambridge: Polity Press).
Giddens, A. (2000), *The Third Way and Its Critics* (Cambridge: Polity Press).
Giddens, A., ed. (2001), *The Global Third Way Debate* (Oxford: Blackwell).
Giddens, A. (2009), *The Politics of Climate Change* (London: Polity Press).
Glasman, M. (2011), 'Labour as a Radical Tradition: Labour's Renewal Lies in Its Traditions of Mutualism, Reciprocity and Common Good', *Social Europe Journal Website* (http://www.social-europe.eu/2011/01/labour-as-a-radical-tradition-labours-renweal-lies-in-its-tradition-of-mutualism-reciprocity-and-the-common-good/, accessed 7 April 2011).
Glennie (2011), 'How the Facebook Generation Keeps People Poor', in *The Guardian*, 5 January 2011 (http://www.guardian.co.uk/global-development/poverty-matters/2011/jan/05/facebook-generation-poor-inequality?INTCMP=SRCH, accessed 13 February 2011).
Goldberg, D. and P. Williams (1988), *A User's Guide to the General Health Questionnaire* (Windsor: NFER).
Goldberg, H. (1962), *The Life of Jean Jaurès: A Biography of the Great French Socialists and Intellectual* (Madison: The University of Wisconsin).
Golden, M. A., M. Wallerstein and P. Lange (2008), 'Postwar Trade Union Organization and Industrial Relations in Twelve Countries', in D. Austen-Smith, J. A. Frieden, M. A. Golden, K. O. Moene and A. Przeworksi (eds) *Selected Works of Michael Wallerstein: The Political Economy of Inequality, Unions and Social Democracy* (Cambridge: Cambridge University Press), pp. 173–204.
Grant, J. (2010), *Co-Opportunity* (Chichester: Wiley).
Greenpeace (2009), *Airplot!* (Video, http://www.youtube.com/watch?v=2JDe3lRvj10, accessed 13 February 2011).
Griffith-Jones, S., J. Ocampo and J. E. Stiglitz (eds) (2010), *Time for a Visible Hand: Lessons from the 2008 Financial Crisis* (Oxford: Oxford University Press).
Griffiths, S. (2010), *Dark Times for Those Who Cannot Work* (www.informedcompassion.com, accessed 11 December 2010).
Groh, D. (1973), *Negative Integration und revolutionärer Attentismus: die deutsche Sozialdemokratie am Vorabend des ersten Weltkrieges* (Frankfurt/Main: Ullstein).
Hall, S. (1998), 'The Great Moving Nowhere Show', *Marxism Today* (November–December), pp. 9–14.
Hamilton, C. (2007), *Growth Fetish* (Sydney: Allen & Unwin).
Hands, J. (2011), *@ is for Activism* (London: Pluto Press).
Harvey, D. (2005), *A Brief History of Neoliberalism* (Oxford:Oxford University Press).
Haupt, G. (1986), *Aspects of International Socialism: Essays* (Cambridge: Cambridge University Press).
Havel, V. (1985), *The Power of the Powerless* (London: Hutchinson).
Hawkes, A. (2011), 'National Audit Office to Investigate UK Tax Deals with MULTINATIONALS' *Guardian*, 19 January 2011 (http://www.guardian.co.uk/business/2011/jan/19/national-audit-office-investigate-multinational-tax, accessed 13 February 2011).
Hay, C. (2007), *Why We Hate Politics* (London: Polity Press).

Healey, D. (1988), *The Time of My Life* (New York: Random House).
Heath, J. and A. Potter (2006), *The Rebel Sell: How the Counter Culture Became Consumer Culture* (Oxford: Capstone).
Held, D. (2004), *Global Covenant: The Social Democratic Alternative to the Washington Consensus* (Cambridge: Polity Press).
Held, D. (2011), *Cosmopolitanism: Ideas and Realities* (Cambridge: Polity Press).
Held, D., A. McGrew, D. Goldblatt and J. Perraton (1999), *Global Transformations* (Cambridge: Polity Press).
Helliwell, J. F. (2003), 'How's Life? Combining Individual and National Variables to Explain Subjective Well-Being', *Economic Modelling* 20(2), pp. 331–360.
Helliwell, J. F. and R. D. Putnam (2004), 'The Social Context of Well-Being', *Philosophical Transactions of the Royal Society of London Series B-Biological Sciences* 359(1449), pp. 1435–1446.
Helliwell, J. F., C. P. Barrington-Leigh and D. Kahneman (2010), 'International Evidence on the Social Context of Well-Being', in E. Diener, J. F. Helliwell and D. Kahneman (eds) *International Differences in Well-Being* (New York: Oxford University Press).
Herr, H. and M. Kazandziska (2011), *Macroeconomic Policy Regimes in Western Industrial Countries* (Abingdon: Routledge).
Hirsch, F. (1976), *The Social Limits to Growth* (London: Routledge).
Hirschman, A. O. (1970), *Exit, Voice and Loyalty. Responses to Declines in Firms, Organisations and States* (Cambridge, MA: Harvard University Press).
Hirst, P. (1999), 'Has Globalisation Killed Social Democracy?', *Political Quarterly*, Vol. 80 Si1 (London: Wiley), pp. 84–96.
Hix, S. (1993), 'The Emerging EC Party System?', *Politics* 13(2), pp. 38–46.
Hix, S., A. Noury and G. Roland (2005), 'Power to the Parties: Cohesion and Competition in the European Parliament, 1979–2001', *British Journal of Political Science* 35(2), pp. 209–234.
Hix, S. and U. Lesse (2002), *Shaping a Vision. A History of the Party of European Socialists 1957–2002* (http://www.pes.org/system/files/images/downloads/History_PES_EN.pdf, accessed 15 November 2010).
Hobbes, Th. (1998) [1641]. *On the Citizen (De cive)*, ed. R. Tuck and M. Silver Thorne (Cambridge: Cambridge Texts in the History of Political Thought).
Hobolt, S. and S. Brouard (2010), 'Contesting the European Union? Why the Dutch and the French Rejected the European Constitution', *Political Research Quarterly*, 1 March 2010.
Hobsbawm, E. (1994), *Age of Extremes: The Short Twentieth Century, 1914–1991* (London: Penguin).
Hopkins, R. (2006), *The Transition Handbook: From Oil Dependency to Local Resilience* (Totnes: Green Books).
Horn, G.-R. (1996), *European Socialists Respond to Fascism. Ideology, Activism and Contingency in the 1930s* (Oxford: Oxford University Press).
Hutton, W. (1997), *The Stakeholding Society* (London: Polity Press).
Huxley, A. (2003), *Brave New World* (London: Vintage).
Iacoboni, M. (2008), *Mirroring People: The New Science of How We Connect with Others* (New York: Farrar, Straus and Giroux).
Imlay, T. (forthcoming), *Practicing Internationalism: European Socialists and International Politics, 1918 – 1960* (Oxford: Oxford University Press).
Imrie, R. and M. Raco (2003), *Urban Renaissance? New Labour, Community, and Urban Policy* (Briston: Policy Press).

Inglehart, R. (1987), 'Value Change in Industrial Societies', *American Political Science Review* 81, pp. 1289–1303.
Inglehart, R. (1990), *Culture Shift in Advanced Industrial Society* (Princeton: Princeton University Press).
Inglehart, R. and C. Welzel (2005), *Modernization, Cultural Change and Democracy: The Human Development Sequence* (Cambridge: Cambridge University Press).
Inglehart, R. and H.-D. Klingemann (2000), 'Genes, Culture, Democracy and Happiness', in E. Diener and E. M. Suh (eds) *Culture and Subjective Well-Being* (Cambridge, MA: Bradford), pp. 165–184.
Institute of Well-Being (2009), *How Are Canadians Really Doing?* (First report, www.ciw.ca, accessed October 2010).
James, O. (2007), *Affluenza* (London: Vermillion).
Johansson, K. M. and P. Zervakis (2002), 'Historical–Institutional Framework', in K. M. Johansson and P. Zervakis (eds) *European Political Parties between Cooperation and Integration* (Baden-Baden: Nomos).
Johansson, K. M. and T. Raunio (2005), 'Regulating Europarties: Cross-Party Coalitions Capitalizing on Incomplete Contracts', *Party Politics* 11(5), pp. 515–534.
Johnson, N. (2010), *Separate and Unequal: How Integration Can Deliver the Good Society* (London: The Fabian Society).
Joll, J. (1955), *The Second International, 1889–1914* (London: Weidenfeld and Nicolson).
Kahneman, D. and A. Deaton (2010), 'High Income Improves Evaluation of Life but Not Emotional Well-being', *Proceedings of National Academy of Science* (USA advance online publication: doi: 10.1073/pnas.1011492107, accessed 10 December 2010).
Kahneman, D. and A. B. Krueger (2006), 'Developments in the Measurement of Subjective Well-being', *Journal of Economic Perspectives* 20(1), pp. 3–24.
Kahneman, D., E. Diener and N. Schwarz (eds) (1999), *Well-Being: The Foundations of Hedonic Psychology* (New York: Russell Sage Foundation).
Karvonen, L. and J. Sundberg (eds) (1991), *Social Democracy in Transition: Northern, Southern and Eastern Europe* (Aldershot: Ashgate).
Kellermann, C. (2006), *Die Organisation des Washington Consensus: Der Internationale Währungsfonds und seine Rolle in der internationalen Finanzarchitektur* (Bielefeld: transcript Verlag).
Kendon, A. (2004), *Gesture. Visible Action as Utterance* (Cambridge: Cambridge University Press).
Keynes, J. M. (2007) [1936], *The General Theory of Employment, Interest and Money* (London: Palgrave Macmillan).
Keynes, J. M. (1971), *A Treatise on Money*, in *The Collected Writings of John Maynard Keynes*, vol. 5 (London: Palgrave Macmillan).
Kinder, D. (1998), 'Opinion and Action in the Realm of Politics', in D. Gilbert, S. Fiske and G. Lindzey (eds) *Handbook of Social Psychology*, Vol. 2 (Boston: McGraw-Hill), pp. 778–867.
Kindleberger, C. P. (1986), *The World in Depression, 1929–1939*, 2nd edn (Berkeley: University of California Press).
King, D. (1999), *In the Name of Liberalism. Illiberal Social Policy in the US and Britain* (Oxford: Oxford University Press).

Kitschelt, H. (1994), *The Transformation of Social Democracy* (London: Cambridge University Press).
Kocka, J. (2004), 'Civil Society in Historical Perspective', *European Review* 12(1), pp. 65–79.
Kowalski, W. (1985), *Geschichte der SAI (1923–1940)* (Berlin: Dietz).
Kroll, C. (2008), *Social Capital and the Happiness of Nations. The Importance of Trust and Networks for Life Satisfaction in a Cross-National Perspective* (Frankfurt am Main: Peter Lang Publishing).
Kroll, C. (2010), *Public Policy and Happiness* (London: Friedrich Ebert Stiftung).
Kronlid, J. (2010), 'Samarbete S-LO bör diskuteras' ['SAP-LO cooperation should be discussed'], *Dagens Arbete*, 5 November.
Krugman, P. (2009), *The Return of Depression Economics and the Crisis of 2008* (New York: Norton).
Kuznets, S. (1971), 'Modern, Economic Growth: Findings and Reflections', 11 December (http://nobelprize.org/nobel_prizes/economics/laureates/1971/kuznets-lecture.html, accessed 10 September 2010).
Ladrech, R. (1993), 'Social Democratic Parties and EC Integration: Transnational Party Responses to Europe 1991', *European Journal of Political Research* 24(3), pp. 195–210.
Ladrech, R. (2003), 'The Left and the European Union', *Parliamentary Affairs* 56, pp. 112–124.
Lakoff, G. (2002), *Moral Politics. How Liberals and Conservatives Think*, 2nd edn (Chicago: University of Chicago Press).
Lakoff, G. and M. Johnson (1980), *Metaphors We Live By* (Chicago: University of Chicago Press).
Landau, M. J., D. Sullivan and J. Greenberg (2009), 'Evidence that Self-Relevant Motives and Metaphoric Framing Interact to Influence Political and Social Attitudes', *Psychological Science* 20, pp. 1421–1427.
Lapavitsas, C. (2010), *Financialisation and Capitalist Accumulation: Structural Accounts of the Crisis of 2007–09* (London: SOAS).
Latour, B. (1993), *We Have Never Been Modern* (Cambridge: Harvard University Press).
Latour, B. (2005), *Reassembling the Social: An Introduction to Actor–Network Theory* (Oxford: Oxford University Press).
Layard, R. (2005), *Happiness: Lessons from a New Science* (New York: Penguin).
Layard, R. (2006), 'Happiness and Public Policy: A Challenge to the Profession', *Economic Journal* 116, pp. C24–C33.
Layard, R. (2009), 'The Greatest Happiness Principle: Its Time Has Come', in S. Griffiths and R. Reeves (eds) *Well-being: How to Lead the Good Life and What Government Should Do to Help* (London: Social Market Foundation).
Layard, R., S. Nickell and G. Mayraz (2010), 'Does Relative Income Matter? Are the Critics Right?', in E. Diener, J. F. Helliwell and D. Kahneman (eds) *International Differences in Well-Being* (Oxford: Oxford University Press).
Lenger, F. (1991), 'Beyond Exceptionalism: Notes on the Artisanal Phase of the Labour Movement in France, England, Germany and the USA', *International Review of Social History* 36(1), pp. 1–23.
Lightfoot, S. (2005), *Europeanising Social Democracy? The Rise of the Party of European Socialists* (Abingdon, Oxon: Routledge).

Lightfoot, S. (2006), 'The Consolidation of Europarties? The "Party Regulation" and the Development of Political Parties in the European Union', *Representation* 42(4), pp. 304–314.
Lind, D. (2010) *Between Dream and Reality*, Working Paper for FES Nordic Countries, Friedrich Ebert Foundation, Stockholm (http://www.fesnord.org/media/pdf/100308_Daniel%20Lind%20english.pdf, accessed 9 November 2010).
Little, B. (ed.) (2010), *Radical Future: Politics for the Next Generation* (London: Lawrence and Wishart; www.lwbooks.co.uk/ebooks/radicalfuture.html, accessed 13 February 2011).
Locke, R. M. and K. Thelen (1995), 'Apples and Oranges Revisited: Contextualized Comparisons and the Study of Comparative Labor Politics', *Politics and Society* 23(3), pp. 337–367.
Lowles, N. and A. Painter (2011), 'Fear and Hope the New Politics of Identity', Searchlight Educational Trust (http://www.fearandhope.org.uk/project-report/).
Ludlam, S. (2005), 'The Trade Union Link and Social Democratic Renewal in the British Labour Party', in S. Haseler and H. Meyer (eds) *Reshaping Social Democracy: Labour and the SPD in the New Century* (London: Print Solutions), pp. 99–118.
Luxemburg, R. (2003), *The Accumulation of Capital* (London: Routledge).
MacIntyre, A. (1999), *After Virtue* (London: Duckworth).
MacMurray, J. (1935), 'The Early Development of Marx's Thought', in J. Needham, C. Raven and J. MacMurray (eds) *Christianity and the Social Revolution* (London: Victor Gollancz), p. 237.
Maggino, F. and E. Ruviglioni (2010), 'Preaching to the Choir: Are the Commission's Recommendations Already Applied?', *Social Indicators Research* 102(1), pp. 131–156.
Magnette, P. (2005), *What is the European Union? Nature and Prospects* (Durham, NC: Palgrave Macmillan).
Mair, P. (2008), 'The Challenge to Party Government', *West European Politics* 31(1–2), pp. 211–234.
Majone, G. (1996), 'Which Social Policy for Europe?', in Y. Mény, P. Muller and J.-L. Quermonne (eds) *Adjusting to Europe. The Impact of the European Union on National Institutions and Policies* (London and New York: Routledge), pp. 123–136.
Marquand, D. (2004), *The Decline of the Public: The Hollowing Out of Citizenship* (Cambridge: Cambridge University Press).
Marsh, M. and P. Norris (1997), 'Political Representation in the European Parliament', *European Journal of Political Research* 32, pp. 153–164.
Maslow, A. (1971), *The Farther Reaches of Human Nature* (London: Pelican).
Mattelart, A. (2003), *The Information Society: An Introduction* (London: Sage).
McCarthy, C. (2010), *The Road* (London, New York: Penguin).
McNeill, D. (1992), *Hand and Mind. What Gestures Reveal about Thought* (Chicago: University of Chicago Press).
Merkel, W. (1992), 'After the Golden Age: Is Social Democracy Doomed to Decline?', in C. Lemke and G. Mark (eds) *The Crisis of Social Democracy in Europe* (Durham: Duke University Press).
Meyer, H. (2007) 'Thinking Globally: The Reform of the European Social Model Is also a Reform of Globalisation', *Social Europe Journal* Website (http://www.

social-europe.eu/fileadmin/user_upload/Authors/Meyer_2-4.pdf, accessed 7 April).
Miller, D. (1999), 'The Norm of Self-Interest', *American Psychologist* 54, pp. 1053–1060.
Misgeld, K., K. Molin and K. Åmark (eds) (1998), *Creating Social Democracy: A Century of the Social Democratic Labor Party in Sweden* (Pennsylvania: Penn State University Press).
Moschonas, G. (2002), *In the Name of Social Democracy. The Great Transformation: 1945 to the Present* (London: Verso).
Moschonas, G. (2009), 'Reformism in a "Conservative" System: The European Union and Social Democratic Identity', in J. Callaghan, N. Fishman, B. Jackson and M. McIvor (eds) *In Search of Social Democracy. Responses to Crisis and Modernisation* (Manchester: Manchester University Press).
Mosley, L. (2003), *Global Capital and National Governments* (Cambridge: Cambridge University Press).
Mouffe, C. (2005), *On the Political* (New York, London: Routledge).
Mulgan, G. (1994), *Politics in an Antipolitical Age* (London: Demos/Polity Press).
National Statistics Online (http://www.statistics.gov.uk/cci/nugget.asp?id=1005, accessed 20 November 2010).
NEF (2002), *Ghost Town Britain: The Threat of Economic Globalisation to Livelihoods, Liberty and Local Economic Freedom* (http://www.neweconomics.org/sites/neweconomics.org/files/Ghost_Town_Britain.pdf, accessed 13 February 2011).
NEF (2008), *Co-Production: A Manifesto for Growing the Core Economy* (http://www.neweconomics.org/sites/neweconomics.org/files/Ghost_Town_Britain.pdf, accessed 13 February 2011).
Nettl, J. (1965), 'The German Social Democratic Party, 1890–1914 as a Political Model', *Past and Present* 30, pp. 65–95.
Noll, H.-H. (2010), 'The Stiglitz-Sen-Fitoussi-Report: Old Wine in New Skins? Views from a Social Indicators Perspective', *Social Indicators Research*, pp. 1–6.
Novek, B. (2009), *Wiki Government: How Technology Can Make Government Better, Democracy Stronger, and Citizens More Powerful* (Washington, DC: Brookings Institution Press).
OECD (2010), *Restoring Fiscal Sustainability: Lessons for the Public Sector* (http://www.oecd.org/dataoecd/1/60/44473800.pdf, accessed 17 January 2011).
Ostrom, E. (1990), *Governing the Commons. The Evolution of Institutions for Collective Action* (Cambridge: Cambridge University Press).
Oswald, A. and S. Wu (2010), 'Objective Confirmation of Subjective Measures of Human Well-Being: Evidence from the U.S.A.', *Science* 327(5965), pp. 576–579.
Padgett, S. and W. Paterson (1991), *A History of Social Democracy in Postwar Europe* (London: Longman).
Paterson, W. and J. Sloam (2005), 'West European Social Democracy as a Model for Transfer', *Journal of Communist Studies and Transition Politics* 21(1), pp. 67–83.
Paterson, W. and J. Sloam (2006), 'Is the Left Alright? The SPD and the Renewal of European Social Democracy', *German Politics* 15(3), pp. 233–248.
Perez, C. (2002), *Technological Revolutions and Financial Capital, The Dynamics of Bubbles and Golden Ages* (Northampton: Edward Elgar).

Petrella, R. (1996), *Le Bien commun* (Bruxelles: Editions labor).
Pilbeam, P. (2000), *French Socialists Before Marx: Workers, Women and the Social Question in France* (London: Acumen).
Platform 51, 'Women Like Me: Supporting Wellbeing in Girls and Young Women', 2011 (http://www.platform51.org/downloads/resources/reports/mentalhealth report.pdf, accessed 12 November 2010).
Polanyi, K. (1944) [2001], *The Great Transformation* (Boston: Beacon Press).
Polanyi, K. (1957), *The Great Transformation* (Boston: Beacon Press).
Pontusson, J. (2005), *Inequality and Prosperity: Social Europe vs. Liberal America* (Ithaca: Cornell University Press).
Popper, K. (1995/1945), *The Open Society and Its Enemies* (London: Routledge).
Porter, H. (2009), 'The Great "Big State" Debate', *The Guardian*, 9 December 2009 (http://www.guardian.co.uk/commentisfree/henryporter/2009/dec/09/big-state-hansard-society-civil-liberties%20, accessed 13 February 2011).
Posner, R. A. (2009), *A Failure of Capitalism: The Crisis of '08 and the Descent into Depression* (Cambridge and London: Harvard University Press).
Powell, E. (1971), 'Speech', reprinted in J. Wood (ed.), *Powell and the 1970 Election* (Tadworth: Elliot Right Way Books), pp. 104–112.
Priewe, J. and H. Herr (2005), *The Macroeconomics of Development and Poverty Reduction: Strategies beyond the Washington Consensus* (Baden-Baden: Nomos Verlag).
Radcliff, B. (2001), 'Politics, Markets, and Life Satisfaction: The Political Economy of Human Happiness', *American Political Science Review* 95(4), pp. 939–952.
Rajan, R. G. (2010), *Fault Lines: How Hidden Fractures Still Threaten the World Economy* (Princeton and Oxford: Princeton University Press).
Rawls, J. (2001), *Justice as Fairness: A Restatement* (Cambridge, MA: Harvard University Press).
Redvaldsen, D. (2011), *The Labour Party in Britain and Norway: Elections and the Pursuit of Power Between the World War* (London: I. B. Tauris).
Rees, T. and A. Thorpe (eds) (1998), *International Communism and the Communist International, 1923 – 1940* (Manchester: Manchester University Press).
Rosanvallon, P. (2008), *La Légitimité démocratique. Impartialité, réflexivité, proximité* (Paris: Le Seuil).
Roubini, N. and S. Mihm (2010), *Crisis Economics: A Crash Course in the Future of Finance* (New York: Penguin).
Ruskin, J. (1860), *Unto this Last* (http://etext.virginia.edu/toc/modeng/public/Rus Last.html, accessed September 2010).
Saeed, A. (2008), 'Between Marx and Mohammed: Class Politics and British Muslims', in Ben Little (ed.) *Class and Culture Soundings Debates* (http://www.lwbooks.co.uk/journals/soundings/class_and_culture/saeed.html, accessed 13 February 2011).
Sanders, W. S. (1918), *Pan-German Socialism* (London: The Labour Party).
Sassoon, D. (1996), *One Hundred Years of Socialism. The West European Left in the Twentieth Century* (London: I. B. Tauris).
Sassoon, D. (2006), 'Socialism in the Twentieth Century: A Historical Reflection', in J. Callaghan and I. Favretto (eds) *Transitions in Social Democracy* (Manchester: Manchester University Press), pp. 15–34.

Scharpf, F. (1999), *Governing in Europe: Effective and Democratic?* (Oxford: Oxford University Press).
Schmidt, V. A. (2006), *Democracy in Europe* (Oxford: Oxford University Press).
Schumpeter, J. (1976), *Capitalism, Socialism and Democracy* (London: Allen & Unwin).
Schwartzmantel, J. (1991), *Socialism and the Idea of the Nation* (Hemel Hempstead: Harvester Wheatsheaf).
Scott, J. (1977), *The Moral Economy of the Peasant: Rebellion and Subsistence in Southeast Asia* (Yale: Yale University Press).
Scruton, R. (2010), *England: An Elegy* (London: Continuum).
Searle, J. (1995), *The Construction of Social Reality* (London: Penguin).
Sears, D. and C. Funk (1991), 'The Role of Self-Interest in Social and Political Attitudes', in M. Zanna (ed.) *Advances in Experimental Social Psychology*, Vol. 2 (New York: Academic Press), pp. 2–94.
Sen, A. (1999), *Development as Freedom* (Oxford: Oxford University Press).
Sen, A. K. (1985), 'Well-Being, Agency and Freedom: The Dewey Lectures', *Journal of Philosophy* 82(4), pp. 169–221.
Sennet, R. (2006), *The Culture of the New Capitalism* (Yale: Yale University Press).
Sennet, R. (2008a), *The Craftsman* (New York: Allen Lane).
Sennet, R. (2008b), 'Labours of Love', *The Guardian* (http://www.guardian.co.uk/books/2008/feb/02/featuresreviews.guardianreview14, accessed 7 April 2010).
Shaw, E. (2005), 'Is the Blair Government Social Democratic?', in S. Haseler and H. Meyer (eds) *Reshaping Social Democracy: Labour and the SPD in the New Century* (London: Print Solutions), pp. 193–211.
Shaw, E. (2008), *Losing Labour's Soul?: New Labour and the Blair Government 1997–2007* (London: Routledge).
Sieyes (1789), *What Is The Third Estate?* (http://www.fordham.edu/halsall/mod/sieyes.html, accessed 13 February 2011).
Skocpol, T. and S. B. Greenberg (1997), 'A Politics for our Times', in S. B. Greenberg and T. Skocpol (eds) *The New Majority: Towards a Popular Progressive Politics* (New Haven, CT: Yale University Press), pp. 104–129.
Sloam, J. (2005), *The European Policy of the German Social Democrats. Interpreting a Changing World* (Basingstoke and New York: Palgrave Macmillan).
Spini, D. (2006), *La società postnazionale* (Rome: Meltemi).
Stevenson, B. and J. Wolfers (2008), *Economic Growth and Subjective Well-Being: Reassessing the Easterlin Paradox*, Brookings Papers on Economic Activity (Washington: The Brookings Institution).
Stiglitz, J. E., A. Sen and J. P. Fitoussi (2009), *Report by the Commission on the Measurement of Economic Performance and Social Progress* (Paris: Commission on the Measurement of Economic Performance and Social Progress).
Swank, D. (2002), *Global Capital, Political Institutions, and Policy Change in Developed Welfare States* (Cambridge: Cambridge University Press).
Sweetser, E. (1998), 'Regular Metaphoricity in Gesture: Bodily-Based Models of Speech Interaction' (Elsevier: *Actes du 16 Congres International des Linguistes*), http://linguistics.berkeley.edu/~sweetser/sweetser.cil.98.pdf, accessed 12 November 2011.
Taylor, C. (2004), *Modern Social Imaginaries* (Durham: Duke University Press).

Tilton, T. (1990), *The Political Theory of Swedish Social Democracy. Through the Welfare State to Revolution* (New York: Clarendon Press).
Tombs, I. (2003), 'Socialists Debate Their History from the First World War to the Third Reich: German Exiles and the British Labour Party', in S. Berger, P. Lambert and P. Schumann (eds) *Historikerdialoge. Geschichte, Mythos und Gedächtnis im deutsch-britischen kulturellen Austausch, 1750–2000* (Göttingen: Vandenhoeck & Ruprecht), pp. 361–382.
Tomlinson, J. (2009), *The Labour Governments 1964–1970: Economic Policy* (Manchester: Manchester University Press).
Tsarouhas, D. (2008), *Social Democracy in Sweden* (London and New York: I. B. Tauris).
UNDP (2010), *Human Development Report* (New York: United Nations).
Van der Hoek, P. (2005), *Handbook of Public Administration and Policy in the European Union* (London: CRC Press).
Veenhoven, R. (2000), 'Well-Being in the Welfare State: Level Not Higher, Distribution Not More Equitable', *Journal of Comparative Policy Analysis* 2, pp. 91–125.
Veenhoven, R. (2004), 'The Greatest Happiness Principle. Happiness as a Public Policy Aim', in P. A. Linley and S. Joseph (eds) *Positive Psychology in Practice* (Hoboken, NJ: John Wiley), pp. 658–678.
Visser, J. (2006) 'Union Membership Statistics in 24 Countries', *Monthly Labor Review* 129, pp. 38–49.
Wagner, M. (2008), 'Debating Europe in the French Socialist Party: The 2004 Internal Referendum on the EU Constitution', *French Politics* 6, pp. 257–279.
Watson, M. (2009), 'Constituting Monetary Conservatives via the Savings Habit: New Labour and the British Housing Market Bubble', *Comparative European Politics* 6, pp. 285–304.
Weber, M. (1918), *Politics as a Vocation* (http://www.ne.jp/asahi/moriyuki/abukuma/weber/lecture/politics_vocation.html, accessed 13 February 2011).
Webster (2006), *Theories of the Information Society*, 3rd edn (Abingdon: Routledge).
Wehling, E. (2010), 'Argument Is Gesture War. Form, Function and Prosody of Discourse Structuring Gestures in Political Argument', *Proceedings of the 35th Annual Meeting of the Berkeley Linguistics Society* (Berkeley: University of California).
Wheeler, R. F. (1970), *The Independent Social Democratic Party and the Internationals: An Examination of Socialist Internationalism in Germany 1915–1923* (Pittsburgh, PA: University of Pittsburgh Press).
Wielgoß, T. (2002), *PS und SPD im europäischen Integrationsprozess* (Baden-Baden: Nomos Verlagsgesellschaft).
Wilkinson, R and K. Pickett (2009), *The Spirit Level: Why More Equal Societies Nearly Always Do Better* (London: Allen Lane).
Williams, L. and J. Bargh (2010), 'Keeping One's Distance. The Influence of Spatial Distance Cues on Affect and Evaluation', *Psychological Science* 19, pp. 302–308.
Williams, R. (1983 [1958]), *Culture and Society* (New York: Columbia University Press).
Wilson, W. (1967), 'Correlates of Avowed Happiness', *Psychological Bulletin* 67, pp. 294–306.
Wolf, M. (2008), *Fixing Global Finance* (Baltimore: Johns Hopkins University Press).

Wordsworth, D. and W. Wordsworth (1986), *Home at Grasmere* (London: Penguin Classics).
WRR, Netherlands Scientific Council for Government (2010), *Out of Sight: Exploring Futures for Policy Making* (WRR: The Hague).
Young Foundation (2010), *Sinking and Swimming: Understanding Britain's Unmet Needs* (London: Young Foundation).
Zittrain, J. (2008), *The Future of the Internet: And How to Avoid It* (New Haven, London: Yale University Press).

Index

Adam, Barbara, 170–1
Agrarian Party (Sweden), 18
agriculture, 203
AirportWatch network, 185
Akerlof, George
  Animal Spirits (with Schiller), 59
Algeria, 20
Allegre, Claude, 173
Allgemeiner Deutscher Arbeitverein (ADAV), 14
Amato, Giuliano, 87
Anderson, Jenny, 8
Andrews, F. M., 126
Animal Spirits (Akerlof and Shiller), 59
Arab spring, 171
Austria
  Cold war neutrality, 18–19
  origins of social democracy, 14
Authoritarianism, *see* paternalism

Bad Godesberg programme, 110
Bakunin, Mikhail, 15
Baltatescu, S., 130
Basel Committee on Banking Supervision, 71
Belgian, 14
Benedict, Ruth, 140–1, 142
Benkler, Yochai, 179
Bentham, Jeremy
  greatest happiness principle, 121, 131
Berger, Stefan, 4–5
Berman, Sheri, 175
Bernstein, Eduard, 15, 40
  best strategies, 52
  democracy and socialism, 39
  democracy as justice, 44
  preconditions of socialism, 49
  war on liberalism, 45
Blair, Tony
  'blue skies thinking,' 174
  communitarianism, 157

freedom and responsibility, 149
Third Way politics, 3, 24, 108–9, 112, 199
what matters, 114
Blond, Phillip, 149
Blue State Digital, 181
Bok, D., 125
Brandt, Willy, 20
  dare more democracy, 6, 30, 205
  Europe for all, 53
  thinking and striving, 199
Branting, Hjalmar, 18
Brave New World (Huxley), 176
Bretton Woods agreements, 39, 40, 110–11
Britain
  'blue skies thinking,' 174
  Climate Change Bill, 184–5
  debt crisis, 149
  dispossession, 139–42
  effect of neo-liberalism, 175
  family life, 146–8
  finance *versus* industry, 144
  income distribution, 67
  Lib-Labism, 16
  Miner's Strike, 142
  modern isolation, 137–9
  origins of social democracy, 14
  post-war Labour victory, 19
  racist right, 148–50
  service sector over industry, 157–8
  social democratic crisis and, 120
  trade unions and, 117
British Airports Authority Ltd, 186
British National Party (BNP), 149, 199
Brown, Gordon
  campaign language, 98–9, 103
  communitarianism, 157
Bulgaria, 14, 128

224

business and industry
  de-industrialization, 21, 144–6
  entering and exiting the market, 77–8
  German manufacturing, 158–60
  global corporations, 78–9, 82–4, 86–7, 202
  service sector over industry, 157–8
  the state and, 81

Callaghan, J., 117
Cameron, David
  the 'big society,' 100–2, 166
  campaign language, 103–4
Campbell, A., 126
Canada, 187
Canadian Index of Well-Being, 123–4
capitalism
  accumulation, 44, 145
  contemporary model of, 5
  debates about, 57–60
  debt and, 62–3
  dilemmas of, 168
  double movement of, 142
  as dynamic system, 43
  environment and, 60
  imbalances of, 58–9
  investment, 61
  level of demand, 61
  monetarism, 40–4
  new production modes, 148
  no longer subject to states, 181
  privatization, 81
  victory over communism, 22
  volatile nature of, 110
  see also capitalism, decent; the market; neo-liberalism
capitalism, decent, 57
  ecological sustainability, 60
  environment and, 62
  financial sector and, 63–6
  innovation, 60, 64
  investment, 63, 64–5
  market excesses and, 72–3
  shared social progress, 60
  stability, 60, 63, 65–6
Carson, Rachel
  Silent Spring, 169
Carter, Jimmy, 97

Castells, Manuel, 190
  capital flow networks, 179
  Communication Power, 184
  The Information Age trilogy, 182–4
  The Information Society and Welfare State, 183
  Rise of the Network Society, 182–3
Castle, Barbara
  'In Place of Strife,' 21
China, 58
Christian democrats
  Cold War era, 19, 20
  common language, 25
  German coalition, 35
Churchill, Winston
  iron curtain speech, 18
citizens
  autonomy of, 201
  of the EU, 50–1
  individuals and state, 198
  protection from corporations, 88
  qualities of, 167
  rights and citizenship, 176
  scepticism of, 196
  sovereignty of, 45–6
  see also civil society
civil liberties, 198
  racism and, 188
civil society
  European civic culture, 207–8
  need for, 85–9
  network autonomy, 184
  state and market, 164
'Civil Society in Historical Perspective' (Kocka), 85
class
  alienated voters, 180
  appealing to all, 21
  economic insecurity, 117
  individualism and, 110, 148
  link to voting, 120–1
  meritocracy and, 199–200
  middle-class concerns, 110, 114
  political representation, 25
  shrinking working class, 29
  trade unions and, 108
  working-class patriotism, 138
Clegg, Nick
  campaign language, 102–4

Climate Camp, 185
Clinton, Bill, 111, 154
Collignon, Stefan, 5
colonialism and imperialism, 20
communication
  competition and the internet, 78
  social change and, 114
  see also network society
Communication Power (Castells), 184
communism
  collapses in Eastern Europe, 22
  defending against, 25
  formation of national parties, 17
  in Western Europe, 21, 22
communitarianism, 8, 162
  'Blue' Labour, 156–60
  in Germany, 158–60
  Third Way politics, 108–9, 112–13
  Third Way politics and, 152
community and local
  within global Europe, 137–42
  people's everyday lives, 7–8
  urban development and, 172
community and the local
  individual freedom and, 167–8
  neo-liberalism undermines, 8
  organization of, 197
Compass group, 3
  'Building the Good Society' conference, 4, 197
Confederation of Socialist Parties of the European Community, 32
Conservative Party (Britain)
  the 'big society,' 100–1, 166
  language frame of, 103–4
  neo-liberalism, 144–5
conservative politics
  EU and, 49
  moral language, 95–6, 97
  paternalism, 104
consumption
  capitalist demand, 61
  decent capitalism, 63
  dispossession and, 141
  globalization and, 148
cosmopolitanism, 8, 152
crime, 112
  drugs, 142–3
Crouch, Colin, 6

Cruddas, Jon, 3
culture, 195
  European civic, 207–8
Czech Republic, 14

Daily Mail newspaper, 187
De Larosière Report, 71
A Decent Capitalism (Dullien, Herr and Kellermann), 6
Delors, Jacques
  'Growth, Competitiveness and Employment,' 35
democracy
  'dare more,' 6, 30, 205
  dealing with the future, 170–1
  defending, 25
  economic foundations of, 44–6
  elected right-wing, 17
  of the EU, 49–52
  the future and, 174
  justice of, 44
  and the market, 80–1, 198
  new politics of, 204–5
  ownership of public goods, 49
  power of trade unions, 110
  principle of, 3
  social democracy and, 52
  strengthening, 165
  see also social democracy
Denmark
  origins of social democracy, 14
  quality of life, 128
  trade unions and, 117
developing world, 20–1
  see also egalitarianism; trade
Diener, E., 125
Dullien, Sebastian, 5
  A Decent Capitalism (with Herr and Kellermann), 6

Ebert, Friedrich, *see* Friedrich-Ebert-Stiftung
economics
  Bretton Woods collapse, 39, 40, 110–11, 115
  deficit and growth, 195
  epochal views of, 143–4
  EU regulation, 34
  Eurozone crisis, 28, 36–8, 69, 115

GDP as success measure, 121–3, 132
global debt crisis, 40, 48, 58–9, 74, 145–6, 149–50
global financial crisis, 195
material progress and, 171
political importance, 5
regulation of, 70–3, 111
social democratic policies, 20, 201–3
state debt and, 69–70
unbalanced, 145–6
utilitarianism, 156
see also capitalism; communism; consumption; the market; neo-liberalism; socialism
education, 69, 187, 198
egalitarianism, 198
distribution of resources, 42, 43
effects of inequality, 59–60
engagement with developing world, 20–1
EU cooperation, 47–9
incomes, 57, 66–9
the market and inequality, 78–9, 80
redistribution of wealth, 47
Social Europe, 205
Sweden's model, 24
'the happy poor,' 130–1
vision and values, 164
wealth and happiness, 127–8
Eight Hour Day campaign, 15
English Defence League (EDL), 148–9, 181, 188–9
environment
civil society activists, 88
climate change, 115
dealing with the future, 71, 73, 170–1, 172
decent capitalism and, 60
energy security, 115, 207
impact on labour, 117–18
issues of, 33
nuclear power, 163
resources, 62
sustainability, 164, 200, 201, 207
values of, 199
see also green politics
Europe
national movements, 138–9

see also Europe, Eastern; European Union; Scandinavia; *individual countries*
Europe, Eastern
collapse of communism, 22
Communist Parties in, 19
quality of life, 128
restored social democratic parties, 23
European Central Bank, 47, 206
European Economic Community, *see* European Union
European People's Party (EPP), 33
European Social Survey, 128, 129
European Union (EU)
common public goods of, 50
democracy of, 49–52
Employment Chapter of Amsterdam Treaty, 33–4
Europarties, 28, 31–4, 37
Eurozone crisis, 29, 36–8, 69, 115
Growth and Stability Pact, 29, 206
integration and policy, 27–31
Lisbon Treaties, 49–50, 51–2
Maastricht Treaty, 34–5, 47
monetary union, 40, 206
policy without politics, 31
political non-cooperation, 47–8
Single European Act, 27–8
'Social Europe,' 34–5, 37, 46–9, 205–8
structures of, 5, 31–2, 35–7, 48–9
Treaty on the European Union, 28

Facebook, 179
family
life in Britain, 146–8
modern isolation, 138
single-parents, 147
Third Way approach, 112
fascism and neo-fascism, 167
defending against, 25
interwar rise of, 17
racist right wing, 148–9
recent electoral successes, 178
financial sector
accountability of, 202
banking system, 64–5
capitalist crises and, 58–9

financial sector – *continued*
  decent capitalism, 63–6
  dominance in economy, 75, 144–6
  investment and, 64–5
  politics and, 196
  regulation and supervision, 66, 71
  in a Social Europe, 206
  stability, 65–6
Finland
  choosing the future, 174
  Cold war neutrality, 18–19
  network society, 183–4, 190
  origins of social democracy, 14
France
  de Gaulle era, 19
  decline of communists, 22
  economic cooperation, 47
  EU social legislation, 35
  French Revolution, 45–6, 179, 180
  hostile to Third Way, 24
  origins of social democracy, 14
  rhetoric *versus* reality, 29
  social democratic crisis and, 120
  workers' movements, 16
Franco, General Francisco, 21
freedom of opportunity, 167–8
Friedrich-Ebert-Stiftung, 3
  'Building the Good Society'
    conference, 4
Friends of the Earth, 184
Fukuyama, Francis, 146–7
the future, 8
  democracy and, 170–1, 174
  expert views of, 176
  fear of, 169–70
  New Labour and, 167
  a right to, 168
  social democratic vision of, 171–5

Gabriel, Sigmar, 31
Galbraith, J. K., 6, 87
  rise of affluent society, 110
Gallup World Poll, 126
gender issues, 33, 201
  socioeconomic changes, 146–7
General Health Questionnaire, 125

Germany
  anti-socialist laws, 14–15
  economic cooperation, 47
  economic imbalance, 58
  effect of neo-liberalism, 175
  first model of social democracy,
    14–16
  income distribution, 67
  the market and the state, 74
  post-Communist, 23
  post-war tensions, 20
  social democratic crisis, 19, 120
  Socio-Economic Panel, 126
  trade unions and, 117
  see also Schroeder, Gerhard;
    Sozialdemokratische Partei
    Deutschlands (SPD)
Giddens, Anthony
  cosmopolitan modernity, 148
  democratic paradox, 171
  the Third Way, 24, 108, 111–14
Glasman, Maurice, 156, 162
globalization
  capital movements, 66, 179
  cosmopolitanism and, 86–7, 160
  economic regulation, 70–1
  labour market and, 59, 68
  the local context in Europe, 137–42
  the market, 62–3
  mitigating impact of, 117
  social change from, 148
  sociopolitical dimension, 160–2
  the Third Way and, 5, 161
Goldsmith, Zac, 185
good society
  defining, 41, 166–7, 173
  disputed utopias, 172–5
  material progress and, 171
  values of, 198–9, 200–1
Gore, Al, 184
Grayson, Deborah, 8–9
Greatest Happiness principle, 121, 131
  see also quality of life
Greece
  debt crisis, 59, 69, 176
  dictatorship in, 21
  transition to liberal democracy, 21

green politics, 115–16
  competition for votes, 195
  Germany Greens nuclear policy, 163
  networked, 182, 184–8
Groh, Dieter, 15–16
Gummer, John, 185
Guterres, Antonio, 35

Hansson, Per Albin, 18
happiness and well-being, *see* Greatest Happiness principle; quality of life
Harvey, David, 145
Havel, Vaclav, 85
Healey, Dennis, 19
health care, 69, 198
Heathrow runway campaign, 185
Held, David, 160
Herr, Hansjörg, 5
  A Decent Capitalism (with Dullien and Kellermann), 6
Hertner, Isabelle, 5
Heyer, Henning, 8
Hirschman, Albert, 48, 49
Hirst, Paul, 181
Homberg, Bodo, 24
homosexuality, 146
  homophobia, 201
Housing Act (Britain), 145
Howe, Geoffrey, 144–6
Human Development Index, 123–4
Hungary, 128
Huxley, Aldous
  Brave New World, 176

Iceland, 176
identity politics, 8–9
  Britain, 149–50
  network society and, 177–8
  post-materialist values, 115
  resistance, 183, 184
  rise of, 116
immigration, 86
  controversies, 150
  political language, 96
  xenophobia, 169
'In Place of Strife' (Castle), 21
The Information Age trilogy (Castells), 182–4

The Information Society and Welfare State (Castells), 183
International Labour Organization (ILO), 68
International Women's Day, 15
Ireland, debt crisis of, 59
Islam and racism, 188
Italy
  origins of social democracy, 14
  social democracy squeezed, 19
  working class strength, 16

Japan
  economic imbalance, 58, 59
  Fukushima nuclear plant, 163
  income distribution, 67
Jaurès, Jean, 15–16, 46
Jospin, Lionel, 35
justice, 164, 200
  democracy as, 44
  as fairness, 42
  social, 52, 200, 207

Kahneman, Daniel, 125, 126
Kautsky, Karl, 15
Kellerman, Christian
  A Decent Capitalism (with Dullien and Herr), 6
Kellermann, Christian, 5
Kennedy, John F., 87
Keynes, John Maynard
  liquidity theory, 43
  money, 41, 42
Keynesian economics
  Bretton Woods collapse and, 39
  limits of, 111
  shift away from, 5
  social democracy and, 43–4
  trade unions and, 110
Kocka, Jürgen
  'Civil Society in Historical Perspective,' 85
Kroll, Christian, 7
Kuznets, Simon, 143

labour
  active policies for, 33–4
  craftsmanship, 159–60, 164
  effect of job loss, 128

labour – *continued*
  environmental issues and, 117–18
  global perspective, 68, 157–8, 161
  income distribution, 66–9
  low-wage sector, 59
  marketplace and, 73
  network society, 186
  policy values, 204
  public sector workers, 5, 29
  self-employment, 72
  social democracy and, 7
  a Social Europe, 206–7
  Third Way disengages from, 113
  women and, 146–7
  see also trade unions
Labour and Socialist International, 16, 17
Labour Party (Britain)
  the active state, 166
  agenda setting, 4–5
  alliance with German SPD, 3
  'Blue' communitarianism, 156–8
  class struggle and, 15
  conservative future of, 150
  dispossession, 139–42
  election losses, 199
  futurity, 8
  identity and belonging, 149–50
  lack of class consensus, 21–2
  loses 2010 election, 27
  New *versus* Old, 154, 155
  reconnecting to public, 30–1
  unbalanced economy, 145–6
  see also Third Way politics
Lakoff, George, 6–7, 163
language
  cognitive transparency, 105–6
  science of, 93–4
La società postnazionale (Spini), 88
Lassalle, Ferdinand, 46
Latour, Bruno, 184
Lawson, Neal, 3
Layard, R. S., 125, 127
Lenin, Vladimir Ilyich, 15, 17
liberalism
  Liberal parties, 25
  socialism as heir to, 45
libertarianism, 98
Die Linke (Germany), 23, 199
Little, Ben, 8–9

local context, *see* community and the local
Locke, John, 41
Locke, R. M., 116
Luxemburg, Rosa, 15, 143

McCarthy, Cormac
  The Road, 168–9
McDonnell, John, 185–6
McGowan, Alistair, 185
Mair, Peter, 28
the market
  abandons people, 141–2
  advantages and drawbacks, 57
  'as much as possible,' 74–5
  assigning a price, 75, 76–7
  capitalism's double movement, 142
  civil society and state, 164
  democracy and, 80–1
  deregulation, 23
  entry and exit, 75, 77–9
  EU integration of, 46–9
  externalities, 77
  failure to manage, 198
  fundamentalism of, 114–16
  globalized, 62–3, 82–4
  information about, 75–6, 79–80
  limits of, 201
  priorities and, 3
  separation from politics, 76, 80–1
  as servant and master, 72–3
  the Third Way and, 5
  volume of activity, 75, 79
Marquand, David, 87
Marx, Karl, 13
  capital accumulation, 44
  competition, 72
  epochs of capitalism, 143
  ideological divisions and, 15
  private property, 41, 42–3
  on surplus, 43
  on volatility of capitalism, 110
Marxism
  changed society and, 52
  one of many influences, 25
Maslow, Abraham, 144
May Day, 15
Mayer, Gustav, 14
media, 196

Mihm, Stephen, 58
Miliband, David, 4
Miliband, Ed, 30
minority rights, 33
Mitterand, François, 111
Mollet, Guy, 20
Moschonas, G., 35–6, 109
multiculturalism, 199, 200
  in local contexts, 138
Myrdal, Alva, 174

Nahles, Andrea, 3
nation-states, *see* national identity and nationalism; state and government
national identity and nationalism, 86, 195
  national exceptionalism, 16–17
  neo-fascist groups and, 188–9
  in network society, 179–81
  new vision of, 181
  socialism and World Wars, 13–14
  see also state and government
neo-liberalism
  challenges social democracy, 22
  the Chicago school, 83–4
  countering, 5
  dominance of, 6, 23, 26, 144–5, 150–1
  economic crash and, 200
  effect on society, 8, 148, 168, 175
  electoral power of, 153
  EU politics and, 49
  fails to deliver freedom, 201
  financial crisis and, 195
  social democracy and, 40, 44
  states and, 81–2, 181
Netherlands
  Cold War era, 19
  origins of social democracy, 14
  pillarization, 16
  Scientific Council for Government, 174
network society
  Castell's analysis of, 182–4
  challenges of, 178–9
  identity politics, 177–8
  national identity and state, 179–82
  political power, 189–90

non-governmental organizations (NGOs), 85
Norway
  egalitarianism, 19
  neo-fascism in, 178
  origins of social democracy, 14

Obama, Barack, 88
  campaign language, 97–8
  financial regulation, 71
  networked campaign, 181
  new technologies and, 177

Palme, Olof, 174
Panhellenic Socialist Movement (PASOK), 21
Parti Socialiste (France), 29
  'Social Europe,' 35
Partit Socialista de les Illes (PSI), 21
Party of Democratic Socialism (Germany), *see* Die Linke
Party of Democratic Socialism (Italy), 22–3
Party of European Socialists (PES), 32–3, 37, 52
  'Social Europe' debate, 34–5
paternalism, 8
  the good society, 166, 167
Perez, Carlota, 143–4
Pickett, Kate
  The Spirit Level (with Wilkinson), 59
Plane Stupid, 185–6
Polanyi, Karl, 142
policy-making
  deficit and growth, 195
  democratic voices and, 51
  EU structures for, 31–2, 48–9
  quality of life framework, 131–3
  Third Way approach, 112
  using quality of life, 124–7
  vision and values, 163–5
  see also politics; social democracy
Polish uprising of 1863, 15
political language
  Brown's mistakes, 98–9, 103
  Cameron's 'big society' campaign, 100–2
  campaigning on values, 96–9
  Clegg's campaign, 102–4

political language – *continued*
  conceptual frames of, 93–4, 95–6
  conservative framing, 95–6, 99, 103–4
  interactive gestures, 103
  moral worldview and, 94–5
  renewal of approach, 7
  of tax, 7
politics
  cyclical nature of, 27
  EU policy-making, 31–2
  Europeanization of, 28
  local/national/global, 8–9
  neo-liberalism's electoral power, 153
  network logic, 189–90
  non-cooperation, 47–8
  rhetoric *versus* reality, 29
  risk and, 6
  self-interest and, 96–7, 99
  separation from the market, 76, 80–1
  voters as consumers, 120–1
  see also community and the local; policy-making; state and government
Popper, Karl, 50
Portugal
  dictatorship in, 19, 21
  economic crisis, 59
Poverty, *see* egalitarianism
Powell, Enoch, 149–50
private property
  monetarism and, 41–3
privatization, 111, 145
pro-tax/anti-cut movement, 182, 187
Proudhon, Pierre Joseph, 15
public goods, 173
  all citizens as owners, 49
  demand and consumption, 61–2
  European, 50
  privatization, 81, 82
  socialism and, 46

quality of life
  critiques of policy, 129–31
  evidence of, 127–9
  measuring, 122–4
  policy advantages of, 124–7

as policy approach, 120–2
  science of happiness, 124
  subjective indicators, 7

racism and xenophobia, 195, 201
  British right wing, 148–50
  neo-fascist groups and, 188–9
Rasmussen, Poul Nyrup, 35
Rawls, John, 42
Reagan, Ronald, 97
rights
  citizenship and, 176
The Rise of the Meritocracy (Young), 176
Rise of the Network Society (Castells), 182–3
risk redistribution, 64
The Road (McCarthy), 168–9
Robini, Nouriel, 176
Romania, quality of life in, 128–9
Rosanvallon, Pierre, 170
Roubini, Nouriel, 58
Rousseau, Jean-Jacques, 173
Russia, 17
Rutherford, Jonathan, 7–8

Sarkozy, Nicolas, 122
Scandinavia
  appeal to middle-classes, 21
  egalitarianism of, 59–60
  public expenditure, 61–2
  strength of social democracy in, 19
  trade unions in, 107
  see also Denmark; Iceland; Norway; Sweden
Scharpf, F., 36
Schmid, Carlo, 46
Schmidt, Helmut, 21
Schmidt, Vivien A., 28, 31
Schroeder, Gerhard
  EU social legislation, 35
  Neue Mitte, 3, 24, 199
Schumacher, Kurt, 20
Schumpeter, Joseph, 72, 143
security, 200
Sen, Amartya, 130–1
Sennett, Richard, 159–60
service sector, 203
  and industry, 157–8
Shaw, Eric, 113

Shiller, Robert
  Animal Spirits (with Akerlof), 59
Sieyes, Abbe, 180, 187
Silent Spring (Carson), 169
Sloam, James, 5
social class, *see* class
social democracy
  in Cold War era, 18–22
  communitarianism, 162
  cosmopolitanism, 160–1
  crisis of, 33, 52, 114–16
  current trade unions relations, 107–8
  defining, 25–6
  democratic commitment, 40
  disconnection from supporters, 5, 114
  diversity and unity of, 24–6
  effects of World Wars, 16
  electoral losses, 27
  electoral strategies, 154–5
  empathy, 104
  Europarties, 31–4, 37
  European integration and, 28–31
  German model of, 14–16
  the good society, 166–7
  historical perspective, 109–11
  internationalism of, 13–14
  Keynesianism, 43–4
  labour movement and, 7
  loss of 'life world,' 140–2
  neo-liberalism and, 40, 81–2
  obstacles of EU structure, 35–7
  pan-European network, 196
  party organization, 155–6
  policy renewal, 33–4
  political language, 95–6, 97, 101
  post-war internationalism, 19–20
  quality of life policy approach, 120–2
  relations with trade unions, 116–18
  revisionism or populism, 29
  sheds Marxist principles, 21
  'Social Europe' debate, 34–5, 37
  structural weaknesses, 153–6
  transparent language, 104–6
  value theory, 174–6
  vision and values, 3, 162–5, 171–5

  see also Labour Party (Britain); socialism; Sozialdemokratische Partei Deutschlands (SPD); Third Way politics
Social Europe Journal, 4, 152
social movements, 196
social security, 203, 206–7
socialism, 8
  origins of social democracy, 13–16
  outlawed in Germany, 14–15
  preconditions for, 49
  as romanticism, 8
  Second International, 15
  social democratic goals, 25–6
  un/realistic, 52
Socialist International, 20–1, 22–3
society
  everyday lives and, 8
  happiness and, 127
  local urban development, 172
  loss of 'life world,' 140–2
society, good, *see* good society
Soundings journal, 4
Sovereignty, *see under* state and government
Soviet Union, 22
Sozialdemokratische Partei Deutschlands (SPD)
  alliance with British Labour, 3
  Bad Godesberg programme, 110
  early electoral roots of, 155–6
  election losses, 4, 27, 199
  engaging with party sympathizers, 31
  in exile, 17
  model organization, 25
  origins of, 14
  quality of life, 133
  'Social Europe,' 35
  supports war effort, 16
  Third Way politics, 84
Sozialistische Einheitspartei Deutschlands (SED), 23
Spain
  decline of communists, 22
  dictatorship in, 19, 21
  economic crisis, 59
  strength of anarchism, 16

Spiegel, Karl Heinz, 3
Spini, Debra
  La società postnazionale, 88
The Spirit Level (Wilkinson and
    Pickett), 59
state and government
  as an agent of the people, 46
  business and industry, 81
  debt and, 69–70
  demand for public goods, 61–2
  economic regulation, 70–3
  individuals and, 198
  loss of economic control, 39, 181
  and the market, 164
  nationalism and, 179–81
  neo-liberalism and, 81–2
  policy debates, 51
  Popper's two types of, 50
  post-national society, 88
  priorities and, 3
  public services and, 201–2
  public spending, 69
  relation to civil society, 164
  sovereignty of, 45–6
  as useful institution, 164
  wealth and happiness, 127–8
  see also national identity and
    nationalism; politics
Stewart, John
  Victory Against All Odds, 185
Stiglitz Commission, 122–4
Stiglitz, Joseph, 123, 132
Stop Climate Chaos, 184
Sweden
  choosing futures, 174
  conservative government, 24
  egalitarianism, 19
  the market and, 175
  middle-class appeal, 21
  model social democracy, 17–18, 24
  neo-fascism in, 178
  origins of social democracy, 14
  reformist socialism, 25
Swedish Socialdemokratiska
    Arbetarepartiet (SAP), 14, 17–18
Switzerland
  origins of social democracy, 14
  quality of life, 128

taxes
  equitable system of, 203
  income distribution, 68–9
  language use and, 7, 94
  neo-liberalism and, 81
  policy values, 117, 207
  pro-tax/anti-cut movement, 182, 187
  unbalanced economy, 145
Taylor, Charles, 172
technology
  economic epochs, 143–4
  environment and, 62
  greening of, 202–3
  innovation, 72, 203
terrorism, 115
Thatcher, Margaret
  communities, 157
  neo-liberalism, 149
  trade unions and, 22
Thelen, K., 116
think tanks, 197
Third Way politics, 84, 195, 199
  Blair and Schroeder, 24
  breaking from, 3
  effect on local life, 141–2
  global knowledge economy, 181
  markets and globalization, 5
  social democratic crisis and, 120
  structural weakness of, 152, 153–6
  trade unions and, 108
  vision of, 111–14
Thompson, Emma, 185
trade
  social externalities, 161–2
  social justice and, 207
trade unions, 7
  class associations, 108
  current situation of, 116, 117–18
  functions of, 109–10
  historical perspective, 109–11
  marketplace and, 73
  Miner's Strike, 142
  moderate demands, 114
  post-war Britain, 21–2
  relevancy of, 7
  social democrats and, 107–8, 116–18, 164
  a Social Europe, 206–7

strength of, 59, 117
Third Way and, 108
tradition, valuing, 8
transport, public, 69
Tsarouhas, Dimitris, 7
Twitter, 179

UK Uncut, 187
United Nations Development
    Programme (UNDP)
    Human Development Index, 123–4
United States
    anti-trust laws, 83
    Consumer Protection Act, 71
    Dodd-Frank Wall St Reform, 71
    economic imbalance, 58
    income distribution, 67
    neo-liberal turn, 111
    politics online, 177
    pro-tax groups, 187
    sovereignty of citizens, 45–6
    Tea Party movement, 177, 181, 189
    Third Way politics, 111, 113
    value-based campaigning, 97
utilitarianism
    economic, 156
    paternalism of, 167
    see also Greatest Happiness principle

values
    of changing society, 146
    civil society, 85–6
    cosmopolitanism, 160–1
    the market and, 77
    in political language, 94–106
    post-materialist, 115
    social and democratic, 195–6

value theory, 174–6
vision and, 163–5
*Victory Against All Odds: How the
    Heathrow campaign was won*
    (Stewart), 185

Wehling, Elisabeth, 6–7
welfare policies, 198
    ageing population, 29
    cuts into, 111
    the good society and, 166
    liberalism v social democracy, 45
    original politics of, 109
    policy renewal, 33–4
    quality of life, 128
    social democratic principles, 39
    taking global perspective, 161
    universalist model, 117
    values of, 204
well-being, *see* Greatest Happiness
    principle; quality of life
Wheling, Elisabeth, 163
Wigforss, Ernst, 172
Wilkinson, Richard
    The Spirit Level (with Pickett), 59
Williams, Raymond, 174
Wilson, W., 126
Withey, S. B., 126
World Values Survey, 126

xenophobia, 169

Young, Michael
    The Rise of the Meritocracy, 176

Zitrain, J., 184